HELL
IF WE
DON'T
CHANGE
OUR
WAYS

HELL IF WE DON'T CHANGE OUR WAYS

BRITTANY MEANS

ZIBBY BOOKS

NEW YORK

I'm With You
Words and Music by Avril Lavigne, Lauren Christy, Scott Spock and Graham Edwards
Copyright © 2002 ALMO MUSIC CORP., AVRIL LAVIGNE PUBLISHING LTD., BMG RIGHTS MANAGEMENT (UK), RAINBOW FISH PUBLISHING, MR. SPOCK MUSIC and FERRY HILL SONGS
All Rights for AVRIL LAVIGNE PUBLISHING LTD. Controlled and Administered by ALMO MUSIC CORP.
All Rights for BMG RIGHTS MANAGEMENT (UK), RAINBOW FISH PUBLISHING, MR. SPOCK MUSIC and FERRY HILL SONGS Administered by BMG RIGHTS MANAGEMENT (US) LLC
All Rights Reserved Used by Permission
Reprinted by Permission of Hal Leonard LLC

Originally published in hardcover by Zibby Books, October 2023
First trade paperback edition, May 2024

Library of Congress Control Number: 2023934634
Paperback ISBN: 978-1-958506-55-4
eBook ISBN: 979-8-9862596-1-1

Book design by Neuwirth & Associates, Inc.
Cover design by Mumtaz Mustafa

www.zibbymedia.com

Printed in the United States of America

10 9 8 7 6 5 4 3 2 1

"I live inside my own heart, Matt Damon."
—Prince, in response to the question
"You still live in Minnesota, don't you?"

AUTHOR'S NOTE

This memoir contains subject matter that may be difficult for readers. Please read with care. There are also details in this book, including names, places, and identifying information, that have been changed for myriad complicated, loving, and fearful reasons. I'm sharing this story to the best of my limited ability, with flawed memories and perceptions, and with the awareness that almost no story ever belongs to just one person.

CONTENTS

Brush Fire

There are endless ways to tell the same story. I could, for example, start this book by telling you about the time when I was seven, or maybe eight or nine, and I discovered a gaggle of baby possums. I could tell you that the mother possum had died, but her babies were still wriggling inside her pouch, so I pulled them out one by one by their tails. Their ears were translucent and their tiny pink hands grasped at their mother's fur. Here is where I could end the story if I wanted us all to walk away feeling nice.

There is, of course, another version. It's not any more or less true. An old man takes his granddaughter out into the field to build a brush pile. The two of them carry branches and trash, throwing stuff onto the pile, lighting it, and watching the fire grow. At some point, the girl stoops to look at something. She stays there for a while, hunched over whatever has captured her attention. When she finally pops up and points to the mess of vermin on the ground, she's beaming. Babies, she exclaims. She moves them all over to a log and then runs back to the house to get a box and a blanket and a few other things the old man can't hear her listing because she's already out of earshot.

When she's gone, the old man goes over to get a closer look. He's never liked animals much, except for his dog. He thinks of the babies getting older and crawling inside his walls, scratching out the insulation, bringing disease. It takes one quick toss and the whole lot of them lands in the brush pile, burns away.

When the girl comes back with a blanket-lined box in her hands, the old man doesn't look at her. She's saying something about feeding them soft oatmeal from a medicine dropper when she realizes they're gone. Maybe she thinks the mother was playing possum and then got up and walked away. She scans the area, sets down her box, lifts the log, and moves the grass around. Finally, her eyes land on the fire. She's silent as she walks over to it. She stares into it, and she must see something because she tries to reach in and then snatches her hand back, yelping. She tries one or two more times before she gives up, sinks to the ground, and wails. The old man keeps loading brush onto the fire because there's trash to burn, and after a while, the girl gets up off the ground and starts loading brush again too.

I come back to this event any time I sit at a bonfire or hold something tiny and precious.

There's another version I could share where I track down the exact year and season, detail what we were both wearing, list the state law my grandfather broke by burning our trash. That's a way to tell a story too, but I'm in a lifelong war between diligence and the wonder of daydreaming, and wonder has always won out. Wonder is more important, for me.

Now I'm going to tell a much longer story. This is just one version, tinted by my fallibility and sympathies and grief. It's complicated and imperfect, like deciding what to do with a pouch full of orphaned baby possums, and I don't have all the answers for the questions it might provoke. Here are the bare-bones details: My mom and I moved around a lot for the first decade and change of my life. Sometimes my half-brother, Ben, was with us, but much of the time he was away with his dad. We stayed in our car, at shelters, and with friends and family. Family included Grandma and Grandpa, Aunt Debbie, Aunt Ginger, Uncle Jon, and Uncle Thomas. I rarely had time to form secure attachments, so characters may appear here as they did to me then: here and gone before you know how to feel.

We lived with so many different people and in so many different places that I can only loosely order the narrative of that time. If I ask my mom, for example, how old I was when Grandpa fell asleep while letting me steer the car, she might say I was six. If I ask my uncle Jon, he might say eight. They each have compelling reasons why they believe they're right. I can't ask my mother, "Why were we at that one shelter with the fenced-in playground?" She doesn't remember, or if she does, it hurts her so much that she doesn't want to. I can't map memories to correlating grades in school because I was almost never there. The truancy officer in one county took her job so seriously that she showed up to the place where we were staying and rapped on the windows while we pretended not to be home—even she couldn't stop my mom from pulling me out of school when it was time to hit the road.

I'm left with little islands of memory. My mom singing along to Toni Braxton's "Un-Break My Heart" with so much emotion that, to this day, I can barely listen to it without getting a lump in my throat. Ben toppling from a stool that he climbed to reach something on top of the fridge, lying on the floor after, alternating between crying and laughing at himself. The time I looked out the car window at a passing semitruck and, in a moment of arbitrary resolve, decided, "I will remember this moment." So clear it's almost painful, but I couldn't tell you when or where it happened.

I often joke that my mind is a Rube Goldberg machine of getting to the point. Let me get going and I will take every available detour. I desperately want to be sure that I'm understood and that I've covered all my bases. Just as desperately, though, I love to luxuriate in the sprawl of a chronicle. It feels good to tell a story, the way treading water and popping bubble gum and putting my hand right in that little cove between my gut and my crotch on those rare nights when I sleep on my stomach feels good.

I'm telling this story the way I need to tell it. I'm also asking you to be here with me. This isn't a small request, I realize. These experiences live inside me, and now I'm casting them into you. Forgive me this human hunger.

CHAPTER 1

The Word Became Flesh And Dwelt

I wake up and I'm scared. I don't know where I am. I say it into the dark: "I don't know where I am." Wan streetlight seeps through the blinds, pinches the backs of my eyes. I hold up my arm to keep it out and repeat, "I don't know where I am." I also don't know when I am, or who I am. I can't think of my name.

"It's okay," says a voice in the dark.

"I don't know who I am," I tell them.

There is quiet and then I am pulled gently back, cradled against a chest, wrapped in warm arms. The arms of my partner, Jeff, I remember. Our bed, our home. I remember myself. I burst into tears that come and come and come and then dissolve into calm. Jeff goes back to sleep. We slot together like a plate cracked down the middle. I want to be still, but my mind can't rest. Cars whoosh by on the street outside our window. The blinds don't block the light. I rattle out of place, out of sync with the slow breathing of sleep.

I get out of bed, pull my shoes on, and go walking. Two blocks up, two blocks over, down the hill, across the bridge, through the unlit park. I make note of my weight pressing my feet into the ground, the air on my skin, how my leg muscles flex and my arms swing. This is supposed to help reconnect my body and mind when I'm feeling like a ghost split into many pieces. When I'm feeling haunted by all the places I've lived and like they're still haunted by me. I try to tell my body, we are here and now. It doesn't understand, but it's satisfied that we're moving.

We move through a park, along the river. I think of walking into the water, settling to the bottom like silt. I think of how cool the water would feel, how dark and quiet.

I still don't know if I believe in souls, but if I have one, its long skirt keeps getting caught in the doors I close behind me. My soul stretches and twists and kinks up, folding over and under itself. Every now and again, my soul and I are pulled back through a door where what happened becomes what is happening. There, I am little and hungry, and dreaming that one day something beautiful will come: a place where my mother and I can live forever.

I walk on. A mile-and-a-half loop and then back out, past the bridge, a stretch of sidewalk with an emergency box blinking help at me, another bridge, a flight of stairs, two blocks down, one block over.

When I get to the front of my house again, I don't want to go inside. Any other time, it's the only place I want to be. After a night walk, though, the house is too still. My body is afraid of being in one place for too long. I go inside anyway, resisting the urge with every step to grab the doorjamb and pull myself back out. I sit in the dark, buzzing with wanting to keep going. I know I could wake Jeff and he would stay up and talk to me, but he's part of my new world and I'm craving the past. I turn on the TV and start a video titled *8 Hours of Driving in the Rain at Night*. The video doesn't show the driver, just the road and the rain, the other cars.

I scoot to the right side of the couch, rest my cheek on the arm. If I squint my eyes, the TV screen looks like a windshield. I wiggle my foot, imagining that the way it makes the couch shake is the engine rumbling. Imagine a weight in the cushion to my left, my mother.

Where are we going tonight? I think to her. I know that speaking out loud would be crossing a line.

Where do you want to go?

I can't get her voice right, not how it used to sound, however many packs of cigarettes ago. I can't get any of it right. We dissipate. The heat vents and the middle console and her hands and face float apart like fog as I try to reconstruct everything.

❦

She made me the navigator. One of those complimentary maps from a truck stop spread out on my lap. I don't know how old I was. The map, when unfolded, was bigger than me. Big enough to use as a blanket or fly out the window as a flag for lost mothers and daughters. Indiana, Ohio, Arkansas, West Virginia, Mississippi—we had a poorly refolded collection in the pockets behind our seats, tokens of all the places we'd tried to run to.

"Get us where we're going, baby," she told me. So I charted the tiny hairlines crisscrossing one another on the wrinkled page and pretended I knew how to read, what any of the symbols meant, or how they could get us where we were going, wherever that was.

"Oh, look." I pointed at an I-80 road sign and then down at the symbol for I-80 on the map, sure that making the connection would be significant in some way.

"Thank you!" she said. She turned on her blinker and got into the next lane. "I'd be lost without you."

It was that voice adults used when they didn't really think you had done a good job, but they knew you needed to feel like you had. What was the word? I'd learned it recently. *Patronizing.*

"I'm not patronizing you!" my mom said.

I didn't realize I'd said it out loud.

"You're my navigator."

It was more than just her voice. It was also the envelope she kept on the dashboard with directions written on it that she glanced at every now and again. When I said we should go one way or another, she got into another lane but didn't actually turn. And when I zoned out while looking at the passing fields or let my head droop down to dream on the landscape of a state, she never woke me up to make sure we were going the right way.

Maybe, though, if she said I was helping, I was helping. It felt good to believe it, like I was taller. She might not need me to read the map, but playing pretend made her happy and I liked imagining us as captain and first mate. So I kept the map out and intermittently pored over it with a visibly furrowed brow before I went back to looking out the window and mouthing the word *patronizing* against my wrist so the skin there brushed against my lips and caught the quiet plosives.

At the next gas station, we got out and stretched, reaching down to touch the gravel under our feet, up toward the power lines, twisting out and then back in toward each other with a new funny face each time. It was important to stretch. Just like it was important to check the back seat before you got in the car and not talk to the cops and wipe front to back. When we finished stretching, Mom went to the phone booth and checked the change slot for forgotten coins.

I sat in the passenger seat and dangled my legs out the open door. From there, I could see her dial a number, twist the metal cord around herself as she scanned our surroundings, stopping on me for a second to grin and cross her eyes, and then cradle the phone between her ear and shoulder to write something on the directions envelope. The booth had words and shapes gouged into the plexiglass or drawn on in Sharpie.

I thought about Ben, my little brother, and how, if he had been there, we would pretend the graffiti was a message for us to decode. Some secret mission that we had to embark on to keep Mom safe.

Back on the road, we were reenergized. This is how it was when we stopped. We'd get back in the car, find the right station, adjust our mirrors and dials while saying "Check. Check. Check," and then off we'd go. We liked squealing out of parking lots and we loved driving next to another car and scanning through radio stations until we found whatever song the other driver was singing. When we passed cow fields we liked to yell, "Moo!" and laugh at how they chewed their cud. To get semis to honk, we pumped our arms. If commercials came on every station at the same time, we repeated them in mocking voices. Or we rolled down our windows and did the wave, starting with her hand straining in the wind all the way to my hand straining against the wind. There were always ways to stay entertained.

She would tell me stories about her life, how everyone had betrayed her, how each day was harder than the last, how the heartbreaks never healed, how her body ached. She told me the story of how I'd been born.

There was a Mexican man. I've never known if by "Mexican" she actually meant Mexican, or if that was the only word she knew to use for people who looked like me and him. The Mexican man, she said, had raped her and gotten her pregnant. I hadn't seen a Mexican man before. The closest I could get was staring at myself in the visor mirror and unfocusing my eyes until my reflection was a light brown blur. I tried to imagine father features inside the blur, tried to love it.

"What's rape?" I asked.

She said the Mexican man was supposed to give her a ride to an appointment, but he drove to his apartment instead and attacked her. She ran from the house without her clothes and banged on doors until an old couple at a pizzeria let her in, gave her a jacket, and called the police. They never found him and she didn't realize she was pregnant with me until months later.

"That's why you're my pretty Mexican princess," she told me. "Also, Mark is not your father."

I forgot about Mark most of the time, and that we were running from him. When we drove, it felt like we were traveling just for the sake of traveling. Where we were going or why didn't matter to me. I never knew, and when I asked, it was only to hear her voice when she answered, "To hell if we don't change our ways!" I wondered if we were just going in big elaborate loops, not headed anywhere at all. I didn't really care, as long as we were in the same car. Mark was not in my thoughts. He was a man I called Daddy, even though he wasn't technically, and who wore a black cowboy hat, and did impressions of old-timey gangsters saying, "Why I oughta," with his mouth pinched up all small and to one side just for my entertainment.

I didn't know we were running. I didn't know he would never let us go. He would follow us to the ends of the Earth.

Sometimes people loved you too much, Mom said, and they hurt you. I didn't put it together that she was talking about Mark, or maybe I did. It gets hard to remember what I knew and what I didn't in light of what I know now. She told me about the other people who had loved her too much or not enough. The first love who had cheated on her. The creeps who wouldn't leave her alone. Her stories made me want to protect her. They made me feel like if anyone came to our car and tried to hurt her, I would jump on them and bite them and scratch their eyes. Her stories made me have to clench my fists because I was too small and I couldn't time travel.

"It'll all be okay," she'd say, but it didn't feel okay, so I pulled my shirt up over my head and cried and could only be consoled by a good song on the radio or salt and vinegar chips.

Running from Mark meant we could only stay in one place for so long, and never with people he knew. The best bet was to stay on the move.

Our car was a big blue station wagon. It didn't have a bathroom or kitchen, but we could fold down the back seats and lay out blankets when we needed to sleep, and use our bags of clothes for pillows. We parked in church parking lots, under clusters of trees, in empty driveways, and sometimes on the side of the road. Mom called it camping.

When it got cold, we found some blankets and slept cocooned together in the back seat. After putting me in two or three shirts, she would hold me close like I imagined koalas held each other. Some nights, when Mom fell asleep first, I rolled over and over, spreading body heat to one side and then the next. I'd touch her face with the very tippy tips of my fingers, gentle enough not to wake her, even though I wanted to. When she was asleep, the world felt muted and strange. I'd climb out of our cocoon and stare out into the dark for dangers.

I liked it better when I fell asleep first. At night, her cigarettes flared up orange in the dark. I'd lie on my side and watch them glow and die, each time closer to her face, so I saw in flashes the round shape of her nose, her bristled reddish brown hair, the scar on her chin from where a dog had almost bitten it off when she was little. Between drags, I could only see her silhouette and the moonlight glowing in the frizz around her head. I couldn't see if her eyes were open and watching me, and I couldn't tell if she could see me watching her. The engine would click as it cooled down, and I'd drift off to its metronome, staring into the black space of my mother's face, clutching her sleeve.

In the middle of the night, I woke up. My mother had her hand on my chest, shaking me. She was saying, "Brittany? Baby, wake up!"

Hearing the fear in her voice, I sat up and looked around. Nobody outside the car as far as I could see, nobody hiding in the back seat. When I looked at my mother to see what had scared her, she was holding her chest and breathing heavily, watching me.

"I just thought. . . ." She didn't finish her sentence, but I knew what it was. Sometimes, she woke up before I did and thought I wasn't breathing.

"I'm breathing," I said, and took deep, extra-audible breaths that sounded like "hee-ho, hee-ho" to show her. Sometimes it made her laugh, but usually not. After a while, she sank down in her seat in relief. Then she sat up and took my wrist, brought my hand to her chest.

My stomach felt uncomfortable sometimes when I touched her, though I didn't remember why yet. All I knew was that, as safe as I felt beside her, my guts felt a different way, like sick scribbles, like being hungry for moving instead of food. I fought the urge to pull away, not wanting to hurt her feelings.

"Feel how hard my heart is beating still," my mom said.

It thumped under her bones, against my hand.

The scare had shaken her too badly to go back to sleep, so she started the car and steered us out onto the road again. These were my favorite times to drive. Almost nobody else was out there. Just us, casting a beam into the void, stopping occasionally to watch some deer run across a field in the moonlight or lie on the warm hood and hunt for shooting stars until the metal underneath us got cold. We loved to listen to this one station that played love ballads and had a host named Delilah whose drop was a soft beat followed by an equally soft voice singing her name. We joined in every time. A soulful chorus of, "Deliiilahhhh."

On this night, we didn't listen to Delilah or any music. I tried to dream my way to sleep again, but I was wide awake. My heart beat fast too. Mom was in one of her quiet moods. When they came, she stared out at the road like it wasn't even there. She wouldn't play any of our games or laugh if I stood and did a silly dance or jumped and bonked my head on the roof hard enough to leave an impression in the cloth-covered foam. Instead, she smoked cigarettes back to back, squinting through every pull.

To keep myself from crawling into her lap and patting her face until she looked at me, I would turn to the window and find something that could be something else. A twisted tree could become a sick spirit that needed freeing. Plump white clouds were ingredients I needed for an enchanted milkshake. Rain drops chased each other and merged or pulled apart in little dramas. Until some bump in the road or the sound of her coughing pulled me back to my seat and sent a shock through my body when I realized that I had drifted so far from her, made a different turn, got too far along the road going in a different direction, a different story.

As an apology, I would lean over the middle console and press my head against her. I will never leave you, I would think into her arm until she shrugged me off or until the buckle started to cut into my ribs. Then I would settle back in against the passenger-side door, lean my neck back to see the landscape, and resolve, though I almost always failed, not to go too far this time.

❧

These days, my mom and I don't have much in common. Not even our memories. On a recent night when I couldn't sleep and couldn't find comfort in the driving videos, I sent her a picture of the title screen for *Unsolved Mysteries*, my go-to sleepless media.

"Guess what I'm watching," I typed.

We used to watch the show together whenever we got the chance. We crossed our fingers at the end of each episode, hoping it would be one where the bolted "Update" plaque slammed on-screen. She'd say, "Fuckin' A, they got one!"

She didn't see my message because she goes to bed early for church these days. The next morning, she responded, "That looks fun." Which meant she didn't recognize the name of a show we used to chant when it was about to come on.

"Remember how we used to watch this?" I asked her, even though I knew already that she didn't. In response, she sent me one of those sparkling images of a teddy bear holding a banner saying that it, or she, loves me.

I kept pressing, called her. "Don't you remember? We watched it all the time! The guy would say—" I made the voice: "What you're about to see is not a news broadcast."

"Oh." I heard in her voice that she remembered, if only faintly. She was quiet and then told me she had to go, had to do something for Grandma.

⊚✝⊚

If you've ever lived out in the country, you know that a single errant crumb can lead to an infestation. A hungry creature comes in, takes the crumb back to its fellow creatures, leads them all to you. It can take a lot of time and effort to get the house pest-free again. You remember that effort. You become more careful of how you eat. Maybe you stop eating anything that creates crumbs, even if that includes your favorite foods. Maybe you grow so afraid of the sound of skittering in the night that you run from your home, shaking out your hair and slapping all over yourself for something that isn't even there. Maybe your daughter brings you your favorite food one day to cheer you up. Maybe you love your daughter, but all you can think about are the crumbs she's going to get everywhere and the fact that she too once fed from your body. Maybe you can't help but notice how hungrily she looks at her own gift. How she waits for your approval, like she might fall apart if you aren't pleased, like she would scatter in the light.

⊚✝⊚

After she remembered *Unsolved Mysteries*, my mother started sending me frequent panicked messages. Not about the show, but about all the fissures its memory had inflamed. About how her body aches, how stressed she is, how she misses driving since her license was suspended, how Grandma won't let a nurse come to the house even though lifting her in and out of her chair is destroying my mother's spine.

"I'm sorry," she'll say, when she tells me about how much she's struggling taking care of Grandma. "I shouldn't be telling you all this."

Still, she tells me about the way they both cry when she cleans Grandma after an accident, the terse arguments they have about elevating Grandma's legs at night. What's worse is when Grandma prays for God to take her home.

"I'm ready," she'll say, holding her knobby hands skyward, as if she can't hear anyone, can't hear my mom saying, "But I'm not ready, Momma."

For some reason, it seems God isn't ready either, so they sit up in that big house on the hillside overlooking the fields and the highway, and they wait.

Mom misses Ben, worries about him. She gets these feelings that he may not be well.

"Your brother's been real heavy on my heart," she tells me. "Can you please call him and see how he's doing?"

I reassure her that he's doing well, but I don't tell her we call each other all the time. It would feel like rubbing her face in how infrequently we both call her. Where conversations with my mother are stilted and full of gaps, my brother and I can spend hours on the phone. He remembers more than Mom, and often more than me.

"Do you remember," I ask my brother, "that time Mom was making a frozen pizza and we ate all the pepperonis off of it while the oven was preheating—"

"Because they were cold and crunchy," he adds.

"And Mom got so mad, she said—"

"You ate all the pepper-fucking-ronis!" he finishes. It's one of our favorites.

"Do you remember," he asks me, "when we drew on those huge pieces of paper?"

"I don't think so. Are you sure I was there for that?"

Sometimes he lived with his dad for months and I didn't see him. It can be hard to remember which memories we shared and which ones we implanted each other in. When I was a kid, I occasionally forgot I even had a brother.

"At that one guy's house we lived with. He was super tall and had red hair and he—"

"Oh!" I interrupt him. "He had that Janis Joplin poster! Yeah! And he gave us that paper to keep us busy so he and Mom could smoke weed."

"What?" When he's surprised, his voice pitches higher, the way Grandpa's used to.

"Yeah, they were smokin' doobers all. the. time. They even offered me some once."

"What the hell," he says. "They never offered me any."

"It's because they knew you couldn't hang," I say gravely.

We are the only ones left who remember. The only ones who get it. The ridiculous, inelegant tragedy of it all. Like that clear hospital mug with the measurement marks on the outside that were supposed to show you how much water to drink, but Mom filled it with Diet Mountain Dew instead—"Caffeine-free," he reminds me. Always caffeine-free—and then it slid off the dashboard and out the window on a wide turn in the middle of an intersection.

"Was it you or me who had to get out and get it?" I ask.

"I think it was me because I remember all the cars honking at me and Mom yelling at them to go fuck themselves."

"Ah, memories," I say.

Lying on my back on the floor or pacing through the house or on long walks through the park, I switch the phone from ear to ear when my face gets too warm on one side from talking for so long. We swap versions of our memories and events that we thought we experienced alone but actually experienced together and vice versa, laughing until we cry, but never crying. When our faces are raw from wiping away tears, we sigh and say some version of "Man, that was messed up."

"Do you remember the time I tried to run away?" I ask him on one call at the tail end of a litany of memories. My stomach aches from laughing.

"No," he says. "When was that?"

"At the Christmas party, at the barn. I must have been ten or eleven. I packed a bag with some chips and Grandma's sweet tea and a book." I'm laughing, but he's quiet. "It was super cold, so I came back after a few hours."

"I do remember that," he says, and there's no humor left. "We were really scared, Brit. We all thought something had happened to you."

"I'm sorry," I tell him, sobered. We pivot and move on, but I realize there is a line. We tell each other our story in a way I could never tell anyone else, but even with him I have to be careful. Especially with him.

⚜

On our next call, Ben tells me about how he broke his foot in his sleep by kicking the wall. He used to kick in his sleep as a kid. Mom and I would wake up with bruises and sore backs. We joked that he was a karate master, but only when he was unconscious. These days, he's animated by nightmares.

After my own nightmares, I don't call Ben. I don't call our mom. I want to. I want to talk about *Unsolved Mysteries* and how the theme song tingled our scalps. I want to talk about our blue station wagon and shooting guns into the sky and perfecting the art of a dramatic exit, but my mother forgot because she needed to, and Ben remembers because his brain forces him to.

I'm in love with the moments that once made the terror of our lives feel better. I can't stop going back. That doesn't mean I have to take the two of them with me. To lie awake with me at night, miles apart from each other, with our hearts all beating too fast in sync, not knowing why. To lose track of then and now and here and not here. To replay memories in our heads like testing gold with our teeth.

I prefer to sit through some feelings by myself. I prefer to haunt my own house, haunt the streets around it, haunt the park, haunt the river. Sometimes I want ferociously to cry with my arms slack at my sides and my mouth wide open, shamble through a grocery store, a library, a courtroom—some place with people who will stop what they're doing and hold me. I prefer not to be touched. I want an astronaut to peer down and witness my unsightly sadness. I prefer not to be looked at. I wish all of the unsolved mysteries were solved. I prefer to be in the dark, where the shape of a thing could be something else. I want to leave. I prefer to be at home.

⚜

I know someone is reading this the same way I know no one is really beside me on the couch on these nights when I can't sleep. To tell this story, I have to pretend I don't know. The way I used to pray in case someone was listening. I never loved the feeling of always being watched, of constant judgment, but now I'm inviting you here. You have a body. You have feelings. I have to acknowledge you before we both go back to pretending we're in the car together. Would it mean anything—would it make you feel loved, or burdened—if I told you that I'm putting my faith in you as much as you must be putting yours in me?

I'm trying to put my body here, pressed between front and back cover like two doors, a place to live forever. But a book is as impermanent as a home. I am different every time I sit down to write. Loving, afraid, angry, hopeful, always shifting. If I waited for my self to settle, it would never be done. Some might say that means I'm not ready. I don't know if I've ever been ready for anything.

Road To God's House

She didn't want to go back home, but money was running out and I was hungry. The car needed gas. Motels were starting to ask for a credit card instead of cash, which meant we couldn't take off in the morning without paying. The last time Grandma and Grandpa had wired us money, we went to the movies and ate White Castle mozzarella sticks and played laser tag. Me, too small to hold my own laser gun, following behind her and scoping out the competition. Now there was nothing left, and they wouldn't send us any more. We were driving on fumes.

To assuage the anxiety of returning home, she peppered the trip with stories. Usually, they started with "I shouldn't be telling you this." Shouldn't tell me about the semitruck driver who she saw beating off, or about the miscarriage she had before me when she fell on her belly ice-skating with her high school sweetheart, or about how Ben was born after a casual hookup's condom broke, or about the time in elementary school when a friend invited her over and then left the room so his mom could pin her down and put a hand up her skirt. She ran out of the house when it was over, to the bridge near her house, and sat under it feeling the rumble of the cars above. When she got home, she expected someone would see it on her, the shame, and know what had happened.

"Everyone just went on like everything was normal, so I tried to too. My grades started slipping. I used to get As and Bs. I think they thought I was just lazy, or stupid." Glazed eyes. "I shouldn't be telling you this."

"It's okay," I told her. "You can tell me anything."

There was nothing I wouldn't want to hear. Nothing I couldn't handle. I think about all of the lewd, helpless stories I absorbed, and I wonder why I don't remember her telling me that we were running from Mark. She gave no reason why we were on the road. I accepted it without question, forgetting about Mark or Ben or anything else.

"My own parents don't believe in me," she'd say, and my heart broke thinking about what that would feel like. What kind of parents wouldn't love their kid, especially my mom! Trees whizzed by, a green blur outside the car, as impossible to focus on as the idea. My grandparents sounded like heartless monsters, so I was surprised when she told me we were going to visit them. Even more surprised when she started telling me stories about how great they were.

"My daddy is invincible." She smiled. "Once, when he took us kids hiking, my sister Ginger picked up what she thought was a stick with a pretty design. When it started slithering and she realized it was a snake, she screamed and Dad ran over, picked up this great big log—like part of a tree that was cut down—and brought it down on the snake. That's when I knew he would always keep us safe."

There were lots of stories like this. He took them with him on revival to West Virginia, where he was from. Beautiful land, all those trees and mountains. He would sometimes see a particularly tempting hill, so he'd stop the car and let the kids out so they could roll down it.

"Mom would say, 'Ray Gene, they're gonna stain their clothes!' but he let us do it anyway." She laughed. I could tell she was remembering those rolls, the green grass, the breathless run to and from the car, sunshine on the top of her head. She was so inspired that we stopped at the next hill we saw and rolled down it.

"Isn't this fun?" she asked me. Hyper light was building in her eyes. I hadn't seen it since the money ran out. I didn't want to dampen it, so I nodded, swatting a bug off my leg. We lay in the grass for a while pointing out cloud shapes, until a car stopped to make sure we were okay. Some people couldn't mind their own business.

"We had this horse trough out back of our house on Meridian, in Indy. He'd fill it up with water and let us play in it like it was our own private pool. I'd jump in with the boys, but your aunt Ginger was a big priss. She wouldn't get in the water and she'd say, 'Ohh, don't splash me! Don't splash me!'"

Waffle Houses and factories gave way to fields outside the car. As we left the city, we sped up. Silos and barns dotted the horizon and then faded into the blur of where we'd been. Cows and horses and goats and chickens plodded around their fenced-in plots of land. *Rural*, Mom called it.

"I don't think it rules," I said. I held my nose. "I think it stinks."

"Those are just cow patties you're smelling. And it's rural, not rule. It means like farmland. Anyway, Dad, your grandpa, used to be gone on revival all the time. During the school year, we couldn't go with him, so we didn't get to see him a lot. When he came home, he'd bring these huge bags of candy and then tease us, opening it just a little and then slamming it shut again, until we were begging him to let us see what he had in there."

That sounded annoying to me. Maybe because I didn't like candy. If someone tried to play that game with me, I would simply cross my arms and wait for them to stop messing around.

"Mom did her best to keep us entertained all by herself when he was gone. She used to be really good at roller-skating, and she would pull us on a blanket around the house." Mom's mouth twitched at the corner. Now she was remembering the floor underneath her, the lumps she felt through the thin layer of fabric, the sound the skates made on the hardwood. "She could skate backward and everything!"

"Does she still skate?"

No, she told me. Grandma had suffered a series of strokes and now her leg didn't work.

"I can't wait to see them," she said. It sounded like she was trying to convince me that this was a good idea. Make me forget how hard we'd been trying to avoid going there, that I'd overheard her telling a friend, "I'd die before I went back there." The way she talked about them now, though, maybe I'd imagined all the other stuff.

"I just can't wait," she said, lighting a cigarette and letting it burn mostly by itself as she drove.

CHAPTER 2

God's House

My mother's parents, my grandparents, lived just off Indiana State Road 67. It was a small, godly home nestled between acres of field on one side and woods on the other. Train tracks ran parallel to the two-lane highway, close enough that the rumble shook the house and rattled the china. My grandparents were in the middle of moving from their little roadside one-story to the giant black barn that loomed on the hillside closer to the woods. I would learn years later that Grandpa sold the little house by the highway to take advantage of a new law that exempted him from paying taxes on the sale income.

When my mother and I showed up, no one answered the door, so she hefted me on her hip and carried me past the line of trees that separated the properties, up the long, sloping driveway, to the barn. The barn was massive and pitch black except for the white metal roof that gleamed in the sunlight and two giant white silhouettes of rearing horses on either side of the front door.

Inside, up the stairs, Grandma and Grandpa were busy with folders and tools. Mom said we'd lived with them when I was a baby, but to me they felt like strangers. Grandma had paper-white skin, black and grey hair styled like a bush, and a little belly. She wore a long skirt, all the way down to her ankles, and leaned on a cane.

"I'm so glad Jesus brought you back to me," she said in a soft southern accent. When she smiled, her eyes crinkled smaller and kinder.

"Who's Jesus?" I asked her.

Her tired face jumped.

"Kristie, you didn't teach her about Jesus?"

"Of course I did, Momma!" my mom said. She nudged me with her knee.

"Oh yeah!" I said, smacking my head like they did on TV. "Jesus!"

I hoped she wouldn't ask me any trivia about Jesus, who, now that I thought about it, did sound familiar. Sometimes, if Mom dropped a lit cigarette in her lap or we got stuck behind a slow car, she would say, "Jesus Fucking Christ!"

Mom urged me forward and I hugged Grandma around the legs. She couldn't bend over, but she patted me on the back with a bony hand.

Grandpa was busy doing something in the hallway, but he put down his tools long enough to come over and greet us. He had thick, slicked-back silver hair, a bulb nose set low on a sun-leathered face, and when he smiled, I saw that he had only a couple of teeth. His clothes were like what someone might wear to an office job, but wrinkled and smeared with dirt and spattered with paint.

"Krissie Lee Ann!" he bellowed, startling me, and wrapped Mom in a big hug. His accent was also southern, but a different kind. Less lilt and more twang. When he hugged me, I smelled Listerine and Old Spice and I wanted him to let go. I didn't like being touched, but it was impolite to say so.

The barn wasn't ready to live in yet, so we stayed the night at the smaller house near the railroad. That first night, as we were lying in the dark in the big bed of the guest room, I asked Mom where we were going next. Grandma and Grandpa seemed nice, and I liked that there was a deck on the side of the house where I could stand and wave at the train as it went by, but something about the way Mom had been quiet since we got there made me want to leave. She laid a hand on my chest, patted, and said, "We're gonna stay here for a while, baby."

We had stayed places before, like in shelters and with friends, but her voice sounded strange, like it hurt her throat to say it. Over the next few days or weeks—I wasn't sure—she slept a lot in that room while I tried to find things to do. TV, Grandma explained, was of the devil, so we wouldn't be watching it here. It wasn't the Pentecostal way.

"Not even *The Simpsons*?" I exclaimed.

"Especially not *The Simpsons*," Grandma said.

The last movie Mom and I had seen in theaters was *The Haunting*. In the scene where a skeleton pops up out of the fireplace, Mom had screamed so loud that other people in the theater had laughed and turned to look in the dark for the unreserved woman. I replayed the movie in my mind when I missed TV.

"What are you doing?" Grandma asked when she caught me sitting somewhere with my eyes closed.

"I'm praying," I lied, and she smiled.

Grandma had me help her cook, or read to me from the Bible, or let me listen to tapes of Christian comedians. There was one I liked in particular where a man told a story from his childhood. His dad had gone outside one morning and found their dog, Puzzums, run over in the street. When he picked the kids up from school, he delivered the news that he'd buried her. They cried and cried, reminiscing about what a great dog Puzzums had been, how she was so smart that she would run to greet them when they honked the horn of their truck three times. As they pulled into the driveway, the kids asked their dad to honk for Puzzums one last time. At the end of the third honk, Puzzums came bounding out to greet them. A miracle! The comedian closed the story by shouting, "Whose dog did my dad bury!"

A long-haired rottweiler lived outside the house. She was Grandpa's favorite dog, but he hadn't named her. He just called her "Dog." I asked Grandma why he hadn't given her a name and she said, "Well, he's from West Virginia."

I nodded like I understood. She told me I could name the dog the way God had let Adam name the animals in the Garden of Eden, so I called her Puzzums, thinking maybe it was a lucky name that would keep her from getting hit by the cars that zoomed past the house nonstop. I liked to sit outside with Puzzums and run my hands through her dull black coat. It was matted in places, clumped up like cocoons hanging off her. All she ever did was lie around in the sun, but I thought she was probably thinking about her puppies. Grandpa had gotten rid of them, driven them out to the country. If Puzzums lay somewhere for a while and then got up, there would be a wet spot under where her face had been. When I told Grandma she must be crying because she missed her babies, she told me, "That's just dog drool."

On the side of the house opposite the highway was a big yard shaded by a walnut tree that constantly dropped bright-green husks. At first, I would gather them because they seemed like magic, but then I realized they made my hands smell like crushed-up pine tree car fresheners. There weren't any toys in the yard, but I could run the length of it or climb on the fence or look up and spin and spin and spin until I got so dizzy that I'd fall to the ground and watch the sky keep spinning while my body hummed.

"Puzzums!" I would yell. "You have to come check this out!"

The yard could only entertain me for so long before I'd go back inside and try to wake Mom up. I wanted to tell her about the spinning and the smells and how Puzzums made a noise that sounded like "Hrrm." I wanted to tell her about the wilds beyond the yard that I wanted us to explore together.

Grandma always seemed to be a step ahead of me. She'd stop me and say, "Your momma's tired. She needs her sleep."

The few times I snuck past her or pretended to be deterred just long enough for her to go back to her own tasks, I'd open the door and wait for my eyes to adjust to the dimness so that I could see Mom under the blankets, breathing slowly, hand curled up beside her face. I would climb onto the bed and touch my fingers to her palm, kiss her on the nose, press my cheek against her cheek. She might rouse just enough to pull me under the blankets and hold me, but I could only stay for so long before I got the gross feeling in my stomach that I couldn't explain yet. I couldn't access the memories that would explain it. Other times, she'd swat me away or not react at all, and I would sit on my knees in front of her trying to beam wake-up feelings to her, waiting for her to smile and jump up and say, "Rahh!" the way she did sometimes if she was already awake when I came to get her up. Eventually, I'd give up and go sit on one of the couches in the living room and make up stories in my head about the swirling designs on the blue silk cushions or the jagged terrain of the ceiling.

Sometimes my uncle Jon, Mom's younger brother, would stop by to help Grandpa move boxes or work on some project up on the hill behind the house. Jon had blond hair, light from working in the sun, and a high-pitched laugh that I loved. I enjoyed his visits because he let me hang off his biceps and did a good Arnold Schwarzenegger impression. He would sometimes try to wake Mom up too, sitting on the edge of the bed and placing a hand on her shoulder.

"Krissie Lee Ann," he'd drawl, imitating Grandpa, and then grin at me as I watched from the doorway.

Mom would grumble and swat his hand away until he gave up, leaning down to kiss her on the head before he left. He'd ruffle my hair on the way out, but his eyes would be red.

One thing that could wake Mom up was church. We had to go as a condition of staying there, she told me. Their house, their rules. Since we didn't have a lot of clothes, especially not any fit for church, Mom had to borrow a dress from Grandma and I had to put on a checkered dress with a belt and poofy sleeves that made me feel like I couldn't move.

"I look like a fucking dweeb," Mom said one evening when we put on our church clothes. She turned in front of the mirror and scrunched her face up, tried shrugging and sucking in her stomach to change how it hung off her. I didn't think she looked like a dweeb, but the dress definitely wasn't something she would normally wear. It was floral with a lace collar and reached all the way to the floor.

"Fuck it," she said finally, and craned her arm back to find the zipper. "I'm not fucking wearing it."

In her underwear, she dug through the duffel bag for something better. I took the opportunity to look at myself in the mirror. My dress didn't look right on me either. It was something about the way my legs stuck out and how the white in the dress contrasted with my skin and made it look darker. Looking at myself was embarrassing. I wanted to change too, but I didn't want to upset Grandma. Mom came back to the mirror in her bra and a pair of blue jeans.

"Does this make my butt look, like, totally big?" she asked me in a voice she called Valley Girl.

"Ginormous!" I said, and she put a hand on her chest in fake shock.

"Kristie, put some clothes on!" Grandma said from the doorway, startling us both.

Mom ducked her head and changed her voice back to normal. "Yes, ma'am. Sorry, Mama."

Grandma shook her head, but looked at me and smiled. "Don't you look just like a little doll baby!"

I put on a smile and gave her a twirl, ending with a flourish like dancers did, with one hand in the air and one on my hip. She laughed and covered her mouth. Mom came back with a plain T-shirt on, ready to go.

"What's wrong with the dress I gave you?" Grandma asked her.

"It didn't fit," Mom said.

"It should have," Grandma said, but she didn't press it, just sighed and shook her head.

Mom wore a somber expression until Grandma turned, and then she winked at me. I glanced at my reflection on the way out, hoping the dress would look less uncomfortable on me this time, but nothing had changed.

Set Me High Upon A Rock

Church was a huge building with a wedge awning over the front doors and a circular mosaic window at the front. The window showed a vivid scene of a dove flying over a green landscape with a blue stream flowing through the middle. Ushers in suits and white gloves posted at the entrance to open the doors and shake hands as we filed in. Inside, the other church members milled and chatted, pastel in the bright lights.

The men all wore suits or at least starched button-up shirts, and the women wore dresses and long skirts, and styled their hair like Grandma's or let it hang down their backs, sleek and straight.

I'd learned that Pentecostal women weren't supposed to cut their hair. Long hair was a glory for a woman, Grandma had told me, and cutting it was a dishonor. Same thing with dresses. Women were supposed to dress like women. God didn't like it when women wore pants. I looked at Mom standing in the vestibule of the church, her chin held up like she was waiting for someone to challenge her blue jeans or short hair.

We were both embarrassing here. I wanted to stand in front of her so no one would look, but I also wanted to get behind her so no one could see me. There was nowhere to hide in the church. Brothers and Sisters—that's what you called people you went to church with—came over to say hello to Grandma and greet me and Mom. Some were old friends who clasped my hands in their pale, papery hands and said, "I ain't seen you since you was just a *little* thing!" or "Look at those eyes!" while I waited for them to let go. Those who had never met me or Mom shook our hands or hugged us. Grandma pushed me forward, saying, "Don't be shy, now. This is Brittany Lee Ann."

"Is she adopted?" they asked.

If she was nearby, Mom said, "No, she's mine," and they apologized and tried to find a place to look that wasn't me or her pants or her hair or me. If she was away somewhere, nodding and smiling as another person told her with a tilted head and raised eyebrows that they were so glad she came back, Grandma leaned in and whispered, "She's not adopted. She's a rape baby." Absolving my mother, she must have believed, of the great sin of consensually coupling with a man outside her race. The white church members made clucking sounds or knelt and tried to make eye contact—I was often being told to look people in the eyes because it showed you were trustworthy—so they could tell me that God loved me no matter what, all children were a gift, etc.

Patronizing, I thought, but didn't say out loud.

When service was about to start, we all filed into the gigantic, high-ceilinged room where rows and rows of pews faced the stage. At the end of every pew, there was a box of tissues, in case God made you cry. Built-in lights beamed down on the drum set snare and piano and purse buckles and blond heads of the congregation. Service started with music so loud it made me and Mom jump.

Everyone else seemed to know the words, so we moved our lips and tried to match the general harmony. Vibrations from the drums hit me in the chest and felt like they might throw off my heartbeat. Around us, Brothers and Sisters raised their hands and turned their faces, begging and thankful, toward heaven. Veins bulged in their necks and foreheads, blue rivers on red land. A few were so moved that they sidled out from the swaying bodies and started running laps around the outside of the pews, pumping their fists, shouting in babble-speak. I wanted to ask Mom what they were saying, but when I glanced up, her face looked the way it did sometimes in the flickering light of a horror movie, pale and drawn.

The music ended and we all sat down. A very pink man came out onstage and started talking into a microphone, dabbing his face occasionally with a handkerchief. He looked to me like a wet piece of bubble gum, and I thought he probably wouldn't sweat so much if they turned off a row or two of the lights up there. The way he spoke sounded almost like singing, but not quite. Extra syllables surged at the ends of certain words. He'd say, "THANK ya, Jesus-uH!" and "The wORD-uh. of GAW-du!" as he paced back and forth across the stage. Occasionally, he would point out at the pews and say something like "I know you know what I'm saying, Brother Wyatt!" People shouted back at him here and there with "Amen!" and "MMM" and more babble words.

I tried to focus on what he was saying, but my mind kept slipping away, up to count the lights, or down to see if I could stretch my legs far enough to touch the pew in front of ours, or inward to tell myself a story about the white bird in the mosaic window above the baptismal tub. The bird was a dove and the green hills it flew over went on forever. That blue water sparkled in the sun and tasted just a little bit like sugar. I would run and tear off my dress, roll down the hills into the water, turn into a dove too, flap, flap, flap up so high that everything got cold and turned to stars in silent black space.

Mom tapped my shoulder and I dropped back into my body. She was standing, sidling out of the pew, so I followed, restraining myself from sprinting out. Back in the vestibule, we let out a big breath and stretched our necks. The preacher's voice was muffled in the other room. I didn't want to go back.

"I need a smoke," she said, and led us through a door and into the night. A light drizzle had started, so we crawled under the detached bed of a semi parked in the lot of the warehouse next door. Crouched like gargoyles on the gravel, we listened to the somehow still audible sound of the preacher inside. My dress made it hard to stay in a crouch, so I bunched it up around my hips. No one was around to see whether I was being ladylike or not.

"It looks like we're popping a squat," I tried, and shot Mom a grin, but she was quiet. She rested the hand holding the cigarette on her knee. Her eyes were locked on the church, but she wasn't seeing it. Wind blew wisps of the drizzle in on us and the cherry got longer and longer on her cigarette until I reached over and tapped her hand, bumping it off. She blinked and looked at me, then smiled.

"You ready to go back in?"

"No."

"Me either."

She flicked the cigarette away and unfolded herself out from under our clubhouse, then pulled me up too and fixed my dress. Before we went inside, I found the red glow of the discarded butt and stomped it dim, then ran back and held her hand as we opened the door and were washed again in the sounds of worship.

I Will Offer Sacrifices With Shouts Of Joy

Church became a regular part of our life. Between playing out-side, reading the Bible with Grandma, waiting for Mom to wake up, helping to carry stuff to the barn, waiting for Mom to wake up, telling Puzzums about my favorite movies and TV shows I missed, and waiting for Mom to wake up, I put on the horrible dress and uncomfortable shiny black shoes and lace socks, and went to church.

To keep myself occupied during service, I played a game where I tried to latch on to the different wavelengths of thought happening at once. In different parts of my mind, I was thinking about thinking, and thinking about thinking about thinking, and about the cicada song outside building and fading, and about my eyeballs moving around behind my eyelids and which way they must roll when I blinked, and about how hard it was to try to focus on it all at the same time. Until it became too much, like trying to hold the reins of too many spooked horses, and I had to give up. I thought, maybe, if I kept practicing, one day I could master it and think of everything at once, on purpose, controlled. I practiced often, and inevitably fol-lowed one thought too far, out into a dream of some feast or falling in love; more proof, I thought, that I was lacking in self-control.

"God knows your thoughts," the preacher would say frequently. He'd deliver this quietly, without his usual flair, making his eyes unfocused so you felt like he could be looking at you, regardless of where you were sitting. This rebuke was so effective on me that I developed a habit of apologizing to God for my daydreams. A ser-mon about the sin of homosexuality or having an unforgiving heart would begin and I would do my best to focus. Before long, my mind wandered and I would catch myself.

Please forgive me, I would think, and still, after so many minutes of impassioned preaching, I was back inside myself, thinking about thinking. Like God, the mind was infinite, and I wasn't disciplined enough to bear witness.

At church, bearing witness meant standing up and saying something into the microphone so everyone could hear. People told stories of miracles, or asked for prayers, or admitted, in a shaky voice, that the devil was trying to whisper in their ear. Then everyone went to the front of the church and prayed on the person who'd spoken. They shouted prayers and cried, grasping and pushing and shaking the person at the center until that person started to convulse and speak the nonsense language that I learned was called tongues. Speaking in tongues was when the Holy Ghost entered your body and let you talk to God in His language. You had to do it at least once before you could go to heaven, like a passcode. I tried to listen from the edge of the crowd and memorize the sounds people made.

"I think I learned a word in tongues," I told Grandma one day over an Oreo McFlurry. "It goes like, shalalalala. Or maybe shanananana." I thought she might be proud of me for being studious about church.

"Tongues isn't a language you learn," she said, wiping a glob of ice cream from the side of my cup. "You have to be entered by the Holy Ghost."

That sounded like possessions from scary movies, but I wanted to feel worthy of being possessed by God's ghost. Praying before bed, I would say shalalalala and shanananana in my head, hoping it didn't mean something rude. Mom prayed with me. We said, "Dear God, thank you for this day. Thank you for everything you've given us. Please help those who need it. Please keep us safe."

I didn't like going to church, but I did want to be good. At first, it all seemed silly and boring. Standing beside Mom in the middle of all that singing and yelling and running, we were surviving it together. The more time we spent there, though, and the more I heard about what was sinful, like doubt and pride and coveting and hatred, the more I felt like maybe I was wrong. I was bad, and church could make me better. Not wanting to be there just meant I wasn't giving myself over enough yet to be fixed. If I tried harder, I felt sure, I would want to be there, but no matter how much I sent my heart out, raised my hands up, thought, "Take me, take me," I didn't feel the match of my soul catching. There was no voice or pool of warmth or divine light. Maybe, I thought, I'm just not able to feel it. Whatever receptor everyone else had that let them be good must not have been in me.

Mom, in her pants and short hair and dark lipstick, was all I needed. We didn't have to stay here and put up with this, I told myself. We were going to blow this popsicle stand before too long anyway. When I looked at her, I felt like she must be thinking the same thing. So, when she took the microphone to bear witness one night, all I could do was sit there and feel the blood move around in me while her voice broke over the speakers.

"I've done a lot in my life that I'm sorry for," she said. "I'm tired of things being so hard. I want to come home."

They closed in on her like locusts, practically carrying her to the stage. I tried to follow, but Grandma put a hand on my shoulder to keep me in place. When someone got saved, she said, sometimes the demons jumped off them and into other people. It had happened in the book of Matthew after Jesus cast demons out of two men and into a herd of swine, and the herd ran mad into the sea and died. She didn't want Mom's demons to jump onto me that way.

As the congregation pulsed around my mother, I caught glimpses of her writhing like the snake my grandpa had killed with a shovel in the driveway, and I wanted to stop them. I wanted to tackle my way through the throng of their holy bodies and save my mom, topple their baptismal tub, knock over the pulpit, punch through the skin of the drums, shatter the mosaic dove window. But I was still afraid that I was wrong, and maybe Mom needed this. She was crying with her mouth wide open and twisted in a puddle shape, but I made myself stand still. Some things that looked like pain weren't. When I got stung by a bunch of bees one afternoon, Grandpa had scraped the stingers out with his pocketknife. The blade had scared me at first, but I stayed still and eventually they were all out. Teeny plugs of my skin open and empty.

When it was all over, the people dispersed and Mom came back to the pews carrying a prayer cloth and smelling like salt. I felt like I couldn't touch her. Her eyes looked watery but calm, and she held her hand limp in her lap. Someone had knelt on it and broken her fingers, but it was okay, she said. She was saved.

Being saved meant she didn't cuss or wear makeup or pants anymore, and we weren't surviving church. We were living it. She woke up early in the morning, brushed her teeth as always, and pulled on a dress with one hand, a little clumsier from the splint. She still smoked cigarettes, but now she read her Bible when she did it. If I tried to make one of our old jokes, she'd chastise me. I'd say, "Sister Phyllis's hair looks like Dracula's," and she would tell me to pray for forgiveness. When I suggested we take one of Grandpa's cars to drive and get some White Castle since our car had stopped working, she told me, "Thou shalt not steal," and that Martinsville didn't have a White Castle anyway, but if we prayed, maybe God would bring us one. If we were lying outside and looking at the stars, I'd ask something like, "How big is space?" and she would tell me only God knew because He created it. I didn't want to talk to God. I wanted to talk to her, but it was like I spoke and all she heard was shalalalala.

Nobody else was unhappy about Mom's new holiness. Grandpa, when he got home from evangelizing, sat down with her on the couch and said, "Honey, I can't tell you how happy it makes me that you let God in your heart again."

"Me too, Daddy," she said, and hugged him around his middle.

When Mom was younger, I learned, she used to be very holy. She had hair all the way down her back. She sang beautifully in the choir, before the cigarettes rasped her voice. Thank God, it could all come back now. I didn't want it to come back; I wanted my mom to come back. I wanted her to headbang to that song about being a bitch and a lover, and walk around in her bra like no one could stop her, and say the word *fuck*, just not at me. Nothing I did worked, though. The only one who could pull Mom away from church was looking for us and was not very far away, though we didn't know that yet. Or we had forgotten. All I knew was that I was alone and my mom was gone even though she was still there.

At night, she held me as we fell asleep, and I felt a war between the sick feeling in my stomach and the desire to cherish this one way we could still love each other. I traced the rough ridges of her knuckles and the part of her splint where the metal met foam and pretended that when she woke up, she would be back to normal and we would leave, or that this was all a con and I just had to keep playing along. But God was so much bigger than me. I was lonely, and my mind kept slipping away until the days smeared into a haze of routine and fantasy. Church lights, hymns, train horn, walnut stench, hairspray, oatmeal, highway house, barn, church lights, hymns, McDonald's, cows in the field, *whose dog did my dad bury*, cane click, Bible pages shuffle, bedtime, church lights, drum thump, white dove, black dog, eternity.

❧

The night Mark finally crept into the house, held a gun to Mom's head in front of her parents, and forced her to leave Martinsville and God and Grandma and Grandpa and Puzzums and me—I can't remember it. Maybe I was sitting on the ground with Puzzums, gripping her fur, or asleep, or so deep in my time-passing haze that I couldn't even register how close my Mom came to having the spirit blown out of her. Maybe my grandfather was thinking about the time he saved his little girl from a snake. Maybe my grandmother was thinking that the devil has many faces. Maybe my mother begged him to take only her and not me, holding out her injured hand, a prayer. Maybe he lowered the gun long enough to ruffle my hair the way he used to and say, "Britterz, it's me. It's Daddy." Maybe I was happy to see him.

What I remember is that, at some point, I surfaced and realized that my mom was gone. I thought she'd left me. Not with a babysitter or in the car while she ran into the store, but truly left me. I searched all over the house, not hearing or seeing anyone—not my grandparents' scared and grieving faces—because there was only one person I wanted. I ran out to the highway, the one that was supposed to take us both away from here, and stood there like there was a plan or an answer. If I was a good girl, I knew, I would pray for her to come back to me. Nothing about me felt good, but I screamed out for her anyway, like God could hear me, or maybe the fields or the White River or a luck dragon.

Grandma couldn't get across the yard with her cane to follow me and Grandpa was gone working or preaching, so she called Jon to come get me before I ran onto the highway and got hit like the dogs whose bodies littered the road into town. When I saw him coming, I tried to run. He grabbed me from behind, let me kick him.

"I know, honey. I know," he said, and cried against the back of my head while I tried to thrash out of his arms all the way back to the house.

When Grandma couldn't get me to calm down, she and Jon put me in the guest room to let me tire myself out. I knew that people didn't like kids who threw tantrums. I'd heard the phrase "You look ugly when you act like that" when I pouted about not getting a snack I wanted at the grocery store. I knew that only brats made a big fuss, and I was supposed to be different. I didn't care. I shook the door and threw myself against the wall, scratched myself like I was full of bee stings, like I was possessed. Even so, as I wailed and beat my arms and legs against the bed that I'd now have to sleep in by myself, I was stricken with awareness of how childish I was acting, like Adam and Eve realizing they were naked. The shame made me quiet, and then my memory goes quiet too.

CHAPTER 3

God's Barn

Once upon a time, there was a beautiful little girl."

I imagined the girl. She had a cherub face, blue eyes, blond hair that fluttered like a thin curtain in the wind.

"Everyone loved her because she had a big heart and she was always polite."

Hands patted her head, her shoulders, her back. She didn't flinch from them; she matched them.

"God saw that she was pure of heart, so He opened doors for her."

Car doors, motion-sensor gas station doors, "Employees Only" doors. Doors with Mom behind them.

It was a story Grandma made up for me at bedtime. A girl, representative of me, went on adventures that Grandma invented in the moment, letting me fill in the actions.

"The little girl walks down a lane and what does she see?"

"A toad on a bicycle."

"The toad on the bicycle rides up to her and says—"

I mumbled something about riding the bike through the swamp. My body was getting heavy. Grandma smiled, taking over the narrative as I drifted away, tucked in on the couch outside the guest room since the bed had been moved up to the barn.

Grandma kissed my head and led us in prayer: "Now I lay me down to sleep. I pray the Lord my soul to keep. His love to guard me through the night, and wake me in the morning's light." There was a version that went, "If I should die before I wake, I pray the Lord my soul to take."

"My momma used to do that one with me," Grandma told me, rubbing her bad leg in preparation to stand. "I'd read a story about a kid who slept with his hand up so God would see him in case of the rapture. I started trying to fall asleep with my arm up too, but I'd jerk awake when it fell down. I wasn't getting no sleep."

After she went to bed, I raised my arm for God, wedging it between the couch cushions so it would stay in place. I missed sleeping next to Mom and being awake with Mom, but I tried to think about Grandma's stories and prayers to distract me.

Mice skittered inside the walls. This close to the field, it was near impossible to keep them out. Grandpa laid out sticky traps and snap traps with peanut butter and cheese. The mice, hungry and clumsy, dragged their broken and stuck bodies around the house, or died behind the fridge and on the bathroom vanity. They left little poop pellets—leavings, Grandma called them—in cabinets and on the counter and blatantly out in the middle of the floor. Grandpa showed me how to prod out the nests they made with the handle end of a broom. Their homes came apart easily. Shredded newspaper packed together, sleeping in stories.

"Go'n now," Grandpa told me when I hesitated to tear them up. He put his hands over my hands and brought the broom down over and over, until they had nowhere left to live. Grandpa's hands curled in a little and he was missing the end of his pinky and ring finger on the right side from an accident with a chainsaw. Born with club hands, Jon had told me, but don't talk about it. They were liver spotted, patches the same color as me. He hated mice, stomped at them when he saw them.

A good tomcat would have hunted the mice and kept their numbers down, but all the cats that came around ended up dashed on the road where the mice then picked through their aftermath with teeny pink hands and black bead eyes. They wriggled around inside the cats' bellies while I watched from the porch, holding on to the slats and believing I was seeing a miracle, a Lazarus cat, until the wound opened and a mouse emerged.

"I'd love to get a cat, but your granddaddy don't want animals inside the house," Grandma confided. "Maybe up at the barn."

The barn was coming along. Grandpa didn't want to spend money on movers. He and Jon moved boxes over little by little so that, sometimes, Grandma would be cooking in the little house and realize we didn't have a whisk anymore. She'd send me up the driveway to look through the barn kitchen. I'd take a shortcut through the grass, climb the fence, jump over the little creek, cross the big yard. Inside, up the stairs, I would climb up on the counters and check each cabinet until I found what she needed.

"Don't be running around in here!" Grandpa would shout as I sprinted past, holding whatever kitchen utensil or book or shampoo bottle Grandma needed. He could never remember my name. He tried a barrage of his daughters' names—Krissie! Ginger! Debra!—until he gave up and just called me Little Girl. By then, I was usually out the door, not wanting to be caught long enough for him to find something for me to do. Pick up sticks in the yard or sweep or blast the fence with a power washer that nearly tore the skin off my foot the one time I got curious enough to turn it on myself. I would get back down to the little house, soaking wet or with twigs and leaves in my hair, hours after Grandma had sent me off for something.

"That man!" she would say, and sigh deeply.

"Does Grandpa perturb you?" I asked her once.

Instead of answering, she started to laugh.

"Where do you even learn these words?" she asked. Still laughing, she had to sit down.

Grandma laughed all the time. Sometimes it was all you could do, she said. She laughed at the funnies in the newspaper. She laughed at the comedians on her cassettes. She laughed at the stories in the picture books she read to me at night. She laughed when I danced like the WB frog with her cane, kicking my legs up high and lifting a pretend hat. She laughed when Grandpa came in the house and shouted, "Deloris Jean! What's that man's number!" and then walked out again, slamming the door before she could answer. She laughed sometimes for no reason at all, bent over the sink, wiping tears from her eyes.

"My momma told me, 'Deloris Jean, sometimes you just have to go in the bathroom and laugh, or you'll cry.'" She held up a crooked finger, imitating her mother.

Her mother was dead, but at least she'd been able to meet all Grandma's children, and had found God before she died. In the end, her mother had stroke after stroke until she couldn't talk or move and her daughters had to roll her over and massage her body to keep her from getting bedsores. She'd been a wonderful woman.

"My parents loved each other, and I mean really loved each other," she told me during bath time. I told her I could do it on my own, but she still stayed in the room to make sure I washed head to toe, the way the Lord intended. "They chased each other around the house, giggling like teenagers. One time, Momma caught Daddy and accidentally pushed him through the screen door in the kitchen. Left a hole there. After Daddy died and Momma got remarried, my stepfather, DC, fixed it, not knowing what it meant to us."

Grandma missed her dad, just like I missed Mom. She was thirteen when he died. The strokes took him long before they would take her mother. On her way to the bathroom one night, she stopped outside his room and heard his death rattle. A croaking sound that sent shivers down her spine. She screamed for her mother, who came in and sent her off to bed.

Three days later, as she arrived home from school, her older sister's boyfriend stopped her at the door and told her, "Your father's gone to happy hunting grounds." My grandmother threw herself across the bed and cried. Cried and cried and cried. She cried as she told the story. What bothered her most, she said, was that her father wasn't saved when he died.

DC, her stepfather, was a cold man, but he took care of them. She learned how to live with him and then, years later, he got sick too, and then sicker, and then sicker. It was bad, she knew, when he went to whip her for some misbehavior and he could barely raise his arm to bring the belt down.

"I cried," she told me, toweling off my hair, "not because it hurt, but because of how weak he'd gotten."

Spare the rod, spoil the child. That was in the Bible. If she or her sisters acted up, my grandmother's mother would send them outside to find a switch. Neighbors out in their yards or peering out the window would see them and know that they were about to be punished. If they brought in a switch that wasn't good enough, didn't have enough branches, they were sent back out to find a better one.

"That's mean," I said.

"That's how you discipline," she responded, and I better behave or I'd find out.

I did behave up until the time she implied that my mom was wild and needed to be straightened out, and I shouted at her, calling her an old bitty. The switch I picked was from the tree out front that had sour red berries that made your mouth numb if you tried to eat them. It was called a hackberry tree, Grandpa told me, and it hacked me up, leaving red welts that stung for a while before they faded to pink and then back to a light tan.

The one time Mom had swatted me on the butt for something, the impact was softened by my pull-up, but it still stunned me. She looked stunned too, and then burst into tears. Lowered herself to the ground, stretched her arms out to coax me in, pulled my hesitant body onto her lap, and cradled me while hot tears dropped on my hair, rolled down my scalp, and met my own. Whenever Grandpa switched me or Grandma rapped me on the leg with her cane or someone at church pulled hard on my arm, I ran away afterward and found a dark place where I could pretend I was back in Mom's lap.

Eventually, I'd come back and sit with Grandma while she worked on Grandpa's checkbook or played a game of solitaire. She had her own deck of cards that she shuffled and then set out on a tray. I sat on the opposite end of the couch and watched her lay out the different piles, flip them over, move them around. Curiosity brought me closer and closer, until I was leaning against her, learning the rules of the game, helping her find the cards she needed.

"This is a jack," she told me, and pointed to the one with a little blond man who had a fancy mustache and a snooty expression. "There's a song, how did it go, oh—" She sang in a warbling voice, *"From a jack to king . . ."*

She covered her mouth. "Your grandpa says I'm an awful singer."

"I think you're a great singer," I told her.

"Jesus don't like it when you lie."

"I'm not lying!" I insisted.

Grandma's voice did warble, but I liked it when she sang. It meant she was happy. She sang in the car on the way to church and on the way home, sang while she cooked, sang when she thought she was alone but I was hiding under the table and watching her drag her bad leg from one room to the next.

I liked hiding. I hid behind doors, under tables, inside cabinets and closets. Sometimes I peered out. Or I just listened to Grandpa talking too loud on the phone or asking Grandma to make him some oatmeal or snapping his fingers for her to hurry up and get him something he needed. No one could see me, except maybe God, who Grandma said was always watching me.

"Even when we're on the toilet?" I asked.

"Don't be vulgar," she scolded.

I didn't mean to be vulgar, but sometimes I couldn't help it. Puzzums would butt-surf in the grass, all hunched over and focused. Or someone would do a big fart in the bathroom. Or a cloud in the sky looked like a butt. I couldn't *not* notice, and it felt like torture to keep it to myself. I craved the improper like I craved mozzarella sticks. I hadn't had either in so long. Grandpa brought home jalapeño poppers sometimes, but they weren't the same, not even close. It was rude to turn down food, so I took them anyway, tried to swallow the cream cheese before I could taste it too much. When I could, I pretended to put them in my mouth but instead pocketed them to feed to Puzzums later. She liked them a lot, gobbled them up without chewing. When I went outside, she nudged my palms with her snout, checking one hand and then the other, and snorting when she found nothing.

"That dog's really taken a shine to you," Grandma said.

I wished Puzzums really loved me for me and not just for jalapeño poppers. At night, when I couldn't sleep, I'd go outside and find her, lean against her side and look at the sky.

"Puzzums," I'd say. "Let's get out of here." I knew she was just a dog and she didn't understand, and that even if she did, she probably wouldn't want to leave. She had everything she needed. Food, water, and people who petted her and threw sticks for her to ignore. Even so, I wished I could ride away on her back, and together we'd find Mom. I wished for it so much that I tried climbing on her once, but she wouldn't move and I climbed down, apologized, and went back inside to lie down on my couch in the dark.

It was hard to sleep sometimes. Coyotes howled sad songs from the fields that cut through my chest. The train rumbled far away, wobbling the china in the kitchen that hadn't been packed yet. Headlights pushed through the window in squares of light that slid across the wall and then disappeared once the car passed. My heart sped up each time one of those cars approached, and I waited for the lights to slow and slide up instead of over as the car turned into the driveway. Ached when they didn't.

It was hard to sleep, but not impossible. According to Grandma, every person was surrounded by guardian angels. To help me fall asleep, I'd picture their loving backs encircling me, facing out in a Spartan formation. A privacy fence of divine bodies. My eyelids drooped and drooped and drooped, and then I was asleep, and there I was in the car with Mom. I smiled at her and she smiled back, turned up the radio, steered us down a long road with no lights except our headlights. Home.

We had to stop for gas, so then we were in a gas station. Too bright, but there she was, walking in front of me down a chip aisle, past the refrigerated drinks, the soda fountain, the coffee. Walking a little fast, turning the corners just before I could catch up. Heading out of the gas station and pausing. But before I could catch up, the doors closed and she was still walking away, not looking back, not seeing that I was stuck inside. I jumped and waved my hands for the sensor to register me, tried to pry the doors open, pounded my fists on the glass, screamed, cried, begged the cashier and janitor and other shoppers, but they didn't care and Mom walked on, got in the car, started it up, drove away.

When I woke up, my heart hammered and I lay still, watching the lights on the wall until my eyelids started to droop, droop, droop, like windshield wipers swiping across our windshield.

Grandma snapped the light on and told me to get up. One of the houses up the hill was on fire. We went outside and looked at it from the porch. The whole hillside was on fire, it looked like, and the flames were creeping down toward us. No, Grandma assured me. It was just the one house, and Grandpa was already up there with the fire department putting it out. It was one of his properties. That nice house with the columns.

"If we were in danger, he would come take us somewhere safe."

What if he didn't make it down in time? What if the fire moved faster? What if it swung from branch to branch like a swarm of screeching chimps and lit the house on fire and we couldn't get away quick enough? Grandma's leg got extra stiff at night and she took a little longer to get around. I imagined trying to drag her away from the flames as they licked at the hem of her skirt. I stood at the window, watching the fire run along the hill, gripping my hair in my fists.

"Okay," she said. "Why don't you go pack a few things and then we'll drive somewhere safe?"

I ran inside and tossed a few toys into a plastic bag. My body thrummed. On the move! Grandma waited by the open door for me, diabetic socks stuffed into her shoes. It occurred to me then that the highway house might burn down and this would be the last time we'd be in it. It felt like a moment in a movie. I took one last lingering gaze around the room and slung my bag over my shoulder.

"I'm really gonna miss this place," I said somberly, and then turned and walked to the car with Grandma. She backed the car up to the end of the driveway and then parked, not even a hundred feet from the house. We turned on the radio to see if the fire was on the news, and watched it rage for a while. I felt silly for having made us leave now that we had a better vantage point and I could see that there wasn't a danger of the fire coming down the hill. Grandma sucked on her dentures and clicked her thumbnails together.

"You want to go up the hill and see how it's going?" she asked. I did. We drove up the driveway, past the barn, and then up the hill to Grandpa's other properties. It was a steep hill, and as we approached, we looked right up into the cloud of red smoke swirling overhead.

"It looks like a cocaine!" I said.

Grandma sputtered. "A what?!"

"A cocaine. You know, like the storm?"

"You mean a hurricane. Don't use that word," she said, but her eyes were already back on the churning smoke cloud. We crested the hill and finally saw the fire trucks, their lights flashing, the jets of water arching into the burning house and the woods beyond. The white columns shone through it all.

"Dear God," Grandma prayed. "Please let them be safe."

That people might be in the house somehow hadn't occurred to me. I prayed with her, a habit I'd gotten used to and tried hard to believe in. As we found out later, after the fire was out and the hillside quiet again, the family who lived there wasn't even home. Away on vacation or out to dinner, not in peril at all.

Grandma let herself laugh then. She laughed as she told Grandpa and Uncle Jon, and her sisters in Alabama over the phone, how I had looked around at the house from the doorway and declared in my little forlorn voice that I was really gonna miss this place. To be the butt of the joke irritated me, as if I was really that sentimental and hadn't been playacting, in part for her benefit, though I didn't say anything because she liked the story so much. The truth was I wouldn't miss that place—I never missed any place—and I didn't when we moved all the way into the barn.

An Accumulation Of Treasures On Earth

At the barn, there was so much more space. There was a hallway that I could run along and get tired before I reached the other end. A stair banister I could slide down. Room after room after room that I ducked in and out of like I was in a *Scooby-Doo* chase scene. An enormous chandelier that looked to me like an octopus with too many limbs all spread out and holding glowing white bulbs, and underneath, a castle-length dining room table with matching chairs. The legs were ornate and swirling and made your eyes water if you hit your knees on them. Behind the table was a window that was so tall, I figured I could stand on my own head five times and still not be as tall as it was. A balcony jutted out from the third floor, where I wasn't allowed.

"Don't you be messing around up there," Grandpa told me, which made me want to go up there worse than almost anything. When he wasn't home, I looked around and saw that it was mostly a bunch of old stuff like film slides that I could hold up to the light and see images of landscapes and people. At the end of the third floor there was an outdoor balcony with a trapdoor that led to a ladder down to the second-floor balcony. I went out, climbed down, then ran back inside and closed the door so no one would know I'd been there.

To my child eyes, everything in the barn was fancy. All of the furniture was imported from France, all with the same design: cream white peaks, like carefully dolloped whipped cream, inlaid with gold flake. Tall china cabinets lined the long hallway, filled with porcelain dolls and plates with delicate blue designs. The glass top of the table that spanned the length of the dining room reflected the light from the chandelier. From the king bed in the master bedroom rose an ornately carved headboard. The plush carpet was a dark red decorated with flowering vines that I looked at when I walked, trying to land with my right foot on the round flowers and my left foot on the star-shaped flowers. I wanted to show Puzzums, but she wasn't allowed inside. Worse, I wanted to show Mom, but she wasn't around, maybe didn't even want me anymore. No, I couldn't think that, couldn't give up on her, couldn't doubt her, had to think about something else.

The barn was so big, which was great for exploring but made it hard for Grandma to get around. To get in and out, she had to walk up the steps to the porch and then up the long flight of carpeted stairs. To get from the bathroom to the kitchen, she had to stop and rest her hand against one of the fancy French cabinets, which couldn't have been very comfortable because the beautiful design was so bumpy. She steadied herself against the banisters that divided up the sections of the hallway, leaned heavily on her cane, and then plopped into a chair or a couch with a big sigh. If Grandpa left moving boxes on the ground that she had to go around, which were increasingly everywhere, she said, "By cracky, Ray Gene!" even if he wasn't around to hear it.

She sent me on errands often, to get a pen or bring her her purse or the phone, or the paper from the mailbox, since Grandpa was always forgetting. The mailbox was across the highway, so I had to check both ways for cars and then dart over, reach up and grab the mail, and then dart back.

The highway wasn't scary, and I wasn't worried about crossing it by myself. For the few seconds I spent on it, my heart beat a little faster, but there was no real danger if the coast was clear. No real danger to play in the grass next to the highway or the little drainage tunnel that went underneath it. So I was surprised when I was playing one day and someone yelled my name in an angry voice. When I looked, it was the relative who was staying with us—a man whose name I won't share.

"You're not supposed to be playing by the highway, are you?" he asked me. The kind of question you weren't meant to answer, not really.

"I'm not *not* supposed to play out here," I said, but he called me a liar and then pulled me by my arm up the side stairs of the barn, inside, and into a bedroom we called the green room for its pine-green wallpaper.

"You could get hit by a car!" he yelled, and took his belt off. My body went cold all over at the sight of the belt sliding out from the loops of his pants. He brought the belt down over my butt and the backs of my thighs. It made people mad when you didn't cry while they whipped you, but I couldn't. I stared at the wallpaper border, up near the ceiling, which showed a scene of horse jockeys and their hunting dogs in the green hills of somewhere far off. He got me across the calves and demanded, "Do you want to end up like one of those dogs on the side of the road?" I didn't answer, but right then I did want to be a dead dog.

Outside the barn was a world of wild for me to explore. Yard that went on forever. Hackberry trees, Oklahoma redbuds, dogwoods, and a peach tree that only ever grew one peach, which the bugs got to before we could. Grandpa's old, broken-down cars, parked in the corner of the property, on which I leapt from roof to roof and hood to hood. The sun made the metal hot under my bare hillbilly feet, and sometimes, when I went to jump, my legs wouldn't let me, and just stayed locked up no matter how hard I thought, Now, okay, now, now! My body wouldn't listen to my brain.

A thin creek, which Grandma called the crick, ran along the fence out front. Salamanders wriggled in the shallow water and over my hands if I kept still enough. A giant crawdad lived in a crag in the crick, and I tried to lure it out with a toy shovel. Frogs plipped and plopped through the mud, which I gathered handfuls of and slathered on the trees that grew along the banks, because I thought it seemed like it might be good for them, full of nutrients. A ritual.

There were all sorts of rituals, not counting the ones we did at church and before we ate and before bed. I had the mud-tree ritual, the ritual where I laid a single dandelion on Puzzums's head exactly between the two brown triangles above her eyes that looked like eyebrows, the ritual where I dropped dots of water through a straw onto the windowsill in the bathroom, the ritual where I blew on the dust motes and sent the particles tumbling and swirling all over, and the dance ritual where I slid in my socks around the polished concrete on the veranda like an ice-skater. Each ritual made me feel like if I did the exact right combination of things, I could conjure something, though I didn't know exactly what. I'd spin and spin and spin around the veranda, circling the wooden stage in the middle that served as the front porch. Bend down, flip one wrist one way and the other wrist another way, rise up, turn my head side to side. Nonsense choreography that I ended with a flourish before restraining myself from looking toward the highway to see if it had worked, brought her back.

Grandma said that spells were magic, and magic was evil. All you could do if you wanted something was pray for it. Like how she prayed that God would heal her and give her back the use of her leg. If we believed God could do it, and that's what He thought was right, she might someday join the Brothers and Sisters who ran around the pews at church when the spirit got so loud inside them.

I prayed with her, but I also set out water droplets and offered mud to the trees in exchange for miracles, just in case. I danced, trying to send extra magic intention through my leg. At church, she went to the front with her cane or walker, depending on how her leg felt, and the congregation laid hands on her, anointed a cloth with oil and pinned it on her dress, shouting into the sky for healing and grace. To show me that all that prayer was working, she had me hold her cane while she went up the stairs at the barn. When she got to the landing, she stood with her arms raised, triumphant. Once, she even did a little hop.

"Grandma," I said. "You're doing it!"

"You see, that's the power of God."

Then she waved me over and braced herself on my shoulder so we could walk to the couch and sit. Her leg didn't hurt, she assured me. It was just heavy. She wore a special booster shoe. To pick it up, we had to drive to the pharmacy in Indianapolis, where, if I stayed close to her in the store while she bought odds and ends, I was allowed to play afterward. People stole little children, she told me. They'd snatch me right up, and she wouldn't be able to chase them down and save me, so I had to stay close. To avoid the temptation to wander, I rode on her lap on the motorized wheelchair.

Once, while we were beeping and whirring through the store, we went down an aisle where someone had propped up a display TV and turned on *A Christmas Carol*. To my surprise, Grandma slowed the chair and stopped under the TV. Maybe she needed something here, I thought. I glanced at her face to see if she was looking somewhere else so I could maybe sneak a peek at the movie, but she was gazing up at the TV. My mouth almost dropped open, but still I waited for her to say something about how ghosts weren't real and Ebenezer Scrooge was going to hell. Instead, she kept watching, so I watched with her and tried to keep completely still, so I wouldn't break the spell. We watched the whole movie, saw Scrooge face the ghosts and weep over his own grave, the family restored, credits. Our necks ached when we finally lowered them and moved on.

"Let's not tell your grandpa about this," she said, and I nodded.

When we weren't at the store or church or at the diabetes doctor where they had all the little plastic model foods on a shelf and a goose outside that charged me when I unwittingly walked too close to its nest, Grandma and I mostly read together on the couch. I cut out coupons and she told me the story of Daniel in the lion's den or David fighting Goliath, how there was no obstacle too big if you had God on your side. Or more cautionary stories, like Samson and Delilah, or Sodom and Gomorrah with Lot's wife, who turned into a pillar of salt for looking back after God told them not to. Some of it sounded pretty harsh, I thought. I had lots of questions, but we weren't supposed to question God.

Questioning meant you were letting the devil get to you. Like how I made a friend at church, but during worship, I swayed to the music and bumped her hip playfully, and Grandma told me that I was a bad influence. If I couldn't be a good child of God, fine, but the worst thing I could do was spread my unholiness. I listened to the stories and clipped my coupons and waited for more fun activities like sewing together, and making sweet tea with cups and cups and cups of sugar, and tea parties.

Grandma loved tea parties. She had a tea set from the Dollar Store and wide-brimmed tea hats with ribbons and flowers that she hotglued on herself. We poured the tea from the little kettle into the little cups and ate Nilla Wafers arranged just so around the saucer. There were even little folded-up fans that we fanned ourselves with, like they did back in Alabama. I said I wished Puzzums could join us, and we laughed at the idea of her in one of the fancy tea hats while she panted in that way that looked like she was smiling.

We were having a tea party the day a voice called out "Hello!" from the other end of the barn. Grandpa left the doors unlocked in case people needed to come in and pay rent or do business, so people were sometimes poking their heads in and shouting to see if anyone was home. This voice sent a jolt through me, though. I looked at Grandma, who was looking back at me. She opened her mouth as if she was about to say something, but before she could, the voice called out again, "Mama?"

I leapt from my seat and rounded the corner, then sprinted down the hallway so fast my tea hat fell off. There in the doorway, Mom. Sun shining behind her, glowing through her rusty brown hair. The scar on her chin. The smile lines around her mouth. She was wearing pants, and makeup, and the splint on her fingers was gone. It could have been weeks or months since I'd seen her, I wasn't sure. I didn't care. Her eyes lit up when she saw me and she opened her arms. I ran, keeping my eyes on her the whole time so I wouldn't lose her, and jumped. The cigarette smell filled my nose, the lavender lotion she used. She kissed the side of my head and my cheek and my eyelids, held me tight and rocked me back and forth. We were leaving, she said, and I should go pack some clothes.

While I picked out the few pajamas I wanted to take—the dresses I would leave behind—Grandma talked to Mom in the next room. Their voices sounded tense, but I was too excited to focus. How easily I turned away from God.

Bag ready, I followed Mom down the hall and out the door. I ran down the stairs, jumping the last few, just so I could run back up and walk down with her again. At the bottom of the stairs, I looked for our car, the blue station wagon with the rust spot on the bumper. It wasn't there, but another car idled at the very end of the driveway. A man's arm hung out of the driver's-side window. Skin on the elbow so dry it looked grey. I followed the arm up to the man inside. His salt-and-pepper beard and hair, the sunglasses, the black cowboy hat. My body felt like nothing, and Mom put it in the back seat. It turned and looked out the back window to where Grandma stood at the bottom of the stairs watching the car drive away. How would she get back upstairs by herself?

We turned out onto IN-67 and the barn moved out of view.

"Quit crying," Mark said. "Aren't you happy to see us?"

I realized I was me, and that I was crying, but I didn't know why. Not yet.

Its Place Remembers It No More

IN-67 stretches diagonally across Indiana like a seat belt. All that time I spent thinking it would take us far away, and it turns out it doesn't even leave the state. It was never an escape route. Years later—I must have been around ten years old—my mother would tell me she tried to walk in front of a car on that road.

"They wouldn't hit me," she told me. "They just kept going. It made me so angry."

What could I say? I pictured her lurching out into the headlights, the sharp swerve, close enough to blow her hair back. Her teeth bared, growling at the receding taillights.

"I'm glad you didn't get hit," I said.

The necessary thing to say. Heartfelt. Limp as the day-old bouquet of wildflowers I'd once picked for her and left on the dashboard.

CHAPTER 4

The Book Of Mark

Mom said God brought Brother Schumacher back to life. He had passed away, from being old or something. They put him in a morgue drawer.

"But God still had work for him." Mom was turned around in the passenger seat. "Before the guy could even start preparing the body, Brother Schumacher sat up, got off the table, and started walking away."

"Was he naked?" I asked. On TV, when people got their chests and skulls sawed open, they were naked under a white sheet. I could see it all. The silver table, the mortician in his lab coat with his mouth open in shock and a saw still whirring in his hand. The retreating, saggy hind end of Brother Schumacher.

"Brittany Lee Ann!" It was rude to talk about nudity during Bible-type stories. Mark snickered from the driver's seat.

The mortician, once he recovered from the shock, scrambled after Brother Schumacher and caught him as he was about to go out the front door of the funeral home.

"Wait!" he called. "You were just dead! We have to get you to a doctor!"

Brother Schumacher only paused with his hand on the door handle and half turned toward the mortician. Mom made her face slack the way a shambling dead man might look and pitched her voice low to quote him: "You couldn't help me then, and you can't help me now."

He pushed the door open and walked back home.

I wondered, still, if he had been naked, how he made it back. Did he call a taxi? Those weren't respectful questions, though, so I kept them to myself. The only peek I got into the aftermath of Brother Schumacher's resurrection was a dentist visit he had some time after.

"When the dentist looked in his mouth," Mom said, eyes wide, "he told him, 'I can't believe this. I've never seen anything like it. Your gums are set. That only happens when someone has died.'"

Brother Schumacher only nodded with a solemn, wise look in his eyes. It killed me that the story ended there. I wanted to know if they could put his gums back and whether the government would find out about Brother Schumacher's miracle and try to weaponize him. Mom wasn't interested in any of that. She told me the story because she wanted me to know that God could bring us back from the worst thing, the very worst thing, if we believed.

"That story is bullshit," Mark said. He'd been quiet throughout the telling except for a sigh or derisive laugh. "People can't come back to life after being dead for days."

"It's not bullshit!" Mom said. Her eyes looked sad, but she smiled at me, like she could make me not hear what he was saying if I just kept looking at her. "God performs miracles."

"Yeah, some man in the sky who can do magic. That's fucking bullshit." He shook his head. "God isn't real."

Mom flinched and turned around in the seat with her head down. "Please don't say that to her."

Mark took a deep breath in. "Don't you fucking tell me what to say." He raised his hand. Mom curled into a ball and sank out of view. "Don't you *ever* fucking—"

There was the road outside, asphalt sliding by. A conveyor belt and cars on it like groceries. Pale yellow grasses zipped past. A blur. Faces of strangers, so many I could never know, if we saw each other again, that I'd seen them before. After Mark raised his hand, it all shuts off. Like someone switched off the TV and the stories went dark. I'm left with the static prickling across my skin, popping in my ears, raising my hair. A reflection of my face in a curved black screen where a narrative was.

WHEN I LIVED with my grandparents, the Bible was supposed to be my one and only reference. Any curiosities I had, however spiritually or morally insignificant, were meant to pass only through the stories found in the thin pages or reverently orated retellings. I couldn't help it that my mental well had been poisoned by beautiful, succulent, evil movies. Before I ever sang a church hymn, I'd watched Pinhead decapitate a man in *Hellraiser* and found it to be a much more moving experience. It wasn't just the entertainment factor either.

When I watched Indiana Jones run from the giant boulder, though I didn't know what a metaphor was yet, I felt the hopelessness of the scene in my body and how it was similar to the way the room felt when Mark yelled at my mom. When Bruce Campbell tried to escape the forest in *Evil Dead II*, screeching to a halt in front of the curled ruins of what was once the road out, I didn't know why, but it pinged inside my mind. The devils howling through the trees.

Any time I was scared or didn't understand something, I was supposed to use the Bible to find answers. Instead, I would reach into my mind and find these scenes. Jack Torrance lurching after his wife and son through the halls of the Overlook Hotel. Sarah Connor resting her head on a picnic table in *Terminator 2* and watching her son bond with the archnemesis who had hunted her in the previous movie. These were my scripture.

IMAGINE YOU ARE being pursued by a great big rolling rock. Like in *Indiana Jones*, but with no music and no plot to assure your survival. You might turn to the rock and scream, "Stop!" The worst thing is that it's a rock and it can't hear you. You spent your whole life learning how to say stop, but now it doesn't matter at all. A rock is just a mass of minerals, and you are just a mass of squishable organs that keep your thoughts moistened. The rock keeps rolling, and you keep thinking, Then what was the use of learning to say stop? And just as the globe overtakes you, it rotates a little farther to reveal, in its pits and crags, what looks like what you would swear is a face.

One Would Think The Deep Had White Hair

The human brain is still fairly mysterious, but one relatively solid theory is that the hippocampus is where experiences metamorphose into memories. The hippocampus is shaped like a sling you might wield against the giant of human experience. It curls through the center of the limbic system, nestled almost affectionately against the amygdala, one of the keepers of emotion. We believe the hippocampus is also a part of our brain that maps our environment and gives us spatial navigation. Perhaps for these reasons, our memories are linked to place and emotion. Most of us remember an event more clearly if our emotions were heightened at the time, and we tend to recall where we were during these events. However, the whole process is much less precise than we might like.

Think of the last time you met someone. Try to recall where the meeting took place, what they were wearing, how the air smelled. Odds are, a number of the details you reconstruct in your mind are incongruent with the material reality of that moment. Your brain will fill in as many blanks as it can, but not always accurately. Especially as time passes, recollections come apart and rejoin with mismatched parts and sometimes vastly different conclusions. We have our mnemonic strategies, our mind palaces, and our rhymes, but we are fallible. Our memory warps, and we are in control and at its mercy in near equal measure.

One of the functions of memory is to keep us safe. Say you are taking a nice walk next to a pond, just trying to practice mindfulness and enjoy your alone time, for once! You're thinking about the serene surface of the water when, suddenly, you hear the distinctive sound of beating wings. You turn and realize, too late, that you've wandered fatally close to the nest of an irate goose. The goose gains on you and pinches the bejesus out of the skin on the back of your arm with its hateful beak, but you manage to escape with your life.

As you rub the back of your arm and look around to make sure no one saw, your hippocampus furiously knits together the sound of beating wings with the pain. When it finishes, it murmurs this new connection against the lips of the amygdala who then converts it into fear. Now, when you hear the sound of beating wings, you flinch and check behind you. Your heart races, preparing you to run. You will remember the experience because your brain has decided it will increase your chances of survival to remember. God bless the brain's heart.

While a strong emotion like fear can cement memories, it can just as easily warp them. If, instead of a goose attack, you were mugged on the way home from work, you might have a harder time shaking the association between the terror of the event and, say, the sound of footsteps behind you. This association might build in your mind until you can't stand to walk in front of another person, not even someone you know and trust. Your brain might replay the memory, stuck in a loop of trying to warn you. A coworker rushes to get into the elevator behind you, and you feel the barrel of the gun at your back again. Someone sidles by you on the bus, and you hear the mugger's voice telling you to hand over your wallet. Each time, your adrenaline kicks in, preparing you. Before you know it, you replay the memory, but now the mugger's hands warp to look like your coworker's hands, the bus driver's hands, your own webbed hands.

We often want more from the mind than it can give us. Resolve, comprehension, focus, realism. We want our recollections to be like a well-kept archive from which we can retrieve exactly what we need when we need it. We want to be able to tell the goose-attack story at parties without someone interrupting us and asking which pond this was, leading us to the realization that, despite the clarity of every other detail, we just don't know for sure. All through the rest of the party and later that night in bed, we wrack our brain to remember which pond it could have been. It would be so much easier if we could call the goose and say, "Hey, remember that time you bit my arm? No, no, I know we said we'd let bygones be bygones, but I was wondering if you remember what pond that was."

It's a rare comfort when another person can confirm a memory. If a bystander witnessed your mugging, you might be able to go to them and ask what they remember. You could check your stories against each other and weed out the incongruencies. Hold out your hands and ask if they're still yours. What the brain can't give us, sometimes, we can give each other. We can fill each other's gaps and hold each other's stories.

For reasons we don't entirely understand yet, our minds love to make associations. Stare at a pine wall and find a face in the wood grain. Imagine a cinnamon bun in the curled end of a banister. Even the hippocampus is named so because of its resemblance to the seahorse. There are certainly evolutionary explanations and Rorschach interpretations for this, but let me release my grip on the refuge of reason for a moment to be charmed by this simple human habit. I love that we are compelled to turn what is into infinite combinations of what has been and what could be. I love that our next instinct is often to share with someone else. And when we encounter something that is like nothing else, we find other ways to make sense of it.

Before we pulled the giant squid out of the deep waters of mythology, through the Sunlight Zone, and into the observation tank of provable reality, we filled in the gaps of what we didn't know yet with tall tales about sea monsters. Sailors recounted their sightings, trying to make sense of their glimpses: tentacle, beak, rolling eyeball. Confirming for each other that what they saw was real, crafting a legend they could steer so the fear of the unknown wouldn't pull them under. Stories can do this for us. It's common practice for therapists to have patients write out their traumatic experiences. When you control the narrative, you get to shape how it lives in your mind.

LIKE LOT'S WIFE, I look back. I'm not sure what or when or where I'm seeing. Just time curling in on itself in the passenger seat. Mark's eyes were brown. I was three years old. I was six years old. We were in the car. We were on top of the park hill. We were in that bright white room. Mark's eyes could have been grey. I am so sure sometimes that Mark's eyes were blue. Mark shatters the story. Like God, He was infinite. We want our memories to be unbreakable monuments, but they are pillars of salt.

When I think too long about the time we spent with him, my body hurts and my mind wobbles like the pressure of a far-off train. Trying to follow a specific memory to any kind of conclusion is like driving toward a semi, blinded by its headlights, compelled by survival instincts to swerve away. No amount of holding the wheel in place can keep you on the road if part of you, however small, wants to survive. Thankfully, there is a lot of me that wants to survive.

ON THE WAY into the store, I reached up and held each of their hands, lifting my feet so they could swing me back and forth. Mark's hand was warm and callused. My mother held on so tight it almost hurt. When they swung me back, I saw the cracked black asphalt stained rainbow by oil, their feet, a sliver of the sky meeting the Earth upside down. On the forward swing, I saw the front doors, the birds' nests built inside the hollows of the sign letters, the blue sky again. The clouds looked perfectly shaped, like the ones from the opening of *The Simpsons*, so I hummed the intro music while I swung.

I liked being what tied us together, the focal point between Dad and Mom where three different people alchemized into a family. When my mother reached for a cart and it sent a static shock that traveled from her finger, through my body, and into Mark, who yelped and let go of my hand, I understood it was a kind of magic that we did together.

I LOVED MARK. I might still love Mark in some room inside myself. He was Daddy. That's what I called him and how I thought of him. When I was around seven years old and I started having growing pains, all I could do was cry and clutch at my knees. They felt as if they were being pried apart with a spoon. Mark sat me on a metal folding chair, propped my legs up on his lap, and rubbed his hands together until they were hot so he could clamp them down over the sore spots. It didn't ease the pain, not really, but it made me feel cared for, which was all I wanted in those days.

As a game, we used to say, "I love you ten times more than you can say today." Whoever said it first won for the day. Most days, I won because I had a singular drive to be the victor, and because I often woke up the earliest and ambushed. I'd point to each of them and shout the phrase. Mark would snap his fingers when I won and say, "Dangit!" Mom would clutch her chest as if she'd been shot and exclaim, "Oh, no!" Even when I lost, it didn't feel like losing.

AT FIRST WE didn't have a home. We slept in the car or in motels, but I hadn't started school yet and they needed a place to keep me all day. There were a few houses that we squatted in, though I didn't know at the time that that's what we were doing. Mark would say we had a new house and when we got there, I wouldn't be allowed to turn on any of the lights or play near the windows. We'd sleep on the floor, the carpet still wet and lined from the shampooer. In the morning, we'd leave through the back of the house, creep to the car, and drive away.

The first place that was ours was a second-floor apartment where a possum lived under the sink. Mom wanted to let the possum stay and so did I, but Mark got rid of it. My favorite part of the apartment was the cubby at the top of the stairs. I liked climbing across the railing to get into the cubby and waiting for Mom or Mark to go past, so I could swipe at them like I was an ill-behaved lion in a cage.

I'm not ready for that part of the story yet.

MARK LOVED *STAR TREK*. Whenever it was on, I had to be quiet. As a toddler, I had sat on his lap and watched the underbelly of the *Enterprise* slide by like it was coming out of the TV and I could reach up and graze it with my fingers. My favorite characters were Worf, whose forehead looked like a mountain range, and Data after he got his emotion chip. Mark liked Riker, I thought, because they looked alike with their dark hair, light eyes, and carefully shaped, angular facial hair. My mother even bought him a *Star Trek* chess set for a birthday, though he destroyed it the next time he was angry at her.

It's funny to me that Mark was a Trekkie. I once found him playing a video game on the computer at his mother's house when I wandered away from the breakfast nook where my mother and his mother were talking. He waved me inside the little computer room and sat me on his lap, showed me how to play. Sounded out the words on the screen for me since I was just learning to read. It turned out to be a medieval role-playing game. Funny how someone like him could also be a nerd.

OF COURSE HE hit me too. Here and there, smacks when I talked back or got out of line or defended my mother. My upper arm in a vise grip. My chin clenched in place to meet his angry eyes. *Grouchy*, I called him behind his back, after he left welts on us. *Moody*, my mother agreed. One moment, he would be giggling and the next he would yank off his belt, beat his fist on the steering wheel, clench his jaw. Cockroaches scattered in the light, but all we could do when Mark turned on us was stay still.

The bathtub must have been at someone else's house. The image of it gets mixed up in my mind with a bathtub I saw in a movie once. A deep claw-foot at the back of a narrow white-tiled bathroom. Big enough for me to pretend I was swimming in it. Not splashing or making noise, because I learned early that the best way to be was quiet. Just lazy strokes, watching the water run down my arms as they arched over and back into the bathwater. Too young to think much of my own nudity. Imagining myself like Baloo the bear from *The Jungle Book* floating lazily down the river with a kid who looked like me riding on his stomach.

I was so lost in my imagination that I barely registered Mark coming into the bathroom and sitting on the toilet lid to watch me. Not even when he stood and approached the tub. It wasn't until he had reached down and started hitting me that I snapped back. I didn't know what I was being hit for, and he didn't say anything, so I closed my eyes and made myself as still as I could.

Another thing I learned early on was that when Mark was hitting you, you let him finish. As he continued to smack me on my back and butt, legs, and chest, my survival instincts overrode my training and my body tried to get away. Water sloshed up each side. My head knocked against the porcelain. I reached with pruned fingers to pull myself up those tall white sides, but the tub was so deep that I couldn't reach the lip, and I think I never got out.

THERE WAS A home movie. A plotless, shaky-camera anthology. I sat on the floor at the end of the bed, watching it with Mark. He liked watching horror movies together, though he always picked slashers while Mom and I favored ghosts and monsters. The part of the home movie that sticks in my mind was of a woman carrying a rottweiler puppy through her house like a baby, its plump grey belly exposed. The puppy howled, so young it was still blind and its cries were more like whistles. It had the same markings on its face as Puzzums. The woman carried it through her house, saying nothing. Then she took it into the kitchen and cut its stomach open.

My hands were at my sides, resting on the floor. I remember the feeling of the blood rushing into my fingers in my left hand. In my periphery, I saw Mark watching me for a reaction. I know the puppy cried. I can see its wrinkled mouth moving, but the memory is silent.

I like to imagine that I have done this muting on purpose and that it's not some automatic mechanism of the brain but my own heroic effort. That I can purposefully sit down for my mindfulness meditation and swim back through time to that dingy room with its cigarette musk and the grainy light flashing from the set. I'm operating by the rules of any reasonable ghost narrative, so I can't turn off the VCR or carry her out of the room. Instead, I kneel beside her. So much smaller than me, and before the cherry birthmarks faded and the sun lightened her hair from black to dark brown. I have to choose between covering her eyes or her ears. There is never a correct decision.

I look at Mark, who is looking at us. Everything that will happen, will happen. The puppy will die screaming. I can't stop this or even take the memory away entirely, but in the face of every inevitability, just doing something is an act of love. I cup my hands over her ears and press my head against hers, promising, I will never leave you.

MUCH LATER, MY mother called him evil. He ruined her life, she said. He got her hooked on drugs. He convinced her to start stripping, to use the stuff they passed around the dressing rooms, to lose herself. He beat her so badly that even his sister begged her to leave. When I was still just a baby, he told her he would kill her if she tried.

"You'll kill me if I stay too," she told him, and walked out. She was only a block away when a van full of men stopped and pulled her inside. They took her somewhere where no one was. She thought she would die. After they left her, she collected what was left of her clothes and started walking. Mark brought flowers to the hospital. He leaned close to her face, as if for a kiss.

"I told you," he said.

He was supposed to be her escape from God, but he saw himself as one. When she first met him, she was a preacher's daughter, tired of wearing dresses and keeping her hair long and being told she was sinful. With him, she had to wear concealing clothes to hide the bruises, her long hair became something he could grab, and everything she did was still a punishable sin. Life was just a matter of submitting herself to one almighty or another. At least the drugs were like a choice. When she took them, I imagine, she could touch heaven. She left her body and all its pain and unholy properties. Nothing on Earth was real.

INDIANAPOLIS MOTELS WERE our haunts. We stayed when we could afford to and sometimes when we couldn't, sneaking out in the early morning without paying, back when you didn't need a credit card to rent a cheap room. Mark and Mom took the bed closest to the door since I was afraid of someone breaking in during the middle of the night. They would protect me, I reasoned, before the intruder could get to me.

The motels were for when they were high, though I didn't know that then. If I try to draw connections, I can remember that on days when we stayed at the motels, they slept heavily, with their mouths open, so far away from me that I could pry their eyelids open and they wouldn't wake up or even see me. They kept the shades drawn, the air conditioner cranked up, and the blankets over their heads. Since I couldn't wake them, I'd sit close to the TV with the volume at 1 and watch Jerry Springer with his spaghetti-water hair and round glasses, or Ricki Lake, who looked like she would have soft hands.

TV could only entertain me for so long, and eventually I would try shaking Mom or Mark, or standing on the bed and saying, "I love you ten times more than you can say today!" It wouldn't work, so I would alternate between watching TV and patting their faces and whispering things like "That lady on the show has a belly button piercing" into their ears until they swatted me away. I tried too, sometimes, sleeping just to pass the time. I'd jam myself between them and try to get tired in the warmth, but my brain was always too daytime to pretend to be nighttime. When I couldn't stand it anymore, I might accidentally pull open the curtains or pretend to be a person knocking on the door. Or jump on their bed, tug on the blankets, and sing, "Wake up! Wake up! Wake up!" until my mother wrenched them out of my hands and told me, "Go swimming or something. I mean, fuck!"

I'd go to the pool and do cannonballs and pencil dives and dog paddle laps until my eyes burned and my head ached. Then I'd go to the front and get myself a cup of coffee with as many sugar packets as I could fit in my hands and the little cups of sweet creamer if they had it. I liked to drink it and watch people and think, We're all here on business. Anything to pass the time so that when I finally went back to the room, they might be up.

I don't know if anyone had told me that you could talk to God by then. If someone had, I imagine I would have all the time, because I was lonely. I might have asked God to please let me breathe underwater, or for a never-ending box of mozzarella sticks, or for better channels on the motel TV. My mom talked to God all the time, to say thank you for the food before we ate, to ask why things were happening, and sometimes for reasons I couldn't understand late at night when I was supposed to be asleep.

"God," she would whimper, and I listened from inside the red dark of my blankets. They were making some kind of magic, I knew, though I didn't understand yet. I felt it in the humid, blurry smell and light in the room. The way the rattle of the air conditioner suddenly sounded important. A ritual, and the only thing missing was me.

Now, I think I know it was a ritual for getting out of your body. It can work even when you don't want it to.

Maybe I was three years old. I could have been four or five or six. Maybe I am always three years old.

Mark must have noticed me being awake that night. I don't know how else it would have started. He must have told me to come over, or maybe he came and got me out of my bed. Maybe I went over by myself. I just don't know. I can't remember. I promise you, I can't remember.

What I do remember is that they made me naked like they were. My mother's eyes were barely open. He showed me what to do to her body. She sat up and showed me what to do to his body. They had me lie on my back. He put a pillow over my face. In case I needed to scream, he said, though I didn't, not the whole time. I just breathed into the pillow and wondered, if I didn't turn my face to the side for air, how long it would take me to suffocate.

I DON'T REMEMBER where we were when my mother told me she was sorry. Her voice was shaking. Mark had drugged her, she said. Otherwise, she would never do something like that. It must have been the next day or soon after.

I can't even see her face. I'm sure I said the words she needed to hear in response, not really knowing what they meant. What I knew was that it was something she wished hadn't happened. Like the time she'd cashed a check and then walked outside and the wind blew the money out of her hands and into the sky, so far away that there was no hope of tracking it down. She'd stood there, clinging to the one bill that she'd managed to hold on to, staring off toward where the rest had gone, whimpering, "God, no. God, please." Like it was impossible that it had really happened. I knew that if I never talked about what happened in the motel again, I could perform a kind of miracle akin to reversing the wind.

To this day, I can't help but get caught up in this kind of magical thinking. Writing this now, I feel like I could go back to the last page and carry my younger self out of the motel before it happened. I would take her to that billboard next to the White River Bridge with the truck on it that had real light-up headlights because it was her and Grandma's favorite. She'd tell me the plot of her favorite *Tales from the Crypt* episodes until I noticed her yawning, and then I'd take her back. By then, Mom and Mark would be asleep, meaning she was safe. Not from Mark, but at least from this one night, which would never happen again. Because I believe Mom, that she would never have touched me if Mark hadn't drugged her. I need to believe that there is a drug strong enough to take your mind so far away from Earth that your body can be possessed and do things that you never would have.

I CAN'T WRITE a story about myself as the sad, quiet child of two drug addicts. That's not how it was, even when it was. To me, sleeping in the car was normal. Better, it was comfy and fun. I loved my bed made of clothes inside a trash bag that I sank into slowly like Uncle Fester from the *Addams Family* movie. I loved the orange glow of streetlights when we parked to sleep and I could poke my fingers into the black plastic until it was puckered all over. I loved the motels and their swimming pools and trashy daytime TV channels. Staying in one place was boring. We got to travel. Nobody could tell us what to do.

When they were high, though I didn't know that's why they were talking so loud and fast, everything was fun. Mark would find big, empty parking lots and do donuts just to make me laugh, and my mom would lean the top half of her body out the window and scream, "WHOOOO!" as the tires squealed and a grey plume rose up around us.

"Let's take her to Chuck E. Cheese," my mom would say, looking over my head.

"Britters, you want to see a circus?"

"The park?"

"Six Flags!"

"Go-carting! I've always loved go-carting!"

We went laser-tagging, roller-skating, to carnivals, to see any movie I wanted, rolled down whatever hill I pointed out as we drove. Everything I did was worth celebrating. Once, on a putt-putt course, I smacked a ball over the fence and yelled "FOUR" like people on TV. Mark lifted me over his head and spun me around, saying I was an athlete. Over his shoulder, at each revolution, I saw my mother on the ground, her mouth wide open, cackling so hard it looked like she was hurt.

HE WOULD KILL for us. That's what he said. That's how much he loved us. When "How Do I Live" by LeAnn Rimes came on the radio, he told us it was our song. The song came out in 1997, so I must have been at least four years old by then. He held Mom's hand, bringing it up to his lips when LeAnn sang the chorus. Outside our car, our motel room, our booth in the restaurant, nothing and nobody else mattered. We would all die without each other.

When Mom got pregnant, he told her she couldn't keep it.

"That's your little brother or sister," she told me, and placed my hands on her flat stomach. Mark put his hands on her stomach too and took the baby away. Afterward, she lay on her side and wouldn't speak. I didn't know how to grieve yet, especially for someone who hadn't been born, but I lay beside her anyway until she was ready to get up.

THE POSSUM LIVED under the sink before we moved in. I wanted to let it stay there, but Mark got rid of it. I didn't think to ask how. For the first time, I had my own bedroom. Right next to theirs. We built a fort out of cardboard boxes for me to sleep in. I decorated with trinkets I'd gotten into the habit of stealing: a lawn gnome from the neighbor's yard, a traffic cone, colorful translucent marbles plucked out of the water fountain on Mark's mom's porch. In my room, in my box fort, I played perverse games. I impaled my doll atop the traffic cone, legs splayed wide, plastic body impenetrable. I drew pictures of Mom and Mark's naked bodies on all the pages of my scrapbook. I lay on my back on the thin cardboard and covered my eyes with my arm, feeling the ghost sensations of that night on my body, seething with anger at the wall in between us.

ACROSS THE HALL from my room was Mark's CB radio room. It was against the rules to go in without him. If I tried, an alarm tripped that sounded like screaming, and Mark came down the hallway in wide strides with one hand raised, eyes hardened. There was the one time he took me into the radio room. The radio was on a desk against a wall, silver and hulking. He sat me on his lap and told me to sing for his friends. I sang "Twinkle, Twinkle, Little Star," embarrassed by my own high-pitched voice.

"Isn't that beautiful?" he asked, rubbing hot circles on my back, and several men crackled through the speakers that yes, I sounded just beautiful.

I was always on Mark's lap, now that I think about it. In one of the earliest memories I can reach, I'm sitting on his lap and looking at a piece of paper where he has drawn stick figures running from falling bombs.

"One," he says, pointing to a bomb in the sky.

"Two," he says, pointing to another.

And so on. Until I got it, in that vague childhood way of under-standing, that things could be counted. He was always teaching me. How to count, how to abbreviate the months, how to run the rub-ber blade of the gas station squeegee across the windshield from top to bottom so the water didn't drip down over your clean swipes. Mark taught me that you could lift the blanket on things and see the legs moving around underneath it, the truth. How to smile with my missing teeth showing, to be disarming, because if you are cute, you can get away with things. How to grasp my neck and say "Ouch" in a mattress warehouse so the owner handed over a stack of bills to keep us from suing. In the apartment, in the bed he shared with my mom, he taught me how to please him.

I'VE TRIED TO write about this before. That room with its white walls and the white blankets. Not the motel room, not that one time with my mother, but their bedroom, many times. I've thought there was only one way to tell it: he took me in the room and hurt me. Any more nuance than that and I would become a co-conspirator, just as culpable as him. I've been ashamed that he didn't drag me into the room kicking and screaming.

Instead, I followed him in there, holding his hand, excited to do something together that made him happy. After, I followed him to the bathroom and sat on the edge of the tub with my belly cramping while he cleaned himself in the sink. It would be two decades before I would find words for the nuance and a therapist would tell me that I didn't share responsibility for the sexual abuse, and that belly cramp would finally unclench.

My mother wasn't home when it happened. I want you to know that. Years later, an uncle would tell me that he babysat me when Mom and Mark were both working. "We taught you," he'd say, "to tell people who asked you where your mommy was, 'She working it!'" Meaning that my mother was stripping. Meaning that, while I was in the white room with Mark, my mother was also learning how to please men with her body.

The dressing room, she would tell me later, was where she really started using. The dancers passed drugs around to cope. She held off for a long time, she says, but Mark encouraged her to use. So they could make more money. Because the drugs made her more pliant. Or because they helped her not think about what they did with me at the motel.

HERE'S A STORY I tell myself: After the night at the motel, Mark and Mom talked about it. She never wanted anything like that to happen again. Okay, he told her, of course. He was horrified too. He was lying. She wasn't. They had to make life better for me, they agreed. He sold more, she danced. We got the apartment. Life was better. I probably didn't even remember, she thought. I clung to her leg when it was time for her to go to work. Dragged, kicking and screaming, begging her not to leave me. To take me with her. That's just how kids are, though. They want their mothers. It broke her heart, but she had to go. Mark gently pried me away and held me so she could leave. As the door closed between us, she looked at her baby in his arms and thought maybe the worst was in our rearview mirror. So blurry now, she's not sure if she really saw anything.

THEY FOUND MY sketch pad. All the pictures of our naked bodies, overlapping in 2D, outlines crisscrossing. Some showed the two of them. Others included me, or some other combination. Did my mother notice the drawings of just me and Mark? Did she think they were simply a cropped version of the ones I'd drawn of all of us? Did I draw any of just the two of us?

"You can't draw pictures like this," Mark told me, squatting down to face me. He held the sketch pad open to a page where the two of them were rendered side by side in crayon. The cartoonish breasts and genitals. "People will take you away from us."

My mother stood in the doorway, biting her thumbnail.

My body burned with shame. It felt obvious, once they'd said it, that it was wrong. To draw dirty pictures. He tore the drawings out of the sketch pad and took them into the other room. Did he keep them?

Instead, they told me, I should draw things like butterflies. The two lumps for one wing and then the other. The long body in between. Maybe a smiling little face.

SOMEONE REPORTED US to Child Protective Services. We were at a motel again when they showed me the letter they'd gotten in the mail, though I couldn't read what it said.

"Now, you have to pay attention," Mark told me. "They're going to ask you certain questions and you have to answer just like I tell you or they'll take you away."

He sat on one bed and Mom sat on the other. I slouched in a chair in front of the two of them, desperately wanting to be done with the mock interview.

"What should you say if they ask you if anyone touches you?"

"You mean, like a hug?" I recited, cocking my head to appear innocent.

"Good. Now what do you say if they ask if anyone has touched your private parts?"

"No, I can wipe by myself."

We ran through questions until I could barely sit still anymore. Don't touch the dolls on their privates. Don't draw bad pictures. Don't tell people I know that sex is when two naked people jump on top of each other like I told Grandma and Uncle Jon, who thankfully just laughed. Play dumb. Be cute. Be disarming.

When he was satisfied, Mark threw his hat in the air and yelled, "Yippee! We're done!" We got pizza and Pringles, and watched a movie. I don't remember what movie.

The actual interview was in a tall glass building in downtown Indianapolis. Mom and I took an elevator to a floor where the windows reached the ceiling. A woman in a suit took me to an observation room with a short drawing table and toys. She told me I could draw while we talked, so I started with the butterfly's wings.

In the elevator back down, I held my mom's hand.

"That was way easier than you said—" I started, but she squeezed my hand to tell me to be quiet. I looked over at the man next to us. He wasn't paying attention. Beyond him, I saw our reflections in the metal wall. The bottom half of my mother and the stranger, and me.

MARK'S SISTER, DANA, was my mom's best friend. At Dana's house, I watched my favorite movies—*An American Tail*, *All Dogs Go to Heaven*, *Titanic*, and *The Pagemaster*—while they sat at the kitchen table playing cards. They alternated between cackling and speaking in lean-in tones. Always engulfed in what was on the screen, I didn't hear. Dana had curly brown hair, bags under her eyes, and a voice that indicated a life of smoking. Her boyfriend, a quiet man with long, thin hair, was named Billy, but I called him Belly for the incredibly round beer belly that protruded from his otherwise skinny frame. Their daughters, Brooke and Kara, were older than me, but they took me with them to the park, to get groceries from the corner market, and to smoke in the gutted car in the alley out back. "Try it," they told me, and handed me the cigarette. I inhaled and then coughed and coughed, launching the peppermint that had been in my mouth into the ashtray with unintended precision.

I was a fun plaything. On command, I would recite lines from movies or sing whatever song they requested. They glued long acrylics on my tiny nails and then laughed until they were on the floor as I desperately tried to remove them to escape the horrible sucking sensation when I touched anything. When I spent the night, Brooke and Kara argued over whose room I would sleep in. Which sister pushed my pajama dress up at night, I can't remember. It didn't make a difference to me. It was routine. My body went soft, to accommodate, whenever anyone touched me. Sometimes, when my mom was putting my shoes on, she had to remind me to flex my foot so it would go in the shoe because I felt the hand on my calf and immediately ceded control.

My mom loved Brooke and Kara. They were like her other daughters, she said. The three of us would pile onto the hood of the car and cling with our fingers between the hood and windshield as she steered us around the potholes that marred the neighborhood.

Between the two of them, I'd watch the sky slide by above, and then I'd turn and look in the window at my mom until she looked back and winked.

"You can't do that in the city," Dana chided when she found out.

DANA'S HOUSE WAS all brown and orange tones. Jalousie windows on the front porch, frosted mirror over the couch, wood-paneled walls. The velvet comforter with the image of a howling wolf on Dana's bed that I ran my hand over, pretending that I was petting the real creature while I told her.

It had been Mom's idea that I go to Dana after I finally said out loud what Mark did in the white room whenever she wasn't home. I don't know how old I was. I can barely remember how she reacted. She said I should tell Dana I was "molested." The word felt sticky and uncomfortable.

I don't know why she had me tell Dana, but I can create a reason if I try. Dana was the person she went to when Mark blackened her eyes or broke her ribs. Maybe my mom saw her as a keeper of terrible secrets. Or maybe she still believed that circumstances couldn't not change when you acknowledged them to someone. It didn't occur to me until I was writing this that my mom didn't tell me not to tell Dana about what she also did. It wouldn't have mattered. I'd already tucked that part away, and maybe she had too.

"You shouldn't make things up" was all Dana said when I unstuck the words about Mark. Her brother could be abusive, but he wasn't that kind of evil.

I don't know how many more times we saw Dana before we fled from Mark for the last time. In my mind, I imagine her sitting there after I left the room, looking at the spot where I rubbed the wolf blanket in the wrong direction and got his hackles up. She didn't think about what I'd told her or about what her daughters tried to tell her, or anything at all. Dust gathered on the glass panes of the jalousie window, on the lip of the ashtray in the bathroom window, on her arms. She just sat there, waiting for the wolf to pounce or smooth out, forgetting the hand that had unsettled it in the first place, and the girl attached to that hand. Until years later, when she sat up at the sound of knocking on her front door. An old friend, visiting with her daughter, so much older now. In middle school, her friend is saying. Isn't she beautiful? Hasn't she gotten so big? Dana can barely hear her. The wolf is howling so loud. She reaches out with both hands and grips the girl's upper arms.

"I'm glad you've grown out of making up stories."

FOR A WHILE, I had babysitters, maybe to keep me from being alone with Mark. There were the people with the long white wraparound couch that I ran along, pretending I was a character in *The Matrix* running on the wall. There was the older man who wore argyle socks and served tea that we both sipped in silence as we stared across the table at each other. There was the single father and his pasty, rambunctious son who always wanted to watch *Alvin and the Chipmunks* movies, which I hated. I don't remember the son's name, just that when we played out back, he had me stand on a stack of plywood and pretended to auction me off.

"Who wants this woman?" he'd say, and I would turn this way and that until he informed me that I was sold or "No one wants you."

In his bedroom, he showed me his Disney books and told me about how, at night, Ariel came out of the pages and danced for him. Then he'd have me lie on the bed so he could push my shirt up and suck on my chest. Once, a neighbor boy came over to play and he offered the boy a turn. I was lying flat with my hands at my sides, waiting.

"I don't think so," the boy said, watching my face, and then he left.

When my mom came back to get me, I reached for her to pick me up and then wrapped my legs around her so the babysitter's son couldn't grab my dangling feet.

"She's mine! *Mine!*" he'd scream, jumping to get me back.

THERE WAS THE boy in elementary school. Must have been in the second or third grade. He forced his hand down my pants on the bus in the bright early morning. I made a feeble attempt to turn away, but my mind slipped off and my body went slack. When I told the school counselor, a white woman with sad eyebrows and pock-marked cheeks, the boy was called to the office.

We know now that children who molest other children are likely victims themselves, mirroring what someone else did to them. If anyone had known better, they might have investigated the boy's home life. Instead, I sat outside the principal's office and listened to the hard thuds of the paddle and the boy's pained wails. I think of his legs as he leaned into me on the bus. Too short to reach the ground.

Bearing The Mark

I used to wonder if it was me. Some quality that made people want to do hushed and unclean things to me. In the swirling childhood years, a neighbor boy would lead me under an abandoned truck bed to "play doctor." A babysitter would fill my mouth with Dawn dish soap while holding my face with her manicured nails pressing into my neck and cheeks. A man in a trailer would spit in my underwear to get me ready for him. Another neighbor boy would drop me into his parents' empty above-ground pool with his pet rabbit and throw rocks at me, forcing me to keep the animal safe with my body as it scratched at me to get away.

I've wondered if there was some kind of weakness they all saw in me. Could it be my skin, my eyes, my hair, darker than theirs, but only slightly so? Was I an exotic thing to experiment on, a curiosity? Did Mark leave a mark on me that let others know I was to be used?

I'm not asking you. I know better than to wonder now, but still, sometimes, I wonder. Without solid answers—without the ability to ask these people what was in their minds while they acted on me—I can only twist assumptions into stories. I can give them reasons or I can take reason from them. They were holding cruelty in their minds, trying it out on a vessel that didn't count. They regret it. They relish it. They hated me. They were indifferent to me. It's because of how they saw me. It had nothing to do with me.

When I say that my father was a rapist, it's doubly true. Mark wasn't biologically related to me, but he was the first person in my life I attached the idea of Dad to. As I got older and tried to figure myself out, it felt like he wrote himself into my body like DNA, stomped up the spiral staircase of my double helixes, dragging his nails across the walls as he went.

All I know about my biological father is that he planted me in my mother against her will. I know that he looked like me, and that I look like him. Black hair, brown eyes, and tan skin. I wonder all the time, though I have guilt about wondering, what his singing voice is like, if we have the same dinosaur knuckles, the same tendency to get out of bed and chug orange juice in the middle of the night, standing in the light of the fridge, always spilling a little on our chest. I want to love him. I want not to want to love him. Sometimes, I close my eyes and cradle my own face and pretend I want nothing.

I used to be afraid that I was evil, that I'd come out this way, maybe because of how I was conceived, that I inherited too much monstrosity, that I was marked like Cain. It was satisfying, in a navel-gazing, scab-peeling kind of way, to imagine that there was something exceptionally terrible inside me. I believed that I could hate myself without hurting anyone. If I was going to sit alone with my shame, maybe, but now I've invited you here. I owe us all a more thoughtful conclusion.

Nothing that happened to me made me monstrous. The only way for me to become monstrous is if I give in to my ugliest impulses. I didn't inherit monstrosity either. Without having met him, all I can really know that I inherited from my biological father are his physical features. I find his eyes, his hair, his skin. These features were monstrous to me growing up. I wanted to have blue eyes like my mother and my brother. I wanted to have light hair and milk skin. I wanted to look like everyone around me, like the people I loved.

Not once in my childhood did I think I was beautiful. Not in my imagination or school pictures or bathroom mirror or spirit. I used to keep my arms crossed behind my back so I wouldn't see the contrast of my skin against my white church dress, and everyone said how polite I was. You can make any connection you want if you're already looking for it.

"He was . . . darker than you," my mother told me one of the few times I asked her what my biological father looked like. A squirm-ing conversation. Race was one of those things we just didn't talk about. In the absence of anything else, I learned about people who looked like me through late '90s and early 2000s media and school-yard jokes. Through the exaggerated fake accents and dramatized shoot-outs and punch lines, I discerned that we were contemptible. It would take me longer to learn how our country saw men who were as dark as my mother said my father was. How there was a story older than me or my father or his father or his father, about how they wanted to claim and hurt women who were as white as my mother. How, regardless of what I knew or how I wanted to be, people saw me as a living confirmation of a hideous American paranoia.

Before I started writing this, I was ready to leave my self-hatred behind without questioning it, like a birthmark that I could keep my shirt pulled down over. Now I'm lifting my shirt to show you the thick brown zigzag splotch above my belly button, where my mother's umbilical cord didn't want to let me go. It's darker than the rest of me, maybe the same color as my father. Maybe he has the same one above his own belly button. It's not beautiful or hideous. Not everything has to be. You get to see it from an angle inaccessible to me, so I'll never really know exactly how it looks to you. I hope that showing you like this means you'll gaze more lovingly than I have.

CHAPTER 5

Confusion Of Tongues

My mom left Mark for good, eventually. We disappeared. To my grandparents' house, to shelters, to whoever would take us in and not report back. We had friends who let us stay with them short-term, for a night or two, or just sit at their table and visit for a while. Their homes flit by in a blur of years and details—puke-colored shag carpet, velvet Elvis portrait, wind chimes tinkling, gritty Kool-Aid, magic pink Pepto Bismol that I chugged after everyone was asleep because it looked like a magic potion, *Aladdin* game on Sega Genesis, fridge that had a freezer drawer full of pop-sicles. I don't remember most of their faces, but their voices filter down from adult heights. They tell me please don't stand on the couch, don't sit so close to the TV, don't eat off the floor, don't put that chicken back after you ate the skin, don't tell anyone, don't stick your fingers in the fan. Mom said that when you were a guest in someone's house, you should be polite, so I tried to be quiet and keep myself inside an invisible square of space where I wouldn't break anything.

"She's so well behaved," adults would say, and I understood that people love a quiet child. If I was lovable, our hosts might let us stay longer.

Children in movies and TV shows slapped cherubic hands against their cheeks in surprise and hid bashful faces behind shrugged shoulders and marched with silly purpose to inane child tasks. I knew that reenacting them would make people love me the way they loved TV children, so I studied commercial kids and movies like *The Little Rascals*. I said, "Uh-oh, silly me!" if I dropped something, or, "Well, how about that!" when I looked at a newspaper.

People laughed and called me a card, but I didn't always get it right. If I acted like Tarzan and beat my chest and yelled, no one was charmed. If, in the spirit of Bart Simpson, I shouted, "Eat my shorts!" the reaction was lukewarm to icy irritation. If I dropped to my knees and wailed, "Ritchie!" into the sky like at the end of *La Bamba*, I got shushed. What I gathered was that loud and abrasive was not lovable, only sweet and demure, cheeky at most. Sometimes, hit by a wave of energy, I wanted to run and jump and sing, but I would be stricken by self-consciousness at how childish I was being, how unlovable.

Some people wouldn't love you no matter how hard you tried, Mom warned me. Some people had hate in their hearts. They would hate you for being different or for having something they didn't. You couldn't waste your time and energy on those people.

Strangers often didn't like me. I can still feel the random scorn. That man in the truck at a red light glaring down at me through our windows like I had done something wrong. The cashier who saw me pinch my finger in the conveyor belt—the black rubber sliding under my hand, the sharp snag—how her face stayed bored, but her eyes looked satisfied. A friend who, when my mom was away somewhere, said, "That kid's freaky."

I was trying to stay very still and look well behaved, resist the urge to kick my feet and feel the thud of my heels against the base of a couch. Another friend laughed and waved a hand in front of my face. "She just sits there." Can't win for losing, as Mom would say. Inside me was something unlovable that I couldn't hide.

In The Rubble Of The Tower

I still don't know how to be charming. I am supposed to be grown up now, at twenty-nine. That means so many things. The clothes I wear, the way I sit, how I answer the phone. What I allow myself to fear. How unhealed I'm allowed to be. It's all supposed to be a certain way. I am a too-long beanpole tilting under its own weight, permanently over- and undergrown, daydreaming in a work meeting about shrinking down small enough to climb inside the outlet by the door, slide along the wires, and pop out of some drainage pipe or chimney into a land where emails and fluorescent lights don't exist.

When I'm in a casual group setting, whole conversations can pass without me contributing a single word. I am content to sit back and observe my friends' faces in the dim bar light, turn the sound of their laughter over in my mind like precious seashells on the beach. You okay? someone will ask, and I'll snap to and make my attempts. Sour notes, too soft-spoken, child-voiced, scrambling to keep up as I overthink and reject versions of what I might say. Talking, finally, but so overwhelmed by the sensation of being looked at that I can't even hear what's coming out of my mouth.

There are rules I am aware of only because I can feel myself failing to follow them. The quiet appraisal of whether I am a peer or a pity. The dismissals. That testing, testing, until I can't stand to be seen. Me, the giant oaf, too big for myself, too quiet to be heard in conversation, too hot around my neck when they lean in and ask me to repeat. What I want is to be a whisp that no one can love or not love, that people can feel but not see, only touch in passing through.

The Whole World Had One Language

There was the crowded, warm apartment where a family lived who looked like me. Brown eyes and hair and skin. A bathroom organizer that I climbed on top of to get away from their dog. Mom, cradling me as I sniffled, my fear of the creature so strong that I forgot to be lovable. Night fell and I wouldn't sleep, worried that if I rested, the beast would get me.

"Hand me that baby." A man's accented voice.

Hesitance, then the sensation of passing from one pair of arms to another—my mother's chapped pale hands sliding away, replaced by olive hands with black knuckle hair. Pulled close, solid chest, cheek against my cheek, warm. Deep timber of his voice, singing in an unfamiliar language. I didn't understand the words to the song, but they felt like love. They put me to sleep. Later, when I asked Mom what the language was, she told me it was Spanish.

"Can you teach me Spanish?" I asked.

"No," she replied after a moment. "I don't know Spanish, but I can teach you pig Latin."

To speak pig Latin, you took the first part of a word and put it in the back, and added an -ay sound. It was easy, but if you could speak it fast enough, no one would be able to untangle what you were saying. When we drove, we spoke in pig Latin, words turned inside out. We had code names for certain restaurants and gas station chains, songs with alternate lyrics. Our own language, protected by ciphers.

I imagined the walkway spiraling around the Tower of Babel had been stretched out and flattened as the tower fell, and we were driving on it, rising on an imperceptible incline, higher and higher, leaving our old language until we were the only ones who could understand each other up in the clouds, up and up, until we flew away like Thelma and Louise, like the end of *Grease*.

"I'm ungry-hay," I'd say.

"Ee-way ont-day av-hay oney-may," she'd respond, her mouth widening to accommodate the strange vowels.

I kept forgetting. It's hard to remember why you can't have food when you're hungry. Like pig Latin, hunger circles in on itself. I'd feel my stomach pinching in and in, rumbling, growling; ask when we were going to stop and get food; be reminded that we didn't have money for food; look inside the cigarette holder for the morsels I sometimes stashed there; be reminded that I ate them, stale and mushy, already; try to focus on something else like the radio or the grain of the dashboard or Mom's breathless humming; feel my stomach pinching in and in, rumbling; etc.

"Goddammit," Mom would snap, eventually, in regular English. "I told you we don't have any money!"

I couldn't keep the information in my head any more than I could keep a meal in my stomach. What I needed was a game I could play that reminded me I was hungry: Press on my stomach, imagine the emptiness as a bubble moving around, a marble maze of intestines. Match the pitch of my stomach gurgles. Imagine someone running alongside the car, dodging road signs, leaping over dividers; cheering them on in my head with a chant that went, *I'm hungry, hungry, hungry, hungry, hungry, hungry.*

It was okay to steal sometimes, especially if you were hungry. We'd go into a gas station under the pretense of needing to use the pay phone. The smell of rolling taquitos and hot dogs and nacho cheese and Subway made our mouths and eyes water. She usually let me put the coins in, but for this trick I would wander away while she punched in the numbers. Navigate my way through rows of clean, packaged food, leather hats, snow globes, shot glasses, VHS tapes of movies about cowboys with crow's-feet, the Dolly Parton discography on cassette.

With a practiced vacant look on my face, I'd open a bag of chips or a tuna salad sandwich or a snack cake and, per her instructions, go to town. If no one stopped me, I could throw the bag away in the bathroom or hide it somewhere. If someone did stop me, I had to act like I didn't know it was wrong, lead them back to the pay phone, where I would confess to Mom, wiping guilty crumbs off my face.

"Brittany Lee Ann!" she would admonish me. "You can't just open and eat food that we haven't paid for! I don't have the money to afford that!"

The employee would usually tell her not to worry about it. They'd laugh together about how kids do the darndest things. We'd go out to the car, me hanging my head and dragging my feet, a criminal on the way to my cell. Once we were out of sight, we'd high-five, and I'd pull out whatever snack I managed to pilfer for her. Usually an iced honey bun. They were her favorite, and she always gave me the last bite.

There were also free samples at grocery stores, which we'd divide and circle like sharks, picking out crackers, cheese, deli slices. We'd pluck a few grapes from the produce section, discreetly open a can of Vienna sausages, make a handheld napkin charcuterie that we'd eat as we walked around, pretending to browse before deciding against buying anything.

Out back, the dumpster held plenty of free food.

"So wasteful," Mom said, heaving herself over the side. "Who throws away a perfectly good container of wings?"

We gorged ourselves and then unbuttoned our pants to make room for our bulging bellies. There was always the looming danger of getting caught. The humorless cashier, the busybody tattletale, one of those security cameras they had everywhere these days. Mom was afraid of the police.

"Pigs," she called them, and gripped the steering wheel tighter any time we saw a car with lights on top or that looked like it could be an undercover vehicle. Sirens made her tense up, made her say,

"Shit, shit, shit, SHIT," even though they usually passed right by or disappeared into the distance. Once, though, when I was at least old enough that I should have been in school, the sirens were for us. Lights flashed, not going around but following our car.

"Hold tight," Mom said, and sped up. We merged onto a long, curving stretch of highway, trees on either side. I clutched my seat belt as she rounded the curve and took a sharp turn down a dirt road. Our car bumped and jostled over the rough terrain, bouncing me in my seat. She steered us off the road and into a clearing, then hit the brakes and idled. We held our breath. Through the trees we saw the cop car zoom by, still blaring its sirens. Not long after, a few more passed with their lights and sirens on.

It was us against the world. She said it to me all the time.

"You and me, Brittany. That's all we have." She delivered this with her hands clenched, white knuckles, on the wheel; into my hair as she held me; through tears; between laughs; over food; in the shower. "You're the only person in this whole world I can count on."

The words made my chest feel big, like she'd knighted me, but sad too that she couldn't trust anyone else. Everyone had let her down or left her. I would never do that, I swore, and I hated those who had.

She had friends, I know, and she must have confided in them. Still, I think there was a part of herself that she never showed people. When we were alone, she wrote poetry in a spiral-bound notebook using her favorite blue ink gel pen. Curled over the page, face far away, glancing up every now and again to think.

"What do you think of this?" she'd ask and read me her poems about feeling alone and powerless, about Mark, about her love for me, about the terrible things that had happened to us. Songs without music.

"That's beautiful," I'd say, meaning it, not knowing yet how paltry my feedback was.

I couldn't read that well when she first started showing me her poems, but I asked her if I could look at the notebook anyway. She let me, and I flipped through pages of her loopy blue cursive, trying to match up the words she recited with the shapes there.

I knew I wasn't writing anything, but I liked to take a pencil and trace the letters on the back of each page, writing her poetry backward. When I was done, I'd show her the blue-grey nonsense.

"That's beautiful," she'd say.

Benjamin

Mom held Ben in her lap and ran her hand through his hair until his eyes drooped. She hummed and rocked, her own eyes closed.

"That's your baby brother," she told me as she laid him down. "You have to look out for him."

I watched him in the back seat when we drove, his body slack with dream. Sunshine settled in his blond curls, the barely visible downy hair on his cheeks, the soft, veined skin of his eyelids. In the visor mirror, through the space between the headrest and seat, I watched him breathe. His hands curled like rose petals, like Fritos, like no reason to ball them into fists.

Mom watched him too, in quick glances at the rearview mirror. Her eyes darted from the road in front of us to the road behind us to Ben sleeping to me watching her watch him. She'd wink at me. When Mom winked, her mouth crooked up on one side, creating creases in her cheek. A wink meant "You and me, that's all we have." It meant I was no baby. It meant we were best friends, conspirators, and nobody could ever get in between us or understand us like we understood each other. We stayed awake, kept a lookout.

The car could get so warm, though, on a good sunny day. A safe, cozy cocoon. I'd rest my head on the door, the plastic heated against my face. Look out the window at blankets of cloud shadows sliding over the land. I'd try to sit up, but my body wanted to be soft, so it would sag against the fabric of the seat, settling into familiar grooves. Until I entered that dark pink space where I could only hear, feel my eyelids, twitch, know that I was drifting. I wanted to stay awake with Mom, to keep an eye on Ben, to see the world come and go, but trying to avoid sleep when it wants you is like trying to stay at the bottom of a pool when your lungs are full of air. I pumped the arms and legs of my mind and still floated away, out of my body, out of the car, up into the sky, my bubbles leaving me, rising, to pop somewhere I didn't know yet.

Scattered Over The Face Of The Earth

Forgetting that I have a brother is as unthinkable as forgetting the sound of your own voice, but there were times in my childhood when I did. Times when the years-long custody battles swung in Ben's dad's favor and I didn't see him for weeks or months. Caught up in my own mind, in the barn, or in the endless tunnel-vision survival drive with Mom, I forgot anything that wasn't right in front of me, including Ben.

There was the classroom icebreaker at one school where we stood every time the teacher read off a fact that matched our lives.

"Stand if you're an only child," she said.

I stood, thinking of driving with Mom.

"Stand if you have a little brother or sister," she said next.

As if I'd been zapped, I remembered Ben, my little brother. Three and a half years younger than me. My best friend. I stood up, hoping no one would notice the contradiction. Hoping he wouldn't feel the betrayal out there, wherever he was.

A Common Speech

I was mean to Ben. Sometimes in the way siblings are mean to each other, but sometimes just to try on cruelty. When we stayed in shelters, I'd claim the top bunk just to win, and then spend the night seething because he was sleeping next to Mom on the bunk below. Seeing our mom love him the way she had previously loved me, as the baby, made my mouth water and my underarms itch.

"You're getting too big to carry," she'd tell me with Ben on her hip, and I would imagine him being left in a gas station while Mom and I drove away.

I didn't have the language yet, but I knew that I had always been at the mercy of adults. Whatever they said, I obeyed, whether I wanted to or not. Now there was this kid who was smaller than me. If I told him to go get me a Sprite from the fridge, he would. If I told him to push me on the swing, he would. Green can sweating on his hands, legs planted in the mulch. I felt like a villain with her henchman, and Ben just glowed with joy to be around me. For all the times I closed him in a cabinet or let him go down a tall slide by himself after I told him I would be right behind, he brought me dandelions and held the end of my blanket cape when we played pretend.

His cherubic appearance and nature made stark the ugliness I felt roiling in me all the time. He was blond and sweet, and I was a dark thing with a gummy smile and a gaze that unsettled people. Still, when we were together, we clicked. He didn't act like I was strange, and I kept him company when the adults were preoccupied. Though my animosity toward him could resurface when our mother let him sit in the front seat or when he was rewarded for sharing and I was deemed a brat, I appreciated his companionship and willingness to follow me where others would not.

Before Ben could talk, we operated on a nonverbal frequency. We explored together, breaking into the shelter storage units or our grandfather's tool shed, climbing among the forbidden items while Mom napped. We found Flintstones Vitamins and ate them all in handfuls, crouched like cavemen. To reach an item from high up, I got on my hands and knees and he stood tippy-toe on my back. He kept watch while I picked locks with a paperclip.

When he got better at talking, Mom taught him pig Latin. It broke my heart. I watched his marshmallow cheeks puff and contract, making sense of the sounds as they rearranged.

"On't-day each-tay im-hay!" I begged her, but he intercepted the message, translated it, stole it. I felt the nose of the car tipping down, declining, but we were still just moving forward. She looked at me in the rearview mirror, apologetic, but with blue eyes that she shared with him and not me.

When she was pregnant with me, she'd told us, she had woken up one night to heavenly bright light shining in the doorway of her bedroom. Once her eyes adjusted, she saw a boy standing there. Blond hair and blue eyes. A vision of the child she would have. Except, she would have me instead and the vision wouldn't come true until her next pregnancy. The story was supposed to be a sign that we were always all meant to be together, but to me it sounded like Ben was God's gift and I was an unfated obstacle.

What Ben and I most wanted was to be around her. We secretly wanted her to ourselves, but always had to share. When she holed up on the third floor of the barn, blowing her cigarette smoke out the little sliding window with her legs drawn up on her chair, we sat on the ground in front of her with our eyes on her face. If she was in the bathroom, and she would sometimes stay in there for hours, we waited outside, singing her songs and drawing pictures to push underneath the door for her. At night, we laid our heads on the hard bone of her chest. Ben on one side and me on the other. She hummed and the sound rattled around inside like summer bugs trapped in a jar. It must have been exhausting to be loved that much all the time. Little hands reaching for hers, tracing the seam on the side of her jeans, pinching the loose skin on her stomach left over from where our bodies had stretched hers. Kneading her and needing her, and she was so tired, so she left, and then Ben and I kept each other company.

When she was gone, we stayed at the barn. The move was done by then, and our grandparents had filled it completely. It had such presence, with its coal-black body and stark white metal roof that, when we said something like "I'll meet you at the barn" or "I must have left it at the barn. Well, it's gone now," we said it like The Barn. A proper noun.

You have to understand The Barn to understand everything else. That place we avoided until we couldn't anymore, always standing in wait for us.

I DON'T WANT to take you to The Barn, but I'm going to. You have to know that The Barn swallowed everything that entered it. Swallowed up light, sound, and time alike. Curdled all of it. Inside The Barn is a mess of years indecipherable from one another, so that when I look back, I see myself at many ages. I look down at my hands on the overflowing, stained kitchen table in a memory and I cannot tell how old the hands are. They could be my hands now.

CHAPTER 6

The Tower

Our grandparents were hoarders, though no one would use that word for years. When we did, we would argue over who was the actual hoarder. Grandpa, whose car overflowed with papers and tools and food wrappers to the point where he couldn't see out any of the windows aside from the windshield and driver's side. Or Grandma, who kept shoeboxes of photos and sent me back inside the gas station for a receipt if I didn't get one. "It's good business" was all she'd say when I asked why, but then the receipts would accumulate all over The Barn amid the coupons and comics she'd clipped out.

The truth is, it was both of them. They had been born not long after the Great Depression ended, and growing up in the shadow of the dust bowl made them want to save everything. Although I had assumed that the mess I'd seen in the house by the highway was the result of being in the middle of a move, once they moved to The Barn and had the space to spread out, everything simply accrued.

The inside of The Barn resembled a stuff city from an *I Spy* book. Everywhere you looked there were sales ads, newspapers, church pamphlets, paperwork, file folders, books, shoeboxes, clothes, toys, toy packaging, bulk foods, tools, crafting supplies, sewing material, disposable cameras, film to be developed, old film slides, miscellaneous chairs and TV trays, tablecloths, disposable flatware, wrapping paper, gift bags, porcelain dolls, collectors' switchblades, board games, card games, puzzles, Bibles, instruction manuals, coat hangers, blankets, pillows, sheets, file cabinets, bassinets, cribs, etc. Every surface was covered except for the ones where we sat or slept or ate, and sometimes even those. Items were added and buried under other items and shifted from time to time, but The Barn never changed. Five or six elegantly decorated fake Christmas trees stayed up year-round, gathering dust and occasionally dropping bulbs that ever so slowly slid from the prickled branches and plunked down beneath, where they stayed. In its unnatural stillness, The Barn was the antithesis of the car. Planted so firmly on its foundation that a tornado had once engulfed it and only peeled away the roof.

The Barn was a monument to what happens when a West Virginia hillbilly makes a lucky investment in a plot of land and gets ahold of some money. The ornately carved moldings gathered cobwebs. The carpets, pocked by furniture indents and spilled food, ended at cheap linoleum tile that was always sticky and spotted with shoe prints. The top of the table was covered in a protective pane of thick glass, but you wouldn't know unless you came for a holiday party, when we were allowed to clear off the two-foot-tall stacks of my grandfather's business papers.

When Ben and I got lice, which happened frequently, Grandma did our lice treatments in the kitchen sink. Eyes stinging, lungs pinched, and scalp raw. Mayonnaise and plastic-grocery-bag caps to suffocate the little bugs. Nearby, the fridge hummed a dirge. None of the counters were clean, and none of the ingredients inside the cabinets ever seemed to add up to a real meal, so we ate a lot of ramen, which my grandfather bought in bulk from Big Lots, with things like mustard and eggs and chips stirred in.

Other than at family parties, we never ate at the dining room table. If we weren't at the Golden Corral, KFC, or a local place called Charlie's that had a stuffed gorilla in a cage out front, we just made a little nest in the trash on the kitchen table where our dish would fit. My grandfather's non-restaurant dishes were always oatmeal with Bacon Bits, bread with peanut butter and syrup, or the ramen noodles, which he called roman nooderals.

The long hallway that spanned the length of The Barn was left dark. Only a few windows let in any natural light, and that was absorbed by the mountains of stuff. To traverse the hallway, you had to walk sideways, sidle through garbage and treasures, inextricable. Amid the smaller items, there were hutches and chests of drawers, imported from France, and a toddler bed that I slept on into middle school in the hallway across from the stuffed couch where Grandma started sleeping after my grandfather discovered Viagra.

Along the hallway were doors that led to the communal bathroom with its claw-foot tub and narrow shower; my grandparents' bedroom, where my grandfather eventually died; and my grandmother's sewing room, which eventually evolved into a craft room that devolved into a storage room. For a while, Mom, Ben, and I lived in the back bedroom, which was technically the main suite. It was the biggest bedroom in the house and had a private bathroom complete with a claw-foot tub, a standing shower, a jacuzzi, two sinks with medicine cabinets, and, of course, a toilet, or, as my grandmother would say, a commode, or terlet. It wasn't really our room, though. For one, my grandfather stored his many imported pieces of furniture in there and we were not allowed to move them around.

Grandpa and Grandma didn't believe in television. We believed in TV very much, though, so Mom hid one under a blanket on the other side of the very large and ornate bed, the headboard of which could theoretically destroy your skull if you leaned back fast enough. One time we were too slow covering it up and my grandfather tore it from the wall and took it outside as my mom chased him, crying, "Daddy, please, not our TV!" Ben and I, both still small enough to fit, crawled under the bed and hid, so we didn't see him get the chain out of his tool room and smash our TV in the backyard.

Without the TV, Ben and I spent most of our time outside. We played in the crick, catching salamanders and poking at the craw-dad crags. Life abounded outside The Barn. There were always cats around, and Puzzums of course. Grandma kept a bag of food hidden, which she would scatter on the porch when Grandpa wasn't home, and which he would scrape away with his foot when he returned.

We gave the cats names like Mamacat and BigBoy, and when they inevitably became swollen with a new litter of kittens, we made a game out of finding their secret birthing spot. Usually, it was under the second-floor balcony or in the storage area that had never been converted from horse stalls and still had a dirt floor and a loft, where I would often climb and dangle my legs and read, or just look out at the field and think. We claimed a kitten for ourselves from each new batch, hoping they would live.

Outside cats had a high mortality rate. We often saw them from the car window on the way to church, dashed on the road. Cats, dogs, deer, raccoons, skunks. Crumpled up like dirty laundry on the shoulder or contorted in the grass. They had been hit by cars, but sometimes they looked like they'd just walked over, lay down in the gravel, and started bleeding.

Only foolish pets got hit, we figured. Puzzums had been living beside that highway for years and hadn't been hit once. She knew what cars did and she stayed away. Other dogs we'd gotten had lasted days or even months running through the enormous yard behind The Barn, but when it wasn't enough, they wandered and turned into bodies. The cats too. We begged our grandfather to let us keep them inside, even just one, but he hated animals in the house. So they kept dying on the highway or getting dragged into the cornfield by scavengers. At night, we could hear the coyotes killing them. Help-less keening that no pillow could block out entirely. Once, when Grandma and Grandpa were away on revival and Ben was at his dad's, the sound pushed Mom and me out of bed.

"What if it's Puzzums?" she asked, peering out through the blinds.

"Not Puzzums!" I cried. I imagined Grandpa's sweet, clumpy dog, surrounded and helpless, stiff with flies around her mouth.

"We have to go save her," Mom said. We got my Grandpa's shotgun from the closet in their bedroom and marched down the driveway. My mother seemed excited, walking fast with the shotgun slung over her shoulder. I had to jog to keep up. At the road, we loaded the gun. There weren't any cars around. I watched the corn and wondered aloud if coyotes ate people.

"Probably not," my mom said. She braced the gun against her shoulder and fired once into the sky above the stalks. It wasn't as loud as I'd thought it would be. The smoke floated up from the end of the barrel and was cut apart by the power lines. When I turned around, my mother was on the ground.

"Knocked me on my fucking ass!" She laughed. I helped her up. Somewhere, a dog started barking. We needed to get back inside The Barn, she said, before someone called the police.

"What about Puzzums?" I asked.

"We scared the coyotes away," she assured me.

They didn't stay gone, though. Carcasses turned up near the edge of the yard, gnawed open and matted with blood. There seemed to be a curse on the animals around The Barn. There was the mouse skeleton I found on the third floor, caught in the ribbons of a type-writer, thin enough in death to slip free. Once, a cousin tied a string around a cat and we found it days later, hanging from a rusty nail. Another time, after my mom failed to pay a man who I later real-ized was her dealer, we found my kitten, a tiny white thing that I'd named Bianca, smashed in the driveway. Next to her, a spattered 2 x 4 and the splotches of blood from where she had tried to run.

Ben and I used to occasionally bring the kittens in and let them sleep on a towel in the jacuzzi. After what Grandpa did to the TV, we didn't want to take chances on contraband, so we lay awake at night, wondering which ones would be left in the morning.

Grandpa was always yelling at us kids for leaving the door open when we came in from outside.

"Shut tha door! You're letting out the cold air," he'd shout. "Were you raised in a barn?"

And we'd say, yes.

Though Grandpa was easy to anger, and though he switched me a few times, and though Ben once saw him sitting on top of Mom and pounding his fists down on her, and though he once shook our bedroom door so hard trying to get in that Mom handed me a knife and told me to use it if I had to, he loved us. We called him Monkey Dad and thought he was zany because he wore a bright orange toboggan all the time. He chased us and, when or if he caught us, picked us up and gave us big sloppy kisses on the cheek.

On days when he wasn't busy working, he let us pile on the hood of the car and then drove us up the steep hill to his properties. He let us ride the four-wheelers along the network of back roads that crisscrossed the fields, and once he even took me to the county fair when Ben was with his dad, and watched with his hands in his pockets as I rode the Magic Carpet again and again, until I couldn't tell my head from my stomach.

Despite his sporadic lack of patience for us, he loved children and he loved giving us presents. Candy, pocketknives, dollar bills. His favorite presents to give to the girls and women of the family included porcelain dolls. The first time he gave me one, I thought I was in trouble. I was in the middle of creating a fort out of an old desk and refolded disposable tablecloths when he shouted, "Little girl!"

Guilty, I dropped the can of green beans I'd been using to weigh down the corners of the tablecloth and turned around. Instead of scowling, he was smiling and holding a long rectangular box. He turned the box and I saw, through the plastic window, a pale white porcelain doll with icy blue eyes.

"I'nt that perty?" he asked me, searching my face for a response.

I didn't like dolls, but I took the box from him with a practiced expression of reverence and replied, "It's beautiful!"

Years ago, Grandma told me, Grandpa had fallen off the White River Bridge while sandblasting. He hit the water so hard, buttons popped off his shirt. His crew stopped working and looked at his bare white belly sticking up out of the water, sure that he was dead. Seconds passed, and then he pushed himself up out of the water and shouted, "Why is everyone just standing around? Get back to work!"

"That's just how he is," she told me. "He can't stand to see someone relax."

Having been raised on a farm, Grandpa was in the habit of rising early. Anyone still in bed would be roused for no reason other than that it bothered him when people slept in. Grandma got up with him and set out his clothes and made his breakfast. After he was gone, she'd make coffee with amaretto creamer and we would drink it together and read the paper. She wasn't raised on a farm, and she treasured the pockets of peace between his meals and intermittent stops at the house for this and that.

The two of them had met when he was a visiting preacher at her church in Alabama. The story was that he was looking out at the congregation, spotted her, and thought, I could never love someone with hooded eyes like hers. She was looking at him and thinking the same thing, but the pastor set them up on a date because they had both been divorced and had children. Their options were limited.

They got engaged and he stood her up at the altar twice before they finally had a courthouse ceremony. She moved with him to Indiana, a state with cold winters where nobody could understand her southernisms. Four children and one major stroke later, she went to her preacher about my grandpa's temper. Divorce was a sin, he told her, and she should stick it out. For better or worse.

And Had Other Sons And Daughters

As a kid, I liked to stand in the driveway and look at The Barn through one eye. I blocked out its surroundings by cupping my hands around my face, and pretended I was looking at an old black-and-white photo. The coal-black wood, white tin roof, and ghostly horses rearing on each side of the front door. Like peering into the past. In a film slide carousel on the third floor, amid images of mission trips and family photos, there was a negative of The Barn. When I held it to the light, I saw The Barn in spirit-blue tones, back when it was first built.

If you reached past me and picked out another slide, you could see Grandpa's father, also named Raymond, facing the camera in ill-fitting jeans and eyes so sunken in, they looked like The Barn. He was a cruel man who once threw a pitchfork at Grandpa and laughed when it stuck in the hind end of a cow instead. He beat on Grandpa's mom and harassed the local women so badly that when my mom got a job at the Sunshine Café in town, a fellow waitress recognized her name and told her, "You know, your grandpa once offered me a pack of beer to give him a blow job."

You could see all of this play out on the slides. Flip through the slides fast enough and you can watch my grandfather grow from a frightened boy with a cowlick, to a young man in army fatigues, to a preacher. Watch the anger jump from his father to him like demons. You might be tempted to flip back and forth through the frames to pinpoint that single slide when he went from someone who needed help to someone who terrorized his family. As if it isn't a sum of bad days and relaxing into coping mechanisms and excuses. As if we don't wear paths in our brains that make it hard to walk anywhere new without constantly stumbling over the old divots. An old camera can only capture so much.

You can't reach back and save him, and you can't cast the anger onto a herd of pigs and send them into the sea, so put down the slides and go out onto the third-floor balcony. From there, you can see all the way up the hill and all the way down the hill. You can see the birds that kept making nests under the lip of the roof, even after Grandpa installed mesh to keep them out. You can see the ashes on the windowsill from where my mother wrote her poetry and chain-smoked, sitting on a hard chair when it was too cold to go out, and the puddle of cigarette butts on the chipped white-painted slats beneath us. You can see the flourishing hackberry trees and the fruitless fruit trees and the crick and the dead cars.

If you relax your eyes until your vision blurs, you can see the echoes of the not-dead cars that my mother left in, and me chasing them all the way down to the highway each time with my arms outstretched, screaming, "Take me, take me with you, don't leave me here," until the times I didn't chase them anymore.

You can see into each neighbor's yard and down to the animal bodies on IN-67. You might see the memory of a girl balanced on the banister getting ready to, bending her knees to, her body letting her, jump. Underneath your feet, there is a trapdoor. You can take the ladder down to the second-floor balcony, walk down the stairs, and leave. I can't. I'm always here, but I'll follow you to the road and point to the spot where Puzzums finally got hit by a car and my grandfather gathered her body in a sheet and carried her to a special hole in the earth, and it was the hardest any of us ever saw him cry.

Building Jon's House

There were reprieves from The Barn. A few times, I stayed with Ben at his dad's house, where the two of them showed me their favorite episodes of *Dragon Ball Z* and the dance they choreographed to the theme music. So in sync that I could forget about the frequent bruises Ben came back with after his dad's weekend visits.

Other times, we stayed with our uncle Jon, who was building his own house up the hill from The Barn. He gave us shovels so we could pretend to help dig the foundation, and let me put on roller skates and roll around the floor when he got it down. Ben was too young to skate, so he sat at the side, clapping as I wobbled by. We had bonfires, visited the Children's Museum, and went paintballing, camping, or to theme parks whenever Jon's kids visited on the weekends. Our favorite place was an indoor playground and arcade named Magic Planet, where Ben, our cousins, and I took turns going down the giant roller slide and getting our fingers snagged or sneaking behind the mesh barriers to spy on the other kids.

Jon had his first kid when he was sixteen, with his high school sweetheart. They got married and Grandpa gave them a little house where they could raise their son together. Before long, they divorced. Jon got partial custody, and then partial custody of his next kid when he married and divorced again a few years later.

"Never have unprotected sex," he lectured us constantly. "I love my kids, but I had them way too young."

I did the math a while back and realized that Jon was around twenty-two years old when he was taking four little kids to places like Kings Island and Six Flags. It makes sense that when he got frustrated with us, he would crook his pointer finger and then bite down on it until his teeth left deep indents. He was still immature, but trying not to yell like Grandpa.

Even though Jon sometimes did irresponsible things, like let us build a potato cannon with a PVC pipe and some of Grandma's hairspray, or drag us on a plastic sled tied to the back of a four-wheeler, he made sure we had childhoods. After working all week in construction, he let us take turns doing pull-ups on his flexed arm. He took us go-karting, swimming, and fishing, not because he was high, but because he understood what it was like not to get to be a kid.

When Mom left and Ben sat at the end of the driveway crying, Jon picked him up and then took both of us to go see the new *Austin Powers* movie. Slightly inappropriate, but well intended and effective.

Jon was the one who tried to tell me early on—I must have been eight or nine—that my mom had an addiction. She had warned me that our family would try to turn me against her, so I refused to listen to him.

"Look in the medicine cabinet," he told me. His eyes were blood-shot, tired and sad, and I couldn't stop thinking of them later when I was alone in the bathroom. I looked in the medicine cabinet. There was a lightbulb burnt on the bottom, some aluminum foil, and little pieces that made no sense to me. None of this added up to drug use in my mind.

When I asked Mom what they were for, her nostrils flared.

"Your uncle fucking planted those there," she said.

Later, when Jon asked me what I'd found, I told him, nothing.

Building Ourselves A City

For a while, when I was in the third grade, we had an apartment. A town house in the middle of Martinsville that Mom's boyfriend at the time paid for so he could see her whenever he wanted. We loved it before we even moved in.

"A place of our own," she called it. Light in her eyes. "We'll sleep on a mattress on the floor until everything is unpacked."

It sounded exciting, like a new adventure, but the day we were supposed to move in, she went without me or Ben, who was at his dad's house. I'd fallen asleep waiting by the door at The Barn. When I woke up, still leaning against the door, and realized it was dark out and we weren't going to spend the first night together on a mattress surrounded by boxes, I stayed there, hating the orange streetlight.

The apartment wasn't really ours. It was hers. Ben and I went over and sat around the big, bulky TV in the living room, and hid in the peculiarly deep cabinets, and lazed on the roof with her while she smoked and the sun set, but when the weekend was over, Ben went back to his dad's and I went back to The Barn. Even the second room, which was supposed to be ours, became more of a storage zone. The promised mattress on the floor stayed there, bare and half covered with boxes, clothes, and toys. Ben and I sat on it playing Nintendo 64, me promising him the next turn but never giving it over. Him, satisfied just to sit with me and watch. We never wanted to leave. It was the first place that was supposed to be just for us.

Mom's boyfriend owned arcade games. He had a few machines that weren't being used, so he let us keep a *Galaga* and *Pac-Man* machine in the corner of the dining room, and a jukebox in the living room. Mom had the high score on *Pac-Man*, and Ben and I took turns knocking each other out of first place in *Galaga*, standing on a kitchen chair so we could reach the joysticks. At night, Mom played "Great Balls of Fire" on the jukebox and danced with me and

Ben standing on her feet, performing wide swings and low dips. Or "Hotel California," dancing by herself, eyes closed, swaying, with Ben and me hypnotized on the couch.

Mom slept through some visits. Locked in her room with blankets tacked over the windows. At church, I had learned about the Veil of the Tabernacle. It was a curtain that kept people from looking at God or the covenant. Only the high priest could pass through the veil, and only once a year with a rope tied around his leg in case he was struck dead and someone needed to pull his body out. Ben and I tried to cross the veil by picking the lock, but when we let light into the room, her voice came out of the mound of blankets, rising from a low moan into a piercing screech for us to get out and leave her alone. We retreated and settled for leaving offerings of drawings and songs and stories outside the door.

To keep ourselves occupied, we wandered the neighborhood, me leading the way and pretending I knew directions. Ben following, usually with a walking stick that he'd found on the ground.

There was a game I liked to play where we acted like we were being pursued. We flattened our backs against a wall or tree, peering before we turned a corner. Any passerby was an enemy. The playground itself was an obstacle course to work our way through. We were spies—mirror roles of the subterfuge that lay over our real lives.

Due to the constant custody battles between our mom and Ben's dad, we knew there were certain things we couldn't talk about. A simple question such as, "What did you do at your dad's this weekend?" felt weighted, no matter how casually intended. Even if I wanted to talk to Ben about how it ached not to be allowed to live at the apartment with Mom, those conversations were off-limits.

Our weekend schedule meant that we saw changes in the apartment in gaps, like trying to read a book in the car at night, glimpsing words only when passing under a light. One weekend there was a new couch, then a coffee table, then a fish tank with one beta fish for Ben and one for me. The next, there was a woman who Mom came out of her bedroom with wearing only a big T-shirt, then the woman was gone. Then a black cat I named Midnight, who slept on my stomach. Then the beta fish died. Then Midnight ran away. Then there was a plasma lamp that Ben and I dared each other to lick. Then the plasma lamp broke and we instead dared each other to turn it on anyway, but we were both too scared that, without the glass dome, the pink lightning would fill up the whole room and kill us.

For a while, Mom's friend Gina lived in the apartment. Gina had an abusive boyfriend, Mom told us, so she needed somewhere to lie low. Gina was nice enough, but Ben and I were more interested in her two teenage sons, Oliver and Evan, who also came to visit on the weekends. Oliver was quiet, with sandy hair and freckles. Evan was, in my opinion, the cooler brother, with spiked black hair and a pierced eyebrow, which Mom called kick-ass. I had a crush on Evan after he showed me how to catch the biggest fish in the pond in *Ocarina of Time*.

In retrospect, having that many people crowded in a small duplex must have been stressful for Mom, but I didn't notice the mounting tension. One day, Gina was cleaning the apartment in the hurried, snatching way that I'd learned was called passive-aggressive. It meant someone was angry but wanted you to figure it out without them saying it. Ben and I offered to help, but Gina gave us both a curt no. When we retreated upstairs to be quiet, Mom found us and handed us a box of toys.

"Go throw these down the stairs," she told us.

Ben reached in and grabbed a stuffed bear.

"Are you sure?" I asked. "Gina seems like she's in a bad mood."

"It'll be funny!" she assured us.

We took the box to the top of the stairs and I half-heartedly tossed a Beanie Baby, which landed with a dull thump halfway down and slumped over.

"No, like this," Mom said, and chucked a plastic shovel up in the air. It spun and then bounced all the way to the bottom of the stairs. "Whoo!"

"Whoo!" Ben said, and followed suit with another Beanie Baby, which went sideways until it wrapped around the handrail and slowly slid down. The image of the little thing on its descent made us laugh, and the hilarity chased out any hesitation I had about joining in. Ben and I lobbed our toys, either not noticing or not minding when Mom walked off. We were laughing and reaching into a second box when Oliver rounded the corner, eyes furious.

"What are you doing?" he demanded. "My mom just cleaned in here!"

The seriousness in his tone lagged a moment behind the fun and, without thinking, we let fly one last toy. Before it hit the ground, Oliver was storming up the stairs. Ben and I ran back toward the bedrooms, but our mom's door was closed and, in a moment of confusion and habitual deference, we bobbed in the doorway of the second room, unsure whether to go in and hide or try to dodge Oliver and run downstairs. Before we could decide, Oliver had us cornered. Without questioning whether Ben would follow, I darted under Oliver's legs and was almost to the stairs when I heard a loud thud. Turning, I saw that Oliver, who had taught us how to climb a narrow hallway by wedging our bodies against the walls and making tiny moves, had pinned Ben by the throat against the wall. Ben's legs were dangling in the air when Mom opened her door. Oliver let go and Ben fell to the ground.

"What the fuck are you doing to my son?" Mom demanded. Her nostrils flared into the clover shape I recognized. It was the shape they took when she got in fights with a boyfriend and told him to pull over, that we would just walk home, even when it was nighttime and home was miles of highway away. The same shape as the time someone on the phone made her so mad that she hung up, spun around, and threw the handset with enough force that, when it barely missed me, it shattered the dome on the miniature bubblegum machine I'd gotten for Christmas.

Now they flared at Oliver, who was holding his hands up like a man confronting a wild bear. From the bottom of the stairs, Gina came running. I remember her hand knocking the Beanie Baby off the handrail, and then I remember nothing, until the static from a walkie-talkie brought me back.

I was at the bottom of the stairs and the front door was open. A cop was in our living room, his walkie-talkie crackling with snippets of information I couldn't follow. Ben sat on the couch, wrapped in a blanket. My brain was still catching up with what I'd seen before, and I felt a rush of panic, even though I could see that Ben was okay. Getting up, I snuck around the edge of the room so the cop wouldn't notice me, until I got to Ben. I stood next to him.

"You okay, Ben Ben?"

He nodded.

The cop gave me a funny look and stopped his bored scribbling on a notepad.

"Did you just call him Bam Bam?"

"It's Ben Ben," Mom cut in. "That's his nickname."

The cop laughed, shaking his head. He looked around our apartment like something smelled bad, like all of this was beneath him, and then he left. After that, Gina moved out and we didn't see Oliver or Evan anymore. It was all ours again, and before too long, it was like it had never happened.

The weekends came and went. Mom got a job in the seafood department at Kroger, where Ben and I could sit in the back and have a tray of cocktail shrimp all to ourselves. We had a dog a few weekends who liked to sit on Ben, Mom said, because she thought he was her puppy. The next weekend, the dog wasn't there. We stayed up all night watching scary movies or cartoons, and fell asleep on the couch. Mom had to quit Kroger, which she hated anyway, because she had cysts on her ovaries that needed to be surgically removed. While she recovered, Ben and I had to stay at The Barn.

Holy Ghost Busters

Our grandparents would have you believe that the only ghost in The Barn was the Holy Ghost, but once, when I was sick with a dangerously high fever, I swore I saw a woman in a 1900s dress walking down the hallway. Another time, I watched a cup move along the flat kitchen countertop. It turned out the counter was wet and it was a suction-based phenomenon that I don't know the scientific words for that made it move, but the initial eeriness of the moment stayed on that counter from then on. Then there was the time we heard a baby crying from the third floor when there weren't any kids in the house other than us.

When Ben and I became afraid of the sounds in The Barn or shapes that could have been creatures hunched among the mounds of flotsam and jetsam, Grandma told us to pray. Steeple our hands and send up wishes. She taught us to say, "Dear God, thank you for this day. Thank you for everything you've given us. Please help those who need it. Please keep us safe." A mantra we whispered to each other as we fell asleep, and still, Ben woke me up in the middle of the night. Eyes wide, glowing pale in the dark.

"Brit," he'd say. "I think I heard something."

"There's nothing out there," I'd grouse and roll over to face away from him.

One night, trying to fall back asleep, I heard Ben's sniffles. Sighing, I sat up and found him staring out into the hall, sucking his thumb. I felt a twinge at his red-rimmed eyes and hiccupping breaths. Most of the time, his crying irritated me. It usually drew Mom to him, cooing and sweeping him up into arms that I was too big for anymore, but Mom wasn't there. The instinct to pull my brother into the warm, protective barrier of my body didn't live in me.

I got up and marched out into the hallway, Ben trailing close behind. Emboldened by my relative courage, I walked with my head held high and my chest puffed out. I scanned the halls and jumped around corners, lifting random items to check underneath and raising my fists, as if ready to battle whatever might rise against us. Yet, as we moved through the pitch-dark, Ben's fear seeped into me. The grandfather clock ticked footsteps into our imaginations. Angels shifted in their paintings on the walls. Tree branch shadows reached for us. All this danger made me feel stronger too. If anything came for us, I told myself, I would jump in front of him and fight. Down the hall, into each room, up the stairs, back down, halting to listen, out onto the veranda, we crept. Ben held on to my shirt, clenching when The Barn creaked or a coyote howled. When we had covered as much ground as we could, we went back to the bedroom. As on other nights, I shut the door and ran my hands over it, my eyes closed. This was one element in a system of magic Ben and I had made up, comprised of rituals and intentions, for when prayer didn't quite do the trick.

"There," I said when I was done. "We'll be safe now."

"Good." He yawned, tired again.

I lifted the blanket and tucked him in, watched his breathing slow and his hands unfurl next to his face. Then I sat up, my back against the hard headboard, keeping watch, my heart beating hard.

Reaching For Heaven

The Barn still had magic back then. A magic that kept the Child Protective Services agents who periodically came to check on us from crossing the threshold. Instead, they met with us outside on the veranda, even when it was chilly. Ben and I knew the script that kept the monsters out and our family together: "No one hits us, we are well fed, everything is okay."

This was its own kind of prayer, but we found more comfort, alone together, in our magic. We distracted ourselves from our mother's absence by creating new rules for our system of devilry. Playing outside, we decided that Ben controlled the wind and the water, and I controlled the plants.

"Hold your hands up and focus," I would tell him, and he did.

The wind blew or the crick water would ripple, and he would look at me with wonder. The evidence irrefutable. I'd nod sagely and then show him how to make potions from the lush vegetation that surrounded The Barn. Pokeweed berries mashed into a rich purple goop, fuzz shaved off mullein leaves, teensy petals plucked from red clovers, dandelion seeds blown off the stem, and goldenrod pollen shaken into a sneezy yellow pile. Whatever was colorful and seemed imbued with power.

Sometimes our games made us spies. When beasts flew overhead, we would flee into the empty cars and water tanks that our grandpa left out in the yard, sun glowing through and warming the thick white plastic that echoed back the pop sounds we made with our mouths. Occasionally, strangers showed up to pay their rent or ask for work, or because they'd seen the giant sign Grandpa put up next to IN-67 that said "Come see the thirteen-bedroom mansion!" Another sign at the end of the driveway retitled The Barn in elegant cursive lettering as The Carriage House. Ben and I watched unwitting tourists as they stepped out of their cars and gazed around at the disorder, probably assuming that the line of cars in the driveway belonged to other curious patrons like themselves.

We watched them go up the stairs, knock, call out, "We're here to see . . . the mansion?" We watched their confusion when they realized that this was it. Their hurried walk back to their car, ushering their well-dressed children along as Ben and I fashioned our hands into makeshift binoculars to watch them click their seat belts, shake their heads, and leave. We sprinkled dirt at the end of the driveway to keep them from coming back.

We both knew we were only pretending, but still, it brought us comfort. With God, on the other hand, that kind of half-belief wasn't allowed. It was damning. I was damned, I knew, because I couldn't believe as much as I was supposed to. I didn't feel the voice of God any more than I felt the trees growing under my hands when I pressed them against the ground and pretended. At church, the lights gleamed on Ben's golden hair and he lost himself in prayer, eyes squeezed tight and head thrown back in worship in a way that I was too self-conscious to do. Another way in which he was innately better than I was. He never asked too many questions that made people sigh, like why did God let Achan's family get stoned for something only he did.

With magic, questions were okay. Ben had plenty.

"What about this one?" he'd ask, holding up a walnut shell.

"The middle is broken. It won't work." I liked being the expert.

"How long do we stir this for?" he'd ask, switching Grandma's good porcelain and wooden spoon to opposite hands.

"Until the pain is unendurable."

"What does that mean?"

"It means you can't stand it anymore."

"Should we have secret, special names?"

"No, that's stupid."

"What do you want to be when you grow up?"

"A mortician."

"I want to be a builder."

"What do you want to build?"

"Houses and buildings and stuff."

Nimrod wanted to build the Tower of Babel to be tall enough to survive if God broke His promise and flooded the world again or worse. I got in trouble for asking what was wrong with having a backup plan. We had to have faith, Grandma chided. I tried to have faith. I closed my eyes and begged faith to live inside me and let me be a good girl. Behind my eyelids, my eyes moved. My thoughts slipped away from faith. I thought about TV. That cartoon where the girl with the long blond pigtails fought aliens and monsters.

"Ben," I said, when I found him later. "Do you want to learn a new spell?"

The Scattering

Then The Barn's magic was stolen.

The human brain is pretty good at defending itself. In the same way a person might block their face when someone raises a fist, the brain will block information if it doesn't think it can handle it right then. In the same way a young girl might shut herself in her room if there are too many people around, the brain will close in on itself if what it's taking in is too much. In the same way a boy being held underwater will turn his head to gasp for air, the brain will pull in any nurturing images it can to save itself from the terror that threatens to drown it.

Everything has to go somewhere. The girl has to come out of her room eventually. The boy's clothes turn up miles down the river. The memories come back years later for no discernible reason. A song on the radio, a smell in the air, a high five mistaken for an attack. On the way to work, you have to pull over and get out of the car, put your hands on your knees, and breathe. Just breathe. It really feels like life should stop after a crescendo like that, after you've time-traveled, but everything keeps moving and you have to too, so you get back in the car and drive to work and sit on your hands while the minute hand chases itself in circles.

TWO WEEKS BEFORE my tenth birthday. Ben was six years old. Grandma sat on the couch across from me, looking through the sales papers for gift ideas. I was playing my Gameboy, which was small enough not to be counted as a TV. The game was *Pokémon*, and I was mad at Ben for erasing my file and making me start all over again. Grandma asked me to check on Ben, who was outside playing.

This moment haunts me. I knew that she meant for me to go outside. To walk down the stairs, across the porch, to the driveway next to the storage shed. To ask him, little brother, are you okay out here? Maybe he would have followed me back inside. Maybe the man in the truck would have seen me and left, or taken me instead. Take me instead.

I didn't do any of that. I sighed and paused the game. I turned to the window I was sitting in front of, looked out, and saw Ben hefting a sheet of plywood on top of two sawhorses. In his training to be a builder, he was always creating clubhouses out of whatever materials Grandpa gave him.

Content with his safety, I turned back around and returned to my game. Still, my body stayed poised at the window. It's there, even now, watching through the glass as Ben finishes his fort and dusts his little hands. As the truck approaches. As the man tells him to get in, that his mom said it was okay, he's going to take Ben to her, to his mom. As Ben climbs up into the truck. As they drive away. I'm still watching out the window, and sometimes, when I try to sleep, my body feels unbearable, like I'm full of too much, like I could run bleating to the sea. My grandmother's sigh of frustration, my brother's screams, the slide of wood, the sirens.

Later, when we realized Ben was gone, I ran outside and looked everywhere. I checked in his fort, lifting up his little makeshift roof and collapsing the whole structure in the process. Destroying his tower, as if it would have kept him safe anyway. I looked in the water tank. The creek and the trees. The side of the house where there was still white paint on the foundation from the time our cousins visited and we all decided to make "art" with old spray cans we found. I checked the tunnel under the road, the horseless horse stalls, the loft, the woods around The Barn. By the time I ran through the enormous backyard for the third time, I knew something terrible had happened. It was true in my stomach, that doom had found us.

My brain flipped through every possible reaction and picked out anger. Don't go off by yourself or talk to strangers. Those were the rules. We knew them. Mom had warned us. Bad things happened to kids, but not us, if we listened. I started a chant under my breath that went, "Stupid kid, stupid kid, stupid kid," over and over as I sprinted through the tall grass and it whipped my arms and face. I don't know how long we looked.

At the bottom of the hill where the road turns out onto the highway, I spotted the ambulance. A crowd of people gathered around it. I ran down the hill, my shoes slapping the pavement, my breath wheezing out of me. Nothing in my brain but getting there. When I reached the crowd, I pushed through and climbed into the open back of the ambulance. I must have told them he was my brother.

A glimpse, of Ben, swaddled in sheets so I could only see his face. Like baby Jesus in the manger, I thought. He opened his mouth, maybe to say my name, but I couldn't hear.

"Did you jump out of the truck?" I asked. All at once, my mind created a story where Ben had escaped from a kidnapper by jumping from a moving truck. Scraped up on the road, but okay.

Don't touch him, someone told me. It would disturb the evidence. I must have looked like I was going to disobey, because I was pulled off the ambulance from behind. By a police officer, I realized. I kicked and thrashed to get back to Ben. I wanted to kill. I wanted to fight everyone in the crowd and pick Ben up the way I had when he was a baby and Mom let me sit on the couch and hold him. His bald little head. The endless string of drool leaking from his mouth.

The ambulance took Ben to the hospital, and the officer took Grandma and me there too. We sat in the waiting room, praying, waiting. When Mom showed up, they led her back through the emergency room double doors. Assuming I could go with her, I followed until a nurse grabbed me by the arm hard enough to hurt. She didn't even speak to me, just tugged me back to the waiting room and threw me into a chair. She shot me that look people gave me sometimes that meant they hated me for reasons I didn't know yet. I watched her walk away, and I hated her back.

For an unbearable amount of time, I stared at the opaque glass divider that separated the coffee station from the play area. A loop played over and over in my mind of the story I'd invented, starting with Ben fumbling with the thin, metal truck door handle, and ending with him just about to hit the ground rushing by underneath.

When they finally let us all go back to see him, I looked for a sign of torment in his face, but he was smiling and joking, buoyant. Even with a black eye, he asked a nurse about her Australian accent, and I just stared at a purplish blotch on his shoulder where the too-big hospital gown hung off. He asked her for a popsicle for each of us. I stood far away and ate it as more people showed up, including his dad. We were all afraid to touch him.

My brother, always making jokes when tension was high, said, "He punched me like this," and did a cartoon swing in the air, mimed his head snapping back, his tongue out, eyes rolled back. His uncle on his dad's side, a hulking ex-Marine with arms covered in tattoos, clapped his hands over his face and left the room. We heard his sobs in the hallways, high-pitched and desperate.

For the rest of the day, I stayed at the hospital while they ran tests and scans, and then someone took me back to The Barn. The police were still looking for the man. I lay awake all night, listening to the sound of dripping in the heating vents. The echoes filled me with terror too real to go exploring by myself. My memory cuts out for a long while after that.

Later, I learned that my birthday came, but when my mom tried to throw me a party, I closed myself in the back room and refused to come out until all the guests had left.

I put the rest together through newspaper clippings and snippets of memory. A woman driving home from work found Ben wandering naked on the side of the highway, picked him up, and called the ambulance. His favorite shirt with the dinosaurs on the front was fished out of the White River days later. The man, known around town as the Reverend for his habit of quoting scripture, was arrested. When questioned, he claimed that he was only reenacting the abuse he'd suffered as a child.

"I thought he was me when I was a little boy," he said in an interview. "I did the same thing that happened to me to him."

In the past, the Reverend had been convicted of arson and spent two years in a mental hospital. Then he'd been arrested again for exposing himself to and abusing several other young boys, but he hadn't been convicted. The boys were too afraid to testify because he told them that he would kill their families if they told anyone.

The Reverend used this same threat on Ben after throwing his clothes in the river and attempting to drown him. Ben, determined to live, had turned his head to the side for gasps of air, again and again, until eventually the man gave up and left him on the side of the road to try to find his way home by following the familiar silo, the billboard, the cow field.

"I called out for you," Ben told me later. "I called out for you to help me."

The day after Ben's abduction, at school, in the middle of class, my body stood up on its own, burning and full of running. I opened my mouth to say something, I didn't know what, but instead I fell apart. My teacher ushered me out into the hallway and let me get some water before going down to the school counselor, who looked at me with soft eyes while I picked at a magnet on her desk.

"How could someone do something like that to a kid?" I asked, though it wasn't really what I wanted to say. There was so much, I didn't even know how to start. I was afraid, I admitted to her, that no one would think what happened to me was that bad now that Ben had been kidnapped.

What I meant, I think, is that it was so easy to understand that Ben had been hurt. Everyone showed up to the hospital with tears in their eyes and their hands wringing, and the doctors told us in medical terms that it had happened. For me, with Mark, there were no doctors and the person I'd told, my mother's friend Dana, had said I was making it up. The most anyone in the family ever said about my own abuse was "You might want to change those pants or the people at the shelter will think you were asking for it" when I wore a pair of stretchy tights. I didn't know how to process any of it, so I focused on my envy of the clarity of Ben's pain.

Of course, there was no clarity. Over the next few years, Ben developed a habit of clenching his entire body and shaking when angry. Until his face and fists turned red. Once, when we rented *Carrie* from the library, he got so upset at the scene where Carrie's mother drags her into the closet that we had to turn it off. Mom sat in the middle of the bed, rocking him as he cried, and glaring at me for choosing such a violent movie. He ran to her crying once after I threatened to throw his coat over a fence during a game of keep-away.

"It reminds him of that man throwing his clothes in the river," she hissed, and looked at me like I was a bug.

I didn't get it. The past was in the past, I thought. All we can do is keep moving. I didn't even understand why my own body went slack and I felt sick when someone reached across me to buckle my seat belt, or why my stomach squirmed at night when I slept next to Mom. How could I understand? I had repressed the memories that should have helped me relate to him.

During the man's trial, Mom rented a motel room just out of town so we could stay away from the chaos. Though Ben wouldn't take showers anymore because he couldn't stand the feeling of water hitting his head, he took a bath while Mom and I sat on the bed and watched the coverage on TV. The man could face over two hundred years in prison, they said, for attempted murder, confinement, and child molesting.

"Fucking bastard," Mom said, and she spat at the screen.

I wasn't allowed in the courtroom during the hearing. I sat outside the heavy wooden doors on a bench across from the Reverend's parents, who had opted out of being in the courtroom during testimony. They stared into their hands, and I stared at them until the court officer handed me a Starburst. I was so focused on tearing the wax paper into tiny pieces, I missed the commotion on the other side of the door when Mom tried to lunge at the Reverend for laughing as he walked past her, saying, "I fucked up your son." She was restrained before she could get to him, and the Reverend's lawyer ended up getting the attempted murder charge dropped by claiming that he had been trying to baptize Ben.

In the end, he got forty years in prison, eligible for parole after twenty. I was in college when they released him. My mom called, frantic.

"He's going to hurt your brother again," she said, her voice wet and clipped. "I just know it."

After we got off the phone, I called Ben.

"I'm not worried," he told me, his voice even. "I can protect myself. I'm a man now."

I closed my eyes and saw the mark on his bare shoulder, the hospital gown slipping down.

THE WORST PART, Ben tells me now, was when our mother retold the account of his kidnapping to anyone who would listen. At the gas station, the grocery store, the welfare office. Details of the worst moments of his life, and he had to stand by like a prop in his own story. Desensitized to the narrative while the reality of what happened congealed inside him. An unendurable chronicle that she couldn't, or didn't, keep in. By the time he tried to talk about what happened in therapy, there was no relief from it. When you can't tell your own account, can't exorcize it, it can get stuck inside you.

"Is that what I'm doing to you?" I ask Ben after he reads my latest draft. "I mean, I'm telling your story too."

"Somebody had to tell it," he says. "I'm glad it's you."

We're on the phone, over a thousand miles apart. Me in Albuquerque and him back in Indiana. He's had a long week, but I can hear in his voice that he's feeling lighthearted. In the background, his friends are laughing. I'm relieved he won't be alone after a heavy phone call.

"If you could go back," I ask, "what would you say to him? Like, if you were in one of those gas stations or grocery stores, and you saw Mom telling the story and your younger self standing there, zoning out, what would you say to him?"

"You mean, like if it was a movie and time pauses and I walk up to that kid and pull him into my temporal bubble?"

"Exactly."

"There's so much I would say to him. God."

My throat hurts and I'm afraid I've pushed too far, but I don't stop him.

"I would tell him, you became a therapist. You learned to love yourself and others around you. This is just a small drop. A few years from now, you will have control over your life. I'd definitely tell him about you and how close we are. Just talk about the beauties of life and why it's worth it. It's always worth it. You don't have to feel trapped like an animal."

Over The Face Of The Earth

The Barn was deemed unsafe for children, so Ben went to live with his dad and I was sent to live with Mark. The details of how or why slip around the edge of my mind like the silver around the sun when I'd try to stare at it. I remember some clothes in a grocery bag, the chain-link fence out front, that blank sensation of being somewhere new, and the way I saw Mark in more detail than I had when I was little. Grey scruff, round cheeks, broad chest, small teeth.

Mark lived in a two-bedroom house next to the train tracks with his new girlfriend and her hyperactive son, Lloyd. There was a big backyard that Mark mowed before making me and Lloyd go out with rakes to scrape up all the grass.

The first day at my new school, they served Salisbury steak in the cafeteria and I told the gym teacher I couldn't participate in laps because of my asthma. Then I sat on the floor and listened to the sounds of shoes squeaking while I buried my face in my knees to hide from the bright fluorescents.

At Mark's house, we ate dinner together and watched movies every night.

"Come sit on my lap," Mark told me the night we watched *The Ring*.

I was too big to be sitting on people's laps anymore, but I did as I was told, my legs dangling down between his. He kept his hand on my back as the movie played, and I tried to pay attention even though I felt like our bodies were magnets trying to get away from each other. When the girl in the movie opened the closet and found her friend crumpled up and discolored, I felt a wash of hot and cold break through me and I wondered, What could happen to a person to make their body do that?

Despite myself, I buried my face in Mark's chest. He laughed and rubbed my back. I wondered if Lloyd and his mom could see us in the flickering light.

AT NIGHT, I slept on the couch in the living room beside the big window that looked out at the street. The train screamed past, and in its rumble, I was able to sleep. I could, Mark offered, sleep in Lloyd's bed if I wanted, and Lloyd would sleep on the couch. I didn't know if Lloyd's mom was okay with displacing her son for another woman's child, and I didn't want to anyway, so I said no thanks. Lloyd resented me for almost taking his bed, I think. As punishment, he would make me play this video game about the Founding Fathers in his room.

In the game, an 8-bit Patrick Henry would come on screen and proclaim, "Give me liberty or give me death," and then you had to defend your colonies from the other players' troops. The game was extremely complicated, and Lloyd refused to explain the rules to me, skipping them when they appeared. Because I didn't know what I was doing, he beat me every round and then, when I said I didn't want to play anymore, he told me I couldn't stop.

Eventually, I would get up and leave the room, even as he called after me to come back and play, and that, really this time, he would explain the rules. I'd go into the next room and try to watch *Pokémon*, but he would scream the theme song over and over so I couldn't hear the show. I begged him to stop. I moved closer to the TV. I tried waiting him out, covered my ears, curled up on the floor, rocked myself.

"Stop it!" His mom would come out of the bedroom she shared with Mark. "Both of you!"

I tried to be good in that house. I did my homework and raked the grass. I washed the dishes, never left my clothes on the bathroom floor. In the mornings, Mark called me into the bedroom for what he called morning lovings, and I'd run and jump under the covers, let him pull me against his bare chest, his bare legs, his cotton underwear, his sleep heat. Mark's girlfriend would leave the room to get ready for work.

I think he just held me and kissed my head and face, my neck. I would come to, alone in the bathroom, waiting for the water to get warm so I could shower for school. Holding the folded towel against my face, I'd whisper-scream into the worn terry cloth.

I thought about Ben all the time, wondered what he was doing at his dad's house. I heard his voice sometimes, whisper-screaming my name from around corners at school and in the house, from the dumpster behind the Taco Bell Lloyd and I walked to sometimes that always smelled like weed. It made my heart race, made me sweat, made me want to run and search and fight.

"What are you looking at?" Mark asked me one day when he caught me staring out through the open kitchen door. There was a little bird outside that had opened its mouth to sing, but instead, Ben's voice had come out, called me Brit, like it was calling for help.

"I thought—" I started, but got stuck at the throat. "I thought I heard Ben say my name."

Saying it out loud made my face hot, made my eyes water, made my fingers tingle and my skin buzz. I tried to back myself into the corner, but Mark pulled me to him and held my face so I had to look him in the eyes.

"Why are you talking about him like he died?" he asked me. "He's still alive."

I didn't have an answer. I imagined the little bird as a piece of Ben's soul that flew all the way from Bloomington to Indianapolis to tell me goodbye. I couldn't tell Mark that. He didn't believe in souls.

"You're right," I said instead. "I'm just imagining things."

This made him happy. He didn't like it when I was childish, like when I washed the dishes and, lost in a trance of bubbles and repetition, started to talk to myself in a lispy voice I'd heard on TV. I didn't realize I was doing it until he came to the doorway and snapped, "Stop talking like that. You sound like a—" And then he called me a word that meant *what's wrong with that kid*, that meant *stop humming, stop rocking, stop pacing, stop looking around the room while you talk to people*, that meant *stop talking so much* or *why don't you talk*, that meant *look me in the eyes, look me in the eyes, look me in the fucking eyes when I'm talking to you*, that meant *do. you. speak. English*.

I thought about lying and saying that I was practicing for a play at school, but all I could do was apologize and smile, wait for his forgiveness. He only looked at me with hard eyes and pushed out a sharp breath of disgust as he passed by and went down into the basement. His disappointment made my joints hurt and my brain scramble for gestures of redemption that I might make. In the water, a serrated knife peeked through the suds. As I washed it, I imagined how easily I could flip it around, give myself liberty and death, fly away, a little ghost bird, whisper-screaming my goodbyes at the windows of my loved ones. Instead, I put the knife on the drying rack with the other dishes and then made a sandwich with Mark's favorite fixings. I put it on a saucer, opened the door to the basement, and descended.

THERE'S SOMETHING ABOUT the basement I can't remember. It could be nothing. When I try to follow myself down the stairs, I see myself at each step, knee bent differently each time, toe planted, heel rising, eyes locked on the sandwich on the saucer, one hand grasping the banister. Then there is a wall, an invisible film, like plastic wrap stretched across the bottom of the stairs through which I can only press my face and take in bleary images: a curtain, a rug, a bed, shapes that must have been something but now don't come together.

WHEN MY GRANDPARENTS found out that I was with Mark, they drove to Indianapolis and took me straight from the elementary school. No time to return to the house for my things or say goodbye. We just bumped over the train tracks that ran beside the school, away. We took I-465, past downtown, where they used to live, off exit 8, where, finally, the road stops being stressful and gets familiar, left onto Kentucky Avenue, which turns into IN-67, past Denny's, the animal hospital, the outdoor theater, the long stretch of road bordered by dense trees, the White River, the gas station and motel, the cow fields, the train tracks, the old house by the road, The Barn. Unsafe for children, but safety was relative. The narrow tunnel in that long hallway. I had nothing to unpack.

WHEN I WAS a kid, I loved going to the grocery store. All that food. Even if we only grabbed a few things, I got excited just being close to the abundance. I wanted to lie on the breads like a big, comfy bed and sweep every iced honey bun into the cart for Mom and get onto the intercom and tell the whole store about the giant squid attack in *20,000 Leagues Under the Sea*. These days, a trip to the grocery store wrings me out.

There are too many colors, too many sounds, too many choices. Way too many people. When I have to buy groceries, I start out fine, thinking of the recipes I'll make and how good everything will taste. Then a glance from another shopper, passing each other once, twice, three times. Following me, wanting to hurt me. That's crazy, I tell myself, but my skin prickles. My back tenses. Throat tightens, lights too bright, can't breathe. Until I am clenching the cart, squeezing my eyes shut, trying to breathe myself back into sanity and prepare myself for the attack that I know is coming.

I get through the store one careful step at a time, as if there is a seven-headed beast made of light right behind me, screaming silently, and it will attack if I make any sudden movements. Grab the bread, the Takis, the spinach. Fleetwood Mac on the loudspeakers. A chill from the refrigerated section. Breathe. Walk. Slide each item over the self-checkout so the cashier will not ask me if I'm okay. More than the beast, I fear making a scene.

Out in the parking lot, wheels clacking over uneven ground. Look both ways, both ways again, cross. The car is right there. Resist the urge to run. Resist the urge to run. Resist the urge to run. Calmly place the bags in the trunk. Return the cart to the corral. Resist the urge to run. Check the back seat. Get in the car. Lock the door. Exhale. Heartbeat pounding through my entire body at once. Safe. Start the car with shaking hands.

CHAPTER 7

A Raging River
Does Not Alarm It

We all came back together, the way we always did. Mom, Ben, and me. We didn't have to live at The Barn anymore, Mom said. She had a new boyfriend, Kurt, who lived way out in the boonies in a biker community. They would keep us safe. Nobody messed with bikers.

To get to Kurt's house, we went up a steep hill off the highway and then followed narrow roads so winding that we got lost the first few times. Kurt himself looked kindly, with round, wire-rimmed glasses and long grey hair that he kept back in a low ponytail. Just inside the front door, he kept a police baton hanging on the wall. He showed it to Ben and me, swinging it out to his side so the inner shafts telescoped out like a car antenna.

Ben and I loved staying at Kurt's. There was a tire swing in the backyard that we pushed each other in, trying to flip over the branch or get a good spin going. Kurt's dogs ran after us, barking, snapping at my loose hair as I swung past. Ben and I would twist and twist and twist the tire until the rope couldn't turn anymore, and then we would each climb on and let it unravel, faster and faster, until all we could do was lean in, our foreheads touching, and hang on.

The neighborhood was nestled between vast woods and a long, wide river that Kurt told us to be careful around because someone had set their pet alligator loose in it earlier that year. It probably hadn't survived the winter, he said, but who knew. Unfazed, we spent most of our time there, slicking the raised bank into DIY waterslides, hacking tunnels and hollows through the brambles to make a clubhouse, catching fat tadpoles, hunting morels, and rowing around in and eventually sinking a canoe. It was like Ben's fear of water went away, at least in that river. I never thought about it, and if he did, he didn't say anything.

We played a game where I would float on my back and Ben would come carry me, light enough in the water to hold. As he took slow, deliberate steps and I let my arms and legs trail limply, he sang the theme from *2001: A Space Odyssey* in dramatic, wordless baritone. If I broke character before he could get me to shore, he'd slide his arms out from under me and let me sink, laugh-bubbles rising out of me all the way to the muddy bottom.

Even when it got cold, there was plenty to do. Kurt had a home computer, and he showed me a game called *The Sims* where I could create a person, or "sim," and then build them a house to live in. He taught Ben and me how to use cheat codes to make extra money and keep the sims' hunger from going down.

When we weren't playing on the computer or braving the cold to play outside, we watched Kurt's giant TV. He had a way of getting free cable that worked as long as we made sure to eject the card from the cable box when we were done watching, so the cable company didn't scramble it.

"We got free fucking cable out here, baby!" Mom said. She spent most of her time in the bedroom, smoking and sleeping. If we wanted to wake her up, we knew to bring her her cigarettes and a cup full of ice and Diet Mountain Dew. Sometimes it worked, but sometimes she would throw off the covers, get out of bed, and stomp around the house grousing about how we never let her rest.

Kurt's room was more like a screened-in porch with the windows all covered in plastic to keep out extreme temperatures. On a bookshelf were potted marijuana plants that I ate a leaf off of on a dare, though I didn't feel anything. A few large cactuses lined the foot of his bed, and I once fell on one and got dozens of its little spines stuck in my thigh.

One day, I brought the morning offering to get Mom up. She was lying on the bed on her back with her eyes open. I tried calling her name, but she didn't respond or even blink. Outside, a cicada buzzed. She looked dead. The cup sweated in my hand.

"Mom," I tried, even though already I felt my mind rearranging itself to not have her anymore. I walked to the side of the bed and set the drink and cigarettes on the bedside table. Her face was still, her eyes wet and looking at nothing. I wanted to reach out and touch her, to see if she was still warm, but all I could do was stare and try to imagine how the world would be without her. Suddenly, she lurched up and shouted, "RAHH!" in my face.

"I got you," she gloated. The blood rushed back to my feet.

"How'd you keep your eyes open so long?" I asked her.

She reached over to the table for her cigarettes. Lit one. Inhaled.

"I learned how to leave my body when I was gang-raped."

She told me how she had floated outside herself and watched the whole thing happen to her from above. Like a ghost watching herself die. Now she could do it on command. Just lie back and leave.

"Try it," she said, so I lay on the bed and let my arms and legs go slack, gaze locked on a spot on the wood-panel ceiling. My eyes burned after a few seconds and I blinked.

"It takes practice," she said, blowing more smoke.

Land Of Us

At night, Ben and I slept in the living room. We could hear the sounds from Kurt's room. Sounds I understood now for what they were. Sounds that made my joints ache and my body want to move. Ben wouldn't understand, I was sure, so I hoped he was asleep. I was surprised one night when I heard him snickering.

"What?" I whispered.

"She keeps calling him Baby," he whispered back.

"So?"

"It's just funny. A biker named Baby." We stifled our laughter in our pillows.

A few times, Kurt took us on motorcycle rides, though I didn't like leaning around curves. How you had to let yourself feel like you were about to fall. How you had to keep your arms around someone as if you trusted them. Mom loved it. We could hear her all the way down the road, over the sound of the bike itself, screaming in rapture when she went on rides. She lifted her arms like she was on a roller coaster. Afterward, her hair and eyes would be wild, and she wouldn't be able to stop moving or talking.

"That was fucking awesome!" she'd say, the same way she did after she did the bungee drop at Six Flags, or rock climbing at the mall, or the Gravitron at the county fair. Stumbling, but elated. Untouched by the headaches I got when I tried.

Mom loved everything about the biker community. She loved being away from civilization, flouting the law, partying. We went to the annual biker get-together at a site way out in the woods called Hog Hollow, where people floated in the pond, naked and zonked, and had sex while driving their motorcycles. Ben and I spent most of the time trying to catch a glimpse of the pond's single albino catfish and daring each other to order liquor from the Old West jail–themed bar.

The very best thing about the biker community was that people were afraid of them. Nobody would hurt us anymore, Kurt assured us. They wouldn't dare. Mom crashed the car into a non-biker neighbor's mailbox once, and they came out, saw it was her, and told her not to worry about it. Our enemies were the bikers' enemies.

"We have people inside," I overheard someone tell Mom one night over a game of cards. "We could take care of that man who kidnapped your boy."

"Did you say yes?" I asked her later.

"I'm thinking about it," she said.

After a few months, Ben went back to his dad and I had to go back to school. The truancy officer who had been hounding us since the first grade didn't care anymore that our family had been through a traumatic event, and not even the bikers could protect us. I took the bus in the mornings to a little school where the playground equipment was rusty and the students always seemed to be look-ing over their shoulders. My class was in a weirdly shaped, carpeted room at the top of a stairwell. On the first day, a girl with braided pigtails leaned over and told me to be careful, that our teacher had once chokeslammed a kid into the wall.

"That wall right there," she said, and pointed near the door.

"What did the kid do?" I asked, but she shrugged.

I watched the teacher for signs of violence, but he mostly seemed bored.

"Can anyone draw a heart on the board?" he asked us. A kid raised a hand and drew a classic heart.

"Wrong," the teacher said. "Can anyone draw a real heart?"

In my mind, I pictured the hearts I'd seen on TV. Pulled from the man's chest in *Queen of the Damned* or plopped into the scale at the morgue in *The X-Files*. I raised my hand. At the board, I drew the main lump and then an approximation of the arteries and valves sticking out of it. When I stepped away, he laughed.

"What's that supposed to be?"

I looked at it, stupid and wrong.

"A heart," I said, wanting to sit back down already.

He turned to the class. "Does that look like any heart you've seen before?"

They shook their heads, intoned, "No," together, and laughed. He waved me back to my seat. By the time I got there, I was gone. I don't know where I went. I spent most of my school career like that. One moment, I would be in the class watching a teacher about to write something on the board, and then, what felt like mere seconds later, the board would be full of equations I couldn't remember having been written and the teacher would be in the middle of a sentence I had no context for. No matter how hard I tried to focus, I would slip away.

Pay attention, pay attention, pay attention, I'd tell myself. Be here. Then someone would be snapping in my face or urging me along the hallway to the principal's office. In the first grade, at a different school, I worked with a tutor. She would come in the middle of class and pull me out to do vocab cards and play Go Fish. I knew I was stupid, and that when the class bully stabbed staples into my leg during reading time, I deserved it. I knew that the first-grade teacher hated me for never finishing the work packets and for humming to myself without realizing it. She looked at me the way people in the store looked at me sometimes, like I was failing some test I never knew I'd started.

One day, the teacher yelled at me for not listening and I felt something warm on my legs. When I looked down, I realized I had peed. She made a sound in the back of her throat and told me to go get some dry pants from the nurse's office and clean myself up. On the way there, my pee cooled on my legs. I imagined running out the front doors and into the cornfield and beyond. Instead, I took the sweatpants the nurse gave me—I tried to tell her that I wasn't allowed to wear pants, but she said it was all they had—into the gym bathroom, where I attempted to wash my underwear and legs and socks as well as I could.

I had my foot hiked up in the sink when a girl from my class opened the door, took a look at me, laughed, and ran back to the class. I knew she would tell everyone. I also knew it wouldn't matter. Nobody liked me anyway. I smelled bad, always had lice, and didn't know how to be around other kids. Not to mention, I was a brown child in rural Indiana. My peers ignored me, made fun of me, or lured me in just to push me away. One girl even asked to come over for a sleepover once, but when she saw the crowded inside of The Barn, she called her mom to pick her up, and then told everyone we lived in filth. Which we did.

Pants-peeing is a common sign of childhood trauma. That's not to say that someone should have known, but I wonder if anyone suspected. After that first accident, I started squatting and peeing at the back of the playground at recess, out by the old, netless soccer goals. I didn't necessarily need to. It just became a habit. The same way I always touched a specific brick on the way to gym class. Another ritual.

I hated school. I faked sick as often as I could, even going so far as pretending to pass out at the bus stop one morning. Once or twice, I hid in the woods all day. I hated the fluorescent lights and loud noises, having so many people around all the time, and feeling stupid and ugly. I went to at least four different schools throughout elementary school. I developed weird, sad crushes that made me a strange thing to my peers and had panic attacks during tornado drills.

The one close friend I made in the fifth grade was a short girl with glasses named Shirley who had also moved a lot and whose parents were also hoarders. I knew we would be compatible the day we both army-crawled away from reading time to rub erasers on the rough carpet and smell the hot rubber friction.

"This is some dead sex," Shirley said, expressing the carpet's perspective. My brain pinged. I hadn't met another kid with the forbidden knowledge of sex or the courage to talk about it. I looked at her again. Her mischievous smile. The groove between her nose and upper lip where I resisted the urge to slot the tip of my pinky.

"Who's your favorite gargoyle?" I asked.

"Lexington," she responded, and my brain pinged again.

We army-crawled back to the reading circle, where our teacher was sniffling through a scene in *Where the Red Fern Grows*. If I sat too close, Shirley didn't appear to mind. Every day at recess after that, instead of peeing out by the soccer goals, I met with Shirley and we raced around in the grass quoting *SpongeBob* and *The Simpsons*, sharing inhalers when we got wheezy. On field trips, we sat together on the bus, even after I threw up because I saw a booger someone had wiped on the back of the seat in front of us.

"My little brother is squeamish, too," she told me once it was all cleaned up. "He blows chunks if you even talk to him about poop."

She didn't seem to notice or care about my social ineptitude or the fact that I smelled like a walking cigarette. Her dad smoked too, she said, but she was determined to get him to quit. We were at the bottom of the social hierarchy, but she endeared bullies with her quick wit. At lunch, when a boy caught me staring into space where his face happened to be, he shot me the infamous annoyed head wiggle and said, "Boo!" As if she'd been waiting for the chance, Shirley shot off, "-bies." The boy blinked and then threw his head back. Boobies! The table laughed, and my transgression was forgotten.

On the day of fifth grade graduation, I was petrified I wouldn't pass, that they wouldn't call my name to come up and get my diploma. More than that, I didn't want to go to what was supposed to be a celebration with a bunch of people who didn't want me around. Shirley was on the other side of the gym because her last name was farther down the alphabet than mine. Throughout the whole ceremony, even after my name was called and I collected my diploma with my heart beating in my head, I sat with my arms crossed over the front of my white floral dress. In photos, I sit among my peers, stark brown and brooding.

At the end of the ceremony, outside the school, Kurt showed up on his bike, in full leather regalia.

"You're gonna be the biggest badass at this thing," he said. "What other kid gets to ride away on a Harley?"

I climbed onto the back and held on. He revved as we sped out. I looked back and saw Shirley watching, a proud glint in her eye. In all the vibration and warm wind, I almost didn't care who else saw. We left the school behind and zipped through cornfields to the wooded road home. Lightning bugs hovered over the grass, glowing green streaks as I held on tightly, grateful to Kurt for this gesture.

Kurt wasn't my dad. I knew that, and I didn't want him to be. Still, I liked the way he told the same story every time he cooked about selling oregano to some guy who couldn't tell it wasn't weed, and the way he fumbled with the remote and apologized the time he tried to turn on a movie for us but accidentally started the porn that had been in the DVD player. I liked that I could tell he didn't know how to talk to Ben or me but tried anyway.

Of course, we left Kurt's eventually. We always left. This time, one of Mom's old boyfriends showed up. He was one we had lived with very briefly, leaving in a storm wherein Mom had flipped him off as we walked out the door and I, very young at the time, had stuck my own tiny middle finger up in mirror rage.

She must have called him. I didn't know why, and I still don't. Mom and Kurt had a fight, so I packed my bags and helped Ben pack his. The ex had brought a kitten to win our favor. We got in the car, took the winding roads for the last time back to the highway, and checked into a motel. Ben slept on the bed farthest from the door, Mom and her ex slept in the other, and I slept on the foldout couch.

I woke up in the middle of the night because the kitten had peed. I slid the soiled cushion onto the floor and curled my legs up to fit on what was left. That's when I heard Mom and her ex. In the dark, I couldn't see what was happening, but I knew. I wondered if Ben was asleep.

The top of my head burned. I reached out for the kitten, which we hadn't named yet, and held it against my chest. Go back to sleep, I willed myself, but the sounds reached across the room and laid too-warm hands on me. I squeezed the kitten closer and felt a rush of anger. Anger with no words.

The kitten let out a little mewl. I could refuse to let go, I thought. I could be horrible. I could keep squeezing. Hurt it. Satisfy the pulsing rage with violence. I considered this, an irrevocable choice, and then I let the kitten loose to totter a few steps away and start plucking its nails in the rough brown fabric of the cushion. I stood up, stomped to the bathroom, and slammed the door.

I wanted Mom to know I was upset. I didn't even know why really, and I didn't think past the satisfying moment of expressing my anger. When she knocked on the door and asked if she could come in, I hesitated before saying yes. Embarrassed, my knees buckled and I sat heavily on the toilet.

"What's wrong?"

I couldn't look at her. "I heard what you were doing."

"What was I doing?" Her voice was sharp now, defensive.

What they were doing made sense in my head as shapes and feelings, but the thought of saying the words for it made me squirm. I pressed the heels of my palms into my thighs.

"What do you think we were doing?" she repeated.

"Sex," I murmured, and wanted to scrape the word out of my mouth.

"We weren't having fucking sex," she said.

I still couldn't look at her. I knew what I'd heard, but maybe I was wrong. Maybe I had imagined it.

"You don't believe me?" she demanded. I didn't answer. "You want to check my fucking pussy?" She hiked her leg up onto the counter. She was only wearing a sleep shirt.

I hadn't remembered the night at the other motel with Mark in years. My brain had tucked it away. Now the memory flooded back and I felt like I was tipping forward and falling off the toilet. My blood jumped from my head to my feet and back.

"No," I said, and the memory returned to its hiding spot.

The next day, her ex drove us to The Barn and dropped us off. I went back to school. Ben returned to his dad's. Kurt left our belongings some time later in a large plastic bag at the end of the driveway. When we opened it, there was a horrible smell. Kurt had peed and thrown up on our things. Mom pulled a bra out of the mess and held it up. On each cup, in red marker, someone had written "REAL SICK."

"Stupid fucker," Mom said, dropping what I realized was actually one of my bras. "That's not even mine."

After that, we moved around a little more. We went to Mississippi to visit our great-uncle, who had chickens whose eggs we collected and ate for breakfast. From there, we took a train to Arkansas, where we stayed on an ostrich farm. The tall birds charged and spread their wings to intimidate us when we approached the fence, so Ben and I kept our distance. We found giant bones while exploring, and the woman who owned the farm told us they were from ostriches. She let us keep a femur. We left after Mom went on a bad date.

"He brought his friend," she told me later, when Ben was asleep in the train seat. "They said they were going to hump and dump me."

"How did you get away?" I asked.

"I told them I have kids," she answered, and kissed my head.

Back in Indiana, we frequented the homes of people who would host us over the years. There was Rhonda, who lived out in a field where the mice flocked inside when it got cold at night. Her boyfriend, Jose, tried to teach me Spanish. We ate chicharrones dipped in hot sauce and practiced vocabulary out of a Spanish-English dictionary.

"She's a natural," he told my mom. "Her tongue was meant to speak the language." The lessons stopped after he accidentally walked in on me getting out of the shower.

"Lo siento!" he'd said, and backed out of the bathroom quickly with his head down. After that, he wouldn't look at me.

There was Theresa, a stout blond woman with glasses so thick they made her look like she had cartoon eyes. She had a daughter my age, named Beth, who I made out with once, but we jumped apart when we heard our moms coming and then didn't talk about it again. Theresa's boyfriend showed up drunk one night, yelling and swinging his fists, and busted the glass light cover in the living room. After he left, Beth and I stayed up scrubbing little dots of blood out of the carpet so Theresa wouldn't lose the security deposit.

There was the distant relative out in the country who had a candy dispenser in his kitchen full of peanut-butter M&M's that Ben and I filled our hands with and then took outside to the underground tornado bunker and crunched in the dark. He kept Coke cans and made things out of them. Little red aluminum planes and frogs and pinwheels.

No matter how far we traveled, we always ended up returning to the godly silence and still air of The Barn. The same year-round Christmas trees, same dead ladybugs in the windowsill, same forgotten orange hat slung over the banister. Whatever solace Ben and I had once found there didn't exist anymore. We were too changed, too old to conjure magic in all that grey. We saw The Barn now as our mom always had. A haunted stake in the ground to which we were all inescapably chained.

Newly adolescent, I balked at facts of my life that I had previously tolerated. The sticky residue that appeared on the undersides of my arms any time I rested them on the kitchen table or really any surface at all. Not being allowed to wear pants. Having to attend church. When my mom put her arm around me or kissed my cheek in public, or when she called me her pretty Mexican princess. Mexican, though we didn't know for sure if I was Mexican or Puerto Rican or what. As far as anyone in my family knew, Mexican encompassed every different kind of brown that I might be.

I didn't want anyone to see me that way because it wasn't how I saw myself. Growing up, when I placed myself in whatever fantasy I was creating, I'd imagined a little blond girl with blue eyes, almost a copy of Ben. When I caught sight of my reflection, my olive skin, black hair, and brown eyes, it was always a moment of dissonance.

To maintain the image of the white girl I wanted to be, I avoided going out in the sun, even when that meant staying inside The Barn. I snuck lemon juice from the kitchen and put it in my baths because I'd read in a magazine that it would make my skin lighter. Locked in the back bathroom, I wielded one of Grandpa's disposable razors against the thick black hair on my arms and legs, my upper lip, the space between my eyebrows.

I knelt, at least twice a week, in front of a jug of bleach and lowered my hair in, holding it there until my lungs and eyes stung, and then kept holding it, a little longer, a little longer, a little longer, imagining my golden halo reward. Instead, my hair took on a strange orange ombre, which I kept up in a clip, mostly to hide it from myself. Still, when I got on the bus before and after school, someone would shout, "Are you a Mexi-CAN or a Mexi-CAN'T?"

"They're just jealous because you're hot and they're racist," Shirley assured me. We shared a stand in orchestra. I had taken up the violin just so we could have a class together. We talked on the phone every day after school about Fall Out Boy, our shared crush on a goth upperclassman, and every single other thought that entered our minds. People called us lesbians because of how much time we spent together. Leaning into it, we held hands in the hallway. I even asked her out, half-jokingly, in the middle of the lunchroom, but she told me to shut up and sit down.

Shirley's calls made The Barn bearable. When we talked, color radiated from the phone, an oasis of joy. Even if we were just taking turns playing songs using the number pad, we spent hours tying up our respective lines, sighing dramatically when another call came in or someone else needed to use the phone. Eventually, one of our phones would beep to alert us that it was dying. We'd say our goodbyes, our mmm-byes, our GUH-byes, our later alligators and after a while crocodiles, our you firsts, no you firsts, our okay for real this times, and then hang up, and then all of that joy would retract, sucked back into the pinpricks where her voice had just been, leaving me to breathe in the spaces between the white grandfather clock's loud ticks.

Estamos Acá Y Ahora

I've started doing mindfulness meditations in Spanish lately. I sit in bed or out on the back patio, pop my headphones in, and close my eyes. A man with a soothing voice tells me to keep mi espalda recta, pero no tensa. I'm pleasantly surprised at how well I understand everything, sometimes so much so that I forget to do the breathing. It's taken me years of daily practice, but I'm now at the level of language proficiency where I can fully comprehend a conversation but can't contribute anything without sounding like a buffoon.

Learning another language is already difficult, but it's even harder when your social anxiety is so potent that you can't speak above the volume of a softly closed door. The idea of pronouncing or conjugating something incorrectly paralyzes me, so I content myself with listening to Spanish podcasts and guided meditations and watching my favorite movies with a Spanish dub. Honestamente, it's lonely.

I moved to Albuquerque in part because I wanted to be around other people who look like me. That might sound a little naive, because it is. When I'm out, sometimes I look down at my arms and the arms of brown people around me and I feel loved, even though we're all strangers. That doesn't mean I feel comfortable enough to attempt joining any kind of community. I was raised seeped in whiteness. Like God and trauma, this is an inextricable part of who I am, informing the way I move through the world and how I express myself. Because I wasn't raised with Mexican culture, I feel like an intruder here.

I haven't figured out this thing about myself. Sometimes, I look in the mirror and I can't even tell how I look. I can tell you that I feel like a mascot for white assimilation. I can tell you that within the last decade, I've stopped plucking my eyebrows and wearing clothes that covered as much skin as possible. I can tell you that, on the rare occasion when I speak in Spanish to someone, they lean in to hear and respond in kind, and I walk away feeling at once ecstatic and like I've told a sick lie. I can tell you that when white people approach me and speak to me in slow, drawn-out English because they assume I don't understand, sometimes I just smile and nod because I don't feel like dealing with it. I can tell you that when I was unpacking after moving a few years ago, I found skin-lightening cream tucked away in the back of a toiletry bin and I cried for the teenage version of myself who slathered it on like a prayer, and then I felt silly for crying because my skin was never really that dark. I can tell you that I set up my ofrenda this year and all of the pictures I put on it were of my white family members, and that I had no pan de muerto because it was sold out at every single panadería nearby. I can tell you that, even though I know it's a common affirmation, I still jumped the first time the meditation guide ended a session by saying, "Estamos acá, estamos ahora." I can tell you that having certainty is sometimes a mirage you create for yourself so you can keep taking steps through the sand.

CHAPTER 8

Where Neither Moth
Nor Rust Destroys

When depression comes for me these days, when I feel the first hint of that sapping pall, I prepare my house as if for a guest. I tidy, plump couch cushions, dust, sweep, wash baseboards, clean mirrors, crawl on my hands and knees to pick up the hairs that fall out of my head behind me wherever I go, knowing how neurotic I look, wishing that I wanted to stop. I pace the house, dizzied, looking for something out of place. I know that my brain is about to pitter to a slow chug, at which point I will only be able to lie on my side thinking of the things I could do to feel better, but having no gumption to get up and actually do them. If nothing else, I will atrophy in a clean environment.

For some indeterminate amount of time, the word *SADNESS* flashes across the marquee of my mind, blocking other more productive thoughts until, eventually, it dissipates. I need only be patient. A particularly tenacious demon may overstay, and on those occasions, I may try to jumpstart myself back to normal the same way I once put on little plays for my mom when she wouldn't get out of bed. Stumbling in her heels, I'd plug in the radio and turn on her favorite CDs, dance and sing, feeling even at that age how her sadness had filled the room with an invisible fog that absorbed and muted my tinny efforts. Now I pick out my own favorite songs and dance to them in the dark. Get my heart rate up, fling my inelegant body hither and yon, an impious exorcism, and then stand there breathing heavily as the sand settles inside me once more.

The point is, depression can become routine. Even when it's Mariana Trench terrible, I know what I'm dealing with. I have tools and strategies. I know my limits and when to ask for help. That said, when that first real bout of bleakness rode in on the coattails of puberty, I was completely waylaid. Until then, I'd always been able to jump into the portal of my mind and leave when I needed to, without even trying. Sure, I'd been sad before, but nothing as intense or prolonged as this. I reached for my mind portal and, in its place, found a sucking chasm.

From the chasm crawled dormant memories that stabbed at me with pitchforks. Flashes of violations, looming faces, phantom sensations on my body. I shook them off, literally, explaining away my twitches as cold chills, my hands over my face as a restrained sneeze. Every moment, though, I felt as if I were being pulled into a black hole in my chest, and rather than clawing and clinging to stay out of it, I wanted to lie down and let myself be dragged, however slowly, into whatever oblivion would make it all stop.

I was eleven when it first hit, and I remember this because a major facet of my angst at the time had to do with turning twelve. In the Pentecostal faith, the age of accountability, when a child becomes accountable for their sin, is twelve. Stuck in the bottleneck of despair, I had decided that I wanted to die, but suicide was an unforgivable sin. The only thing I dreaded more than being alive was going to hell. Though I had distanced myself from the faith, I couldn't shake that ingrained fear. My solution was to give myself a literal deadline, to end my life before I turned twelve, before it could be counted against me.

Grandma and I still spent time together, but there was tension between us now over my insistence on wearing pants, my reluctance to go to church, and my immoral moodiness. She was the utmost authority in my mind on the word of God, so I went to her with my first biblical question in years.

"If someone younger than twelve commits suicide," I asked her, "do they go to heaven?"

She was reading the paper, but she set it down on her lap and took off her glasses. I'd intended to ask casually, but I realized when it was out of my mouth how obviously about me the question sounded.

"No," she said, after a long moment. "It's still an eternal sin."

I nodded, but I felt like she was lying, which was also a sin. She knew what I was asking, but some things just weren't talked about.

"You are the apple of my eye," she told me instead. Offering me a reason to stay. I hated myself that it didn't feel like enough.

She would never tell the apple of her eye if there was a loophole through which to slip out of this world. The pause before she'd answered told me that the answer was yes. I just had to get it done before I turned twelve. I tried to leave with a bunch of pills from the medicine cabinet, but they turned out to be aspirin. I tried jumping from the balcony. I tried cutting my arms. At the end of each attempt, I told no one and immediately began planning the next.

The night before my twelfth birthday, inspired by a character in a book, I tried slowing my breath gradually until it was so slow that my heart would stop. Lying flat on my back, body slack, I pulled in slow breaths and let them eke back out. My head swam, my limbs tingled, and my heart slowed but would not stop. The clock on the bedside table crept from 9 p.m. to 10 p.m. to 11 p.m. Seeing midnight approach set my heart racing, undoing all my hard work. I tried to start again, but the hour came, and then it was too late. If I didn't want to spend eternity falling, burning, and gnashing my teeth, I was resigned to live, to remember, to The Barn with its dust motes and cold, wet silence.

Unwilling to accept that reality, I tried to think of contingency loopholes. Baptism washed us clean of our sins, so if I hired a hitman to shoot me the moment I emerged, reborn, from the water, I would be forgiven for hiring the hit on myself in the first place. Another fast pass to heaven was dying to save someone else. I could dive in front of a spiked road roller, shoving someone out of the way at the very last second before my soul got squished out of me like a spectral glob of toothpaste.

Outlandish, desperate, last-ditch grabs at salvation. Out of options but not out of desire to die, I went to my mom.

"I feel like I'm a book," I started, "and I still have so many pages left, but I just want to close it."

It wasn't even what I wanted to say. It felt too small, too trite, for the heavy grey miasma that made it impossible to imagine a future. She pulled me close, the way she used to when we slept in the back of our station wagon, and cried into my hair. I wanted her to hold me, but when she did, my stomach squirmed.

She looked for a hospital for me. We visited one in Indianapolis, but during the introductory appointment, when I asked if I could bring my radio and they said no, Mom broke down.

"Are you serious?" she shouted. "She needs her music!"

Downstairs, in the cafeteria, we ate sandwiches and looked everywhere but at each other.

"We'll find you a better place," she said.

The hospital I ended up in was called Meadows. During our first visit, a kid my age screamed in the next room.

"Mom," he cried. "Please don't leave me here."

My own mother looked at her hands. We didn't have other options. With Medicaid, we could afford two weeks. They took my clothes and checked me for sharp objects. Mom hugged me goodbye, and then they led me into the facility, where a nurse took my blood without looking at my face. When I told her that I felt a little woozy, she replied coolly that she hadn't taken enough blood for me to feel dizzy. They led me to an empty bedroom at the end of a hallway. When I settled in to sleep, I noticed the names gouged into the nightstand. Without sharp objects, I wondered how they had been carved.

During the stay at Meadows, I read a book that I'd brought with me about two teenage girls who became pregnant even though they were virgins. One would give birth to the second coming of Jesus and the other would birth the Antichrist. I read it every second I had time between meals and activities. At night, while children in the rooms around me were restrained to their beds, I sat on the desk next to the window and angled for moonlight to see the words. I was obsessed with the idea of an evil baby. That someone could come out already twisted, irredeemable.

The group therapy room was right next to the time-out room. If a kid acted up, they were strapped into a jacket and locked in the room. All throughout group therapy, we would hear the thuds of the kid throwing their body against the wall. In gym class, we were given a tote full of balls and set loose. I learned to stay out of the fray after I reached for a ball and got scratched in the face. At meals, I sat next to a little girl who couldn't have been older than four. When she couldn't get her milk carton open, she wailed and threw her food. After a few times of this, I opened it for her.

"You're only rewarding her tantrum," an aide told me.

I felt like I shouldn't have been there. There was nothing wrong with me. Actually, I felt great. I sang in the shower, ate all my food, and painted in art class. An aide called me out of nap time one afternoon and asked me why I was even there.

"I don't know," I told him, and I really didn't anymore. Maybe it hadn't been all that bad.

"What's going on at home?" he asked.

"My grandpa yells a lot," I said, though it felt inadequate.

When the end of our insurance coverage came, Mom picked me up in the middle of group therapy. An aide came in and pulled me out, told me I was going home. I skipped down the hall to get my stuff. Outside, I hugged Mom and leaned against her shoulder while she signed some papers. It was like I had been washed of the dread I was feeling all the time.

Not long after, she left again. I watched her drive away, and then I went and sat next to Grandma, who was sitting on the couch, reading her Bible. If I'd been younger, I would have asked her when my mom would be back. She didn't know any more than I did. The truth settled in my chest, a yawning, windy cavity. She would always leave me. I slid onto my side and rested my head on Grandma's lap, though I knew there would be no comfort in it. While I cried, she patted my head and read to me from the Book of Job. Everything that hurt us, she said, was a test.

Have You An Arm Like God

It's painful to doubt God after a religious upbringing. A slipping terror that I would deal with years later, but that day, on the couch with my grandma, I was experiencing a much more painful version of losing my religion.

Family and friends had tried to tell me that my mother was addicted to drugs, but I never believed it. Even after the time I overheard her telling a boyfriend on the phone, "Drugs make me feel good, Mike! I don't care! I want to keep feeling good!" Even after Ben told me he helped her tie off. Even after my violin went missing and, when I gathered the courage to ask her if she knew where it was, she paused for a minutes-long second before telling me no. Even after the day I found her on the third floor of The Barn, slumped on the couch, her hand palm-up in her lap, fingers curled just enough to keep a small silver pipe from rolling onto the floor the way the lighter resting beside her foot must have. Her chest rose and fell with slow, heavy breaths. I pressed her shoulder and said her name. Mom. She didn't respond.

"Mom!" I said, louder, and the sound of my own voice scared me. I realized I hadn't spoken all day.

My mother opened her eyes, first one and then the other a second slower. They were red and swam across my face without seeing me in it. Her head rolled to the side and she tried to push herself up, but sank back down, like she was sliding in mud, and fell back asleep.

I picked up the pipe, still warm, and set it on the clothes piled on the couch. Then, crouching down, I took my mother's arm and put it over my shoulder.

"Come on," I said, and stood. Almost as tall as her at that point. She came with me, tilting too far, almost toppling, but I shifted and kept us upright. With a hand around her hip, I led her through the doorway to the first room. We shuffled and wobbled until I was able to lower her into a sitting position and get my hand on the back of her neck to ease her down. I took care not to disturb the canopy that she and Ben had constructed out of a sheet, which now billowed gently over our heads in the low setting of the box fan. She smacked her lips and scrunched her nose, flinching from some unseen irritant while I lifted her legs onto the bed and pulled off her shoes.

I tried folding her hands together on her chest, the way cartoon men napped with their hats over their faces. She looked like she was posed in a coffin, so I moved them to her sides. When I looked up, her eyes were open again. Still red and swimming, but, and maybe I was looking for it, lucid. Like she wanted to say something and couldn't get it out. Her jaw wiggled and her lips came together to make some kind of consonant. Suddenly, I was scared, or something like scared that made me want to leave the room before she could say whatever it was that she was trying to say. It felt like whatever she said in that moment would be the real truth.

Her eyes drooped shut again. I sat on the bed for a second, watching her breathe, waiting for her to look at me again or jump up and scare me. When she didn't, I went back to the landing and found the pipe and her lighter. The residue on the pipe looked like nothing, just burnt-up, undefinable gunk. I carried them back into the room, glancing at my mother through the sheer, white fabric of the canopy.

On the ground near the closet, barely hidden behind a roll of carpet, was a duffel bag. Inside there were Ziploc bags, but the contents of those looked like nothing too. Like there were shapes and colors inside, but none that I could look at directly. Like if I did look, they would be the real truth too, so they stayed swallowed up by the duffel, just beyond the reach of the light from the window.

I zipped up the duffel, slung it over my back, and opened the tiny door in the back of the closet that led to the inside of the roof, where the only things were some old Christmas decorations that seemed too clumsily stored to ever be useful again. Unsettling dust and crunching something that sounded breakable under my knee, I buried the duffel in the decorations. Then I was outside, in the backyard, still digging, but this time in the dirt instead of old tinsel. I didn't remember coming outside or starting to dig. On the ground beside me were the pipe and lighter. I pushed them into the hole I'd dug and scooped earth over the top.

It wasn't the last time I'd find her stash. Eventually, the evidence outweighed the denial and I finally let the truth settle in. Even after she returned, and left, and returned again, I couldn't go back. Though I'd never said it to her face, I stopped believing in her. At a sixth-grade orchestra performance, as I scanned the crowd, aware of how pathetic and cliché scanning the crowd for an absent parent was, a classmate asked me where my mom was.

"Probably off doing crack," I said, surprising myself. I wanted to take it back. It felt like a betrayal. It was a betrayal. My guilt burbled alongside the concert anxiety and anger. By the time my mother showed up again and told me, "I'm so sorry. I wouldn't have missed it for the world," I didn't have the energy to tell her it was okay the way I had so many other times.

My mother's patience for my lack of blind, limitless forgiveness ran out quickly. "Your sister is acting like a typical teenager," she told Ben in front of me. They had started playing craps together regularly. The sound of the dice shaking and rolling grated on me, mostly because I was sure she was doing it extra-loud to get under my skin. Join us, Ben would offer, but I never did. I recognized in the way he followed her around and gazed lovingly at her when she spoke that he was still deep in worship. There was nothing I could say to warn him that one day his heart would be broken. Especially not while she was whispering in his ear that I had now turned on her too, the way she'd always known I would. Because I had slipped away, she held him even tighter. It was them against the world.

Can Your Voice Thunder Like His

There was a time when heartbreak clouded my understanding. Now I know that addiction isn't a matter of weakness or moral failing. Our mother didn't choose drugs over us as much as she was possessed and controlled by a hunger in her brain that was as committed to owning her as Mark or the church. The drugs overactivated her basal ganglia, which meant she couldn't feel pleasure from anything else anymore. They sensitized her extended amygdala until everything outside of being high felt so miserable that she was using not to feel pleasure but to escape the pain. Her prefrontal cortex, already damaged from years of trauma, stopped working to control compulsions or assess risk. I couldn't expect her to pull herself out of that cycle any more than I could expect her to pull herself out of an open grave with broken arms and legs.

When I first started going to therapy in earnest, I was disheartened by the advice that I should go to a "happy place" when my flashbacks came. A happy place, and many of the other basic coping strategies I was being taught, felt too similar to prayer. Like rituals I had to perform just because, and whether or not they worked depended on how committed I was to believing in them.

It wasn't until I complained to Ben about the ineffectiveness of the happy place that I got any clarity. The amygdala, he told me in the voice he uses when he gets a chance to bring up his degrees in psychology in casual conversation, is where fear lives. It's like the caveman part of our brains, left over from a bare time when fear and aggression were all we had use or room for, when brains were needed only for survival. The amygdala operates in images and feelings too ancient for words. If you see the shadow of a hackberry branch and your amygdala turns it into a monster arm stretching out to snatch you from your life, it will not help you to think the words, "This isn't real. It's just a tree branch." Instead, you have to show your amygdala an image of something comforting. A beach, a serene pond, a hackberry branch full of bijou ruby fruits. Falkor following our car, circling the telephone poles when Mark cracked his knuckles against the middle console. This is the amygdala's language, how it comes to trust that things are okay so it can turn off the valve releasing panic into your body.

Once I knew the scientific rationale behind the happy place practice, I trusted it, which allowed me to actually employ it. When a therapist recommended deep breathing, I asked her to break down the physiological process. When I started getting patches of goose bumps on just one arm, I researched horripilation and the sympathetic nervous system.

My mother and I loved to watch horror movies together, especially stories where mothers saved their children from monsters. We reveled in moments when the movie moms held their children, limp and sweaty but now free of whatever evil had nearly taken them away; when wild-eyed mothers with strong arms brandished weapons and said things like, "Don't touch my child, you son of a bitch!" My mother would lean forward in her seat, take in every mannerism and line of dialogue, gathering clues for how to be strong. We liked that the horror genre had clear rules. Never split up. Don't open that door. Once you know the name of a demon, you have the power to make it leave.

This last rule is very important. If I could cast out all my mother's agony by flinging holy water and reading the names of neurological processes out of the psychology books I've accrued in my quest for control, I would. Even though I know a savior complex is not just gauche but downright selfish, I would try. But life doesn't follow the satisfying narrative structure of a horror film. I can't exorcize my mother's demons. I can only name them, and hope to understand.

I want to be unselfish every day. I want, every day, to be able to look at my mother and everything she's done, and see what I know to be true: she experienced early head trauma and abuse, she suffers from disorders that disallow her from participating in the same reality as those around her, she is tortured by addiction, she has a good heart and soul inside a pained body.

Some days, though, it's hard to be generous. It's hard not to feel anger for the child I was. Even as I remember her brushing back my hair and telling me, "You were such a beautiful baby," I feel my limbs made achy by the effort to shrink myself, see the way she stiffened when I leaned against her, hear the hard edge of each word she spat when my presence was too much. She preferred sometimes not to be touched.

My mother lived in extremes. She could be fully dedicated to giving me a life she didn't have and couldn't give me, to granting me confidence, to being my best friend and teacher. Then she would remember that she never asked for this, she was still so young, too young, it's not fair, this kid wants too much. I learned that, while one day I could ask for "anything in the whole wide world," on another I should not say a word, not even if I was hungry or my stomach hurt. I remember her, and see myself, in extremes: generosity or reproach, affection or revulsion. I am trying to live somewhere in between. I'm still trying to live here.

How Often I Have Wanted

There is an apocryphal version of the death of Judas. In the story, Judas, full of remorse about Jesus's crucifixion, runs home to tell his wife that he plans to take his own life. He wants to do it before Jesus is resurrected and comes to punish him. Laughing, Judas's wife says that Jesus is as likely to rise from the dead as the chicken she's cooking. On cue, the chicken rises and crows, frightening Judas out of the house and all the way to the tree where he hangs himself.

These are the questions that used to get me in trouble, but I do wonder if the chicken used the opportunity to get away. Did it hop down from the counter while Judas's nameless wife chased after her husband? Where would it have gone, and would it have been imbued with higher sentience through the process of resurrection? If so, what did it think about being brought back to life just to prove a point? Would that awareness diminish its sense of self-worth?

Lately, I've been thinking about getting chickens. I've done extensive research on different breeds, upkeep, equipment, and the nearest veterinarians who practice poultry care. I've even picked out names: Johenn Sebastian Bawk, Ludwing van Beakthoven, and Brittany Jr. Chickens are underestimated intellectuals. They have their own complex system of communication, a rudimentary ability to count, and a capacity for empathy. I have a frequent fantasy of going out in the early morning and seeing three plump little biddies waddling toward me as fast as they can. The only reason I haven't hatched my plans yet is because of the imperious terms of my lease, which dictate that I am not allowed to have any joy in my life.

"Will you write me a letter saying they're my emotional support animals?" I ask Ben on the phone after finding a website for custom chicken helmets.

"That would be unethical," he, a freaking narc, says.

"So, what? I should just die?"

"Oh my god," he gripes. "Why are you trying to rent and have livestock?"

"Because I know they'll love me back!" I cry, but I know he's right. It's unlikely that any landlord will let me own chickens without extorting me to within an inch of my life with pet fees. If I want to have chickens, I'll need to buy a house. Every day, I look at listings for houses priced for people who have either generational wealth or really good credit. I've never given much thought to homeownership before, because it felt impossibly far off, but now I'm ravenous. My mouth waters at the sight of a fixer-upper with a spacious, privacy-fenced yard. I fantasize about spackling and tearing out carpeting. I'm afraid of how much I want.

To be honest, I'm afraid of the chickens too. Not just that I'll kneel to refill their water and they'll peck my sensitive and vulnerable belly button, but also of the terror that comes with loving something. I have recurring nightmares about the windows in my house opening by themselves, forcing me to run from room to room and close them so my little cat won't get out. When I wake up, she's usually next to me, sleeping on her back. I reach out and pet her and she peeks through one eye to see if I'm going to be cool or if this is one of those pats that will culminate in me pressing my forehead to hers and telling her that I'll tear the Earth apart with my teeth if anything ever happens to her. I don't know why I want to quadruple that neurosis, but I do.

At twenty-one, I had a tubal ligation, meaning I'll never have children. When I told certain members of my family, you'd think I betrayed them for thirty pieces of silver. Motherhood was a gift I'd wasted, an obligation I'd turned from. I was selfish, and I'd stolen the grandbabies and nieces and nephews that could have been. All condemnations that fell on me like weak slaps from a weak little baby that I'll never have. A small scar inside my belly button, a promise.

I've told my mom, too, but she forgets, and it's too difficult to rehash every time she asks when I'm going to give her grandbabies and tells me no, the cat doesn't count. To distract her, I tell her that I'm thinking of buying a house so I can get chickens. She's delighted by the idea. It reminds her of the stories my grandma told her as a child about the mean rooster that chased her through the backyard every day when she came home from school. So mean, she'd flee up the hill behind the house and hide in the outhouse until it left, then creep toward the back door with the hole in the screen, braced for that terrible crowing.

"Remember that time we stayed on a chicken farm?" my mom asks when I call her to talk about how chickens like listening to music.

"The one where we collected their eggs in the morning?" I respond on cue. It's a story she loves, and we revisit it often. I can see the crisp Mississippi morning, standing outside the coop together, pointing at how they threw their heads back to drink water. How their waddles jiggled with the effort. How my mom laughed until she had a coughing fit.

"Yeah," she says. "You kids loved it there."

We did. We loved the train ride there, daring each other to stand between cars, one foot on each side of the coupler. We loved the Osage oranges that looked like alien brains littering the ground. We loved the pineapple upside-down cake our great-aunt made us. We loved competing to see who could spell Mississippi the fastest, speeding up the cadence until we gave up on the letters and started making up words to go with the tune.

M-I-S-S-I-S-S-I-P-P-I

If-you-don't-leave-me-a-lone-you're-goin'-to-die

Don't-you-think-it's-so-sad-that-chi-ckens-can't-fly

When-we-go-back-on-the-train-we-won't-say-bye

There's an apocryphal version of my life where I have a child. She's a restart of myself, with huge brown eyes and the same cherry birthmark on her left temple that will fade by the time she's a toddler.

Many nights, she'll ask to sleep next to me, and on many nights, my stomach will twist in discomfort. Her nightmares will be inherited, shifting images of terrors she doesn't understand, and I will be helpless to reach in and stop them. Watchful through the night to make sure she keeps breathing. She'll want and deserve everything, and I'll have only what I have. Her mind will be a delicate Rube Goldberg machine of understanding the world and herself, and I an imperfect marble rolling with good intentions toward levers and baubles that could fall in any direction.

I am so full of love, it overwhelms me. It's terrifying and unsustainable and matched, at times, by my fear. According to a questionable translation of his own noncanonical gospel, Judas Iscariot was Jesus's most-beloved companion, so devoted that he agreed when Jesus asked Judas to betray him to the soldiers. I wonder if he thought about saying no. How love and sacrifice can be selfless and selfish in equal pace. A kiss at dawn, the rooster's crow still ringing through the air, and Judas ran home, silver spilling from his hands like promises. The scent of cooking chicken, soon to be stolen from his nose.

Does The Rain Have A Father

My family was self-aware, in a good-humored kind of way, of our spectacle. A common utterance was "Somebody oughta write a book about us," delivered with a deep sigh and an eye roll. Usually after some occurrence like Grandpa getting pulled over for driving in reverse on the highway because the furniture he was carting on top of his car covered the windshield. Or someone filing a restraining order against someone else and then breaking it a week later because forgive and forget, pray about it, family is family.

Everyone loved everyone else, and nobody missed holiday parties. Grandpa had the kind of family patriarch power that meant he could show up at someone's house in the early morning and tell them he needed help with something, and that person, even as they complained, would rub the sleep out of their eyes and pull on work boots. Everyone commiserated about the tyranny, but no one questioned him to his face.

"That man treats my mother like garbage," Jon would say in disgust, but Grandma wouldn't let anyone try to intervene. My grandfather used her as a secretary and kept a meticulous ledger on the wall of all the money he gave her for groceries and other expenses. Once, she fell while coming up the driveway and couldn't get up. When he found her lying on the ground some time later with Puzzums curled up at her side, he stood over her and asked, "Honey, what are you doing on the ground?"

"Oh, just taking in the sights," she quipped.

My mom was his baby girl. He'd sing a little song to her that went, "Krissie Lee Anne, Krissie Lee Anne, come on over, and don't stop 'til you git here," and she'd go to him and kiss his cheek, call him Daddy. Throughout all her disappearances and reappearances and disappearances, he took her in and gave her work and fought her battles. If someone in the family let me stay with them when she left, he made sure that they relinquished me when she came back. I lived with all of my aunts and uncles at some time or another.

Anyone who tried to keep me, or otherwise help, my grandfather blocked. Anyone who went against him was removed from the will or lost whatever gifts—cars, home loans, mercy from his wrath—he had bestowed on them. I learned quickly not to get used to my family's hospitality, but to treat each stay like a sweet reprieve.

When I was in high school, my grandfather died and we all went back to The Barn to see his body before it was taken away. It was well after midnight and we milled around in the long hallway as if unsure of where we should be without him there to bark orders. When the paramedics loaded him onto the stretcher, my mom followed them all the way out, leaning over his body and wailing. My aunt Ginger stayed folded in half on the couch outside his bedroom, reaching down every now and again to scratch lines in the dry skin where her skirt ended. Jon and Thomas hovered on each side of my grandma, who had a general air of holding it together.

Ben and I met at the top of the stairs as I was on my way out. I can't remember if we talked or hugged, just that we stood for a long time next to the cubbyhole beside the stairs that we had once climbed inside to hide from Grandpa's rages. Now we were too big to fit.

CHAPTER 9

Sanctuaries

J on took me in the most times, and took Ben in later when it was his turn to try to escape. His house was unfinished and out in the woods. Prone to starting but never finishing projects, Jon lived amid treasures, tools, and exposed wood. When I lived with him in middle school, wires hung from the ceiling in some places and we had to use pliers to turn the upstairs shower on, but we got along well. I came in from school and watched movies on his big TV until he got home late at night from his job as a construction worker and fell asleep next to me, sitting up. On the weekends, my cousins came to visit. Ben too. We still went camping and did fun stuff, though Jon was slower than he had been when we were young, and he wore a back brace while driving. When my cousins and Ben left, I could see him droop, so I'd make chili out of whatever was in the kitchen or heat up some canned beef stew.

"Bert," he'd say in the mornings, over a thermos of dangerously strong coffee, "you ain't half bad."

If he wasn't too tired after work, we would go to the video store in town and rent movies. Usually a raunchy comedy or cheesy horror film. I loved watching movies with Jon because he laughed easily and uproariously, stamping his foot, pointing, and crying. All it took was a man falling down a flight of stairs or an especially over-the-top slasher scene and he would crack up. It was infectious too. I'd start laughing along with him and then I wouldn't be able to stop, not even after Jon inevitably fell asleep halfway through.

Mom showed up after a while and took up residence on the couch in Jon's living room. She slept most of the time, and rapidly escalated to screaming if something woke her up. When she was awake, she scratched herself constantly and picked at her face. She developed a tic in her neck and began praying in a quick, quiet voice to the sky before every drink or bite of food. I barely recognized her most of the time, and if I expressed concern, it turned into an argument that ended only when I went into the bedroom I was staying in and locked the door.

At night, when Jon got home, I heard her telling him, "She's being so horrible to me, Jon. All she does is give me attitude."

I wanted to defend myself, to tell Jon that she was lying about me. I couldn't confront her, though. It was a line I still couldn't cross.

Jon pulled me aside after a few weeks.

"I'm so sorry," he said, his voice catching. "I can't have her living here. I don't want her around my kids. I don't want her in my home."

I knew she wouldn't leave without me, so I left and went back to The Barn with her. The next time she left, I moved in with my aunt Ginger and uncle Steve, and their six blond children in Kentucky. They flipped houses, though I didn't know that's what they were doing at the time. All I knew was that they would live in a big, beautiful house for a few years and then move and repeat. Their house in Kentucky was an old Victorian with an unfinished attic that they said would be my room when they fixed it up. It was summer, and since there was no school to keep us all occupied, Ginger walked us to the library almost every day or took us to a nearby river to swim.

The youngest was still a baby, and I would carry her, plucking red buckeye flowers from trees we passed to brush across her forehead, a little magic to keep her safe from growing up.

Steve had a temper, and when he was home, we were all careful. The children stopped playing running around and laughing games and instead spent their time with games they could play quietly, blond heads bent down over a Game Boy or puzzle. Like there was a storm inside the house and the rain was falling too hard to hear one another. Once, I accidentally knocked over a pane of glass in the living room, and he called me stupid in a voice so loud, I thought I'd shatter too. He could be funny, but also cruel. Every night, he wanted steak for dinner, so Ginger would press one inside their George Foreman grill, and I would watch the yellow fat melt and dribble into the grease-catching tray, and although she was rail-thin—prominent cheekbones, hard nose, and long, dishwater-blond hair piled on top of her head in the style of the Pentecostal women of our family—she almost never made one for herself.

I liked Aunt Ginger and the way her eyes closed when she smiled or when she periodically stopped to scratch the inside of her ear with her pinky finger. If her children were being irritating, she would say things in a clipped typewriter voice. If they were being really irritating, she held their faces gently and called them nicknames, like honey or beebee, in a voice so sweet it made my spine tingle.

My aunt Ginger liked to have me sit on the trunk at the end of her four-poster bed in front of a mirror and brush the tangles out of my hair and smile at the reflection of my face. She'd call me Pretty Pocahontas and tell me about how they dressed me when I lived with her and Steve as a baby.

"I used to put you in the most adorable outfits," she'd say, looking away from my thrift-store blue jeans and Mom's T-shirt hanging to my knees. "You were my little doll baby."

She showed me a photo album that had professional pictures of me as a baby in frilly, brightly colored and loudly patterned dresses with billowing white petticoats peeking out and matching head-bands and shoes. In one, Ginger held me in her lap and smiled up at the camera. I did look like a doll with my gigantic brown eyes and coal-black hair. After a few pages, the pictures of me ended and were replaced by pictures of their children, all blond hair and blue eyes in outfits that were nicer than anything I owned.

For a time, Ginger told me, she and Steve thought they couldn't have children. They were thrilled when my mom asked them to adopt me. They filled the nursery they had started to accept would never be used with clothes and toys for me. Right before they could sign the adoption papers, my mom showed up with Mark and said she wanted me back. Mark threatened to hang Steve from a tree across the street if he called the cops. There was nothing they could do.

"I wish she would have let me raise you," she said, and gazed at my face like I had died.

At night, we all slept in front of box fans to cool the Kentucky sweat off ourselves, spoke goodnight prayers into the grated wind to hear our voices metallic and holy and loving. When I closed my eyes, I imagined I was lying in a dry prairie with the breeze passing over and against me. I rarely slept in that house, in the blue dark with streetlights that flickered on only often enough that I feared what I might see in the next illumination.

My sleeplessness started as an issue of too much heat. It became an issue of too much thought the night after we found a broken baby bird on the front steps.

"Must have fallen from the tree," Ginger said, and we gathered around the bird and tried to mourn. That night, looking out the vintage-glass window that always appeared as if it had just been rained on, I imagined the small thing falling, its mother diving frantically to catch it, but unable without arms or hands or language to say goodbye. Or maybe she hadn't been there at all, and the small thing had plummeted alone. Dried up under the southern sun and peered at by children.

Grandpa hated Steve and wanted Ginger and the kids closer, so he showed up and pounded a "For Sale" sign that he'd made into the front yard of their house. People from the church showed up to help them pack, but Ginger burst into tears when she saw us putting clothes into the wrong boxes.

"That's not where those go!" she cried, and sat on the floor to sort them all out, folding each little shirt and pair of pants carefully. She always wanted things to be clean and particular, and they never were. Once, when she'd asked me to bring her the laundry, I'd stood in the doorway of the bathroom holding the hamper and watched her adjust the towel on the rack over and over, her eyes far away, muttering a prayer under her breath. Now she prayed under her breath again while the church volunteers and I stood around, unsure of how to help.

Steve and I joked about stuffing me in the back of the U-Haul, but when the time came to leave, I was sent back to The Barn.

There was a brief time in the seventh grade when I thought I might move in with Shirley, who was still my best friend. Her family was moving two hours away to be closer to her mom's grandparents.

"I wish I could come with you," I said over the phone.

"Then come!" she said. "My parents love you like another daughter."

In the weeks leading up to the move, we talked about how we would decorate our room and share clothes, and how we would get a second chance at making an impression as cool goths at our new school. We even told people at our current school that we were leaving together. The few friends we had gave us hugs goodbye on the last day, but when I got back to The Barn and announced my departure, Grandma informed me that I couldn't just take off across the state with my friend.

"But why not?!" I demanded. The rules had been so loose before and I'd lived so many places. I couldn't understand why I wasn't allowed this move.

"You just can't!" Grandma told me.

All at once, the silliness of our plans dawned on me. Even though I hated her right then for telling me no, I laid my head on Grandma's lap and wept. She didn't pat my back this time. This wasn't a test of God, just an adolescent gloom.

I called Shirley to tell her the bad news and we said our weepy goodbyes, promised to call every day. I hadn't known I could miss anyone as much as I'd missed my mother, but when Shirley was gone, I slipped further into a depression that only lifted when she picked up the phone and said, "Yyyellow!"

She had been my best friend since the fifth grade, a relationship whose ending I had forgotten to fear. I'd watched her grow from a four-foot-nine kid with round glasses, brown hair, and an earnestly donned *Rainbow Brite* T-shirt to a four-foot-nine teen with stylish square frames, dyed black hair, and that same *Rainbow Brite* T-shirt, now worn ironically. She'd been into The Barn, gazed upon its mess and said only "This is just clutter. My house is *nasty*." She made Ben feel welcome when he hung out with us, and never brought up his kidnapping even though everyone at school knew about it. She'd seen my mom come home high, hair and eyes wild, ranting about the fight she'd been in and the man whose knees she'd smashed with a bar stool. Despite everything, she didn't stop talking to me or treat me like the trashy mess I feared I was. I loved her, accidentally and irrevocably, and then she was gone too.

Next, I moved in with my uncle Thomas. He lived a few miles away in a small house with a spare room, where I slept on an air mattress. My favorite thing about living there was his endless supply of frozen yogurt and a computer with internet access. Once he showed me how to set up a Myspace account, I spent hours after school each day customizing my profile and chatting with Shirley and the latest boy I had a crush on. His name was Clay. We went to the same middle school. He had sandy brown hair and blue eyes, and I was sure I was in love with him.

Eventually, Thomas asked me to move out because his friend needed a place to stay and he didn't want me living with another grown man. Back to The Barn, but at least now I had a boyfriend. We talked on the phone all the time, passed notes at school, and went on dates to PG-13 movies.

"I wish we had a special place where only we could go," we'd tell each other in dreamy voices. We broke up and got back together, as middle-schoolers will, but he told me he loved me. I loved him back. His older brother dropped him off after school when my mom wasn't around, and we made out until his mom got off work and picked him up. One night, in the middle of our usual kissing session, the front door opened.

"Hide," I told him, and went to see who it was. My mom came in with a man I didn't know. Her eyes were clear and she was smiling.

"This is Tony," she said.

"Hiya," said Tony.

She continued, "We're going to go stay at his house. It's really nice, Brit. Three bedrooms, two and a half bathrooms, a *dishwasher*—?"

The phone rang. She picked it up.

"Hello . . . ? Clay? I don't—"

I signaled to get her attention.

"Just a second." She covered the mouthpiece.

"Clay is here," I confessed, wringing my hands.

"Oh," she said, waving my concern off, then put the phone back to her ear. "He'll be right out."

Clay came out of his hiding spot and greeted my mom and Tony.

"You don't have to hide next time," she told him, waggling her eyebrows.

When he was gone, we packed some clothes and got in Tony's truck, a bouncy old thing where I had to sit with my legs on either side of the stick shift. His house was far out in the fields, down a series of winding roads just like Kurt's had been. It really was nice. The carpet was plush and white, and the backyard was enormous.

"This is your room," he told me, and led me to a room with its own personal bathroom.

I looked at Mom to confirm this was real.

"Yeah," she said, nodding enthusiastically. "Isn't this freaking awesome?!"

Tony was a single man with no children and a big house all to himself. He would love to take care of us, he said. Even Ben had a room for his weekend visits. I was cautious at first, but he proved to be a bit of a goofball at the very worst. He was bald and grey, with a disproportionately round belly and a habit of scratching his inner ear with his keys.

"I hope you kids know I love your mom," he told Ben and me. I believed him. What I wondered was whether Mom loved him back. They seemed to have fun together. Mom seemed happy, if not a little exasperated sometimes.

"He takes for*ever* to cum," she told me one day while deep-frying some Tater Tots. "Ah, but he's sweet."

As a middle-schooler, I was old enough for her to talk to me about these things without apologizing anymore, though I hadn't told her that Clay and I had started having sex in my new bedroom while she slept on the other side of the house. It felt like something I wanted to keep for myself, and I wasn't sure how she would react. This was a new realm, one that I wasn't sure would be included in our "talk about anything" rule.

It felt good to be wanted. Like the final step in showing him that I loved him. We spent the summer having sex, riding in the back of Tony's truck, and swapping mix CDs. Even when I started at the high school and he, a year behind me, was still at the middle school, we talked on the phone every night and saw each other on the weekends. Even after Mom and Tony inevitably got into a big fight and we moved out, Grandpa let us stay in one of his unrented houses, where Clay and I were close enough to walk along the train tracks to each other's houses.

I try to remember what that time was like and how I felt. How he was. Sun beating on the top of my head as I walked, balancing on a train rail. Field stretched out to my left, highway on the right. In the distance, his figure grew closer until I could see his sandy hair and small mouth, and that space in my chest that had felt like a vacuum for so long was full. Hey, we said, smiling, when we reached each other. Hands clasped or knocking each other off-balance on the way back to my little house. Up the steep hill, through the back door, into my bedroom. He wrote a sweet message on my headboard in lipstick that I owned but never wore. If I fell asleep, I woke up to his gaze, soft and loving, on my face.

In the winter, he broke up with me over the phone. I begged him not to go and then I didn't eat for a week. I went to school and came home, a husk. When I found out he was dating someone else, I slept under my bed and pulled out handfuls of my hair.

"He's an asshole," Mom said. She knew how I felt. Her first love had cheated on her. The first time she cut her hair was after the breakup.

"I always loved your long hair," he told her. "It breaks my heart that you cut it."

They were even. She offered to take me for my own haircut, or to drive me over to his house if I wanted.

"We could egg him or shit in a bag, set it on fire, and leave it on his porch," she suggested.

"That's okay," I said. All I wanted was to blow away like a leaf. She kept trying, driving me two hours to Shirley's house and making my favorite food, her specialty casserole that had Doritos crushed up in it. At the store, she'd point to random boys my age and say, "Oh, he's cute." She mixed us extra strong piña coladas and played music loudly, grabbing my limp hand and urging me to dance with her and Ben. When I failed to cheer up after more than a month, her patience grew thin.

"Tell me what you're feeling!" she'd plead when I burst into tears in the middle of an episode of *Scrubs* that I'd once watched with him. What I felt like was the strained tissue in the middle of mitosis, a word I'd learned in science class, but I didn't know how to verbalize the image of a cell splitting, and I was too tired to try.

"Tell me!" she repeated when I said that I didn't know how to talk about it. "Tell me!" Until she was yelling, clenching my arms, forcing me to the ground as if she could command me to speak. She let go, stood, and went to her room without saying anything else.

"You want to be honest with each other?" I asked her the next time. "Okay. You have an addiction, don't you?"

It was the first time I'd ever said it out loud. The words felt unnatural. Her lip curled.

"I hate everyone," she said.

This was something she declared often, but always with the addendum that I wasn't included in "everyone." I was the only one she could count on. The only one who really loved her. The only one in the whole world.

The addendum never came. Only her eyes, blue and severe, fixed on me. I felt something in my chest like an engine knocking.

"Even me?" I whispered.

She was silent, and then suddenly she was still silent. Our membrane furrowed, tugged, and then severed, and we were two separate daughter cells.

We kept our distance from each other. When I cried in the shower, she no longer knocked on the door and asked if I was okay. Ben offered what comfort he could in the form of making me ramen and picking bundles of flowers that he left outside my room, but he was also on his way out. Another custody hearing came, and when he and Mom got home from court, she went into her room and slammed the door.

"What happened?" I asked him.

"I wrote a letter to the judge that I wanted to live with Dad," he said, shaking.

We looked toward her bedroom, where we could hear her cussing and throwing things. The door swung open, startling us both.

"You wanna live with your fucking dad, Ben?" she screamed. "You want to leave me?"

"I'm sorry," he said, crying.

"Don't even worry about visiting," she continued. Her nostrils flared. "You don't ever have to see me again."

"Mom," I said, holding my hands up, "this doesn't mean he doesn't love you."

"He sure doesn't fucking act like it," she spat.

"Let's sit down and talk," I offered.

"I don't want to talk!" She pointed severely at Ben, whose head hung. "Your brother betrayed us."

"No," I said, "he didn't."

She didn't respond, but went into his room and started throwing things into the hallway.

"You don't want to live under my roof," she panted, "guess you don't want anything I buy you."

"Mom, please!" Ben sobbed.

"Stop!" I shouted. "You're scaring us!"

She dropped what was in her hands and stepped toward us. I felt my body tense in preparation, but she stomped past us and back into her room, where we heard more clattering.

"Fuck!" she yelled. "FUCK!"

I ushered Ben into his room and locked the door before she could change her mind. Ben tried to pick up some of his things, but gave up and plopped down on his bed to weep into his hands. I sat beside him and put my arm around his shoulders. Sliding onto his side, he laid his head on my lap.

"I'm sorry!" he wailed.

"You don't need to be sorry," I said, and ran my fingers through his curls. Closer to brown than blond now, darkening with age the way his father's had. We stayed that way until his dad came to pick him up, and then I was alone with Mom in that tiny house my grandfather had loaned us.

Mom refused to come out of her room for a while. I knocked on her door with mugs full of Mountain Dew and asked her to come out, but she only mumbled that she just wanted to sleep.

"You want to watch a movie?" I asked through the door.

"Not right now," she responded, her voice raspier than usual.

I wanted her to be okay, but I knew not to push. We nursed our heartaches on opposite ends of the house, passing quietly on the way to the bathroom or kitchen, drifting through the grocery store.

In the spring of ninth grade, Clay called me. He'd just gotten a cell phone and wanted to give me the number.

"You're welcome to call me," he said, so I did. It was awkward at first, but then we talked like old times. I told him about Ben leaving.

He told me about getting the new *Grand Theft Auto*, and invited me over to play. I went, and my hands shook almost too much to hold the controller. He was still with his new girlfriend, but I was happy, in a jittery, sickly way, that he still wanted to be friends.

"Clay and I are talking again," I told Mom, hoping she would get excited for me the way she sometimes did about a B on my report card or a witty comeback I'd made to a school bully. A "Hell yeah!" and a high five. Anything to see her perk up.

"That's great, baby," she said, but there was no energy in it.

Mother's Day was coming up, and I was determined to make her feel better. I cleaned the house, dusting the TV and the individual horizontal blinds, vacuuming, washing the windows, and scraping the hardened spots off the kitchen counter. The house felt almost new by the time I was finished, so I nearly screamed when Aunt Ginger asked if she could come over and do laundry with all six of the kids the night before Mother's Day. She'd moved in at The Barn to help take care of Grandpa since he'd been diagnosed with dementia, and the washer there was broken.

They heaved in several jumbo trash bags full of clothes and set up camp in the living room. The house was small, so the wet heat from all our bodies and the laundry stuck to the walls and windows and dripped down in rivulets. We opened the doors and let the clouds of steam curl out and dissipate in the cold night air, but we still couldn't touch anything without coming away with a damp hand.

Mom stayed in her room for most of the night, coming out once to use the bathroom and dodging the kids as they chased each other. I flinched and corralled them back to the living room to let them pick out a movie. All the ruckus must still have gotten to her, though, because she came out of her room a while later and said she was running to the gas station to get some cigarettes.

When Ginger had finished all her laundry, she asked me to thank my mom when she got back, and hefted the bags out to her car again. The house was quiet. I sat down for a second to take a breath, and then set about cleaning again. I wiped the condensation off everything I could reach, vacuumed again, and put the furniture my cousins had moved back into place. When I was done, I took a shower and went to bed.

As If They Were Not Hers

When I got up the next morning, my mother wasn't home. She might have gone to church for the Mother's Day service with my grandma, I thought. I was grateful that she didn't wake me up and make me go too. I sat down at the table to work on a handmade Mother's Day card. It felt childish, but she'd always said, "I'd much rather have something you and your brother made than some cheesy-ass Hall-mark card from the store."

There was a box of brownie mix at the back of one of the cabinets. I didn't like brownies, but she did, and I figured we could bake them together when she got home. We needed groceries, but there were enough ingredients for brownies.

Overnight, the walls and windows had accrued more condensation. I wiped them off again and closed her bedroom door so her room wouldn't get sweaty. The day stretched out and turned to another night. I stood her card up on the table so she would see it when she came in, and went to bed.

When I got up to go to school, the card was still there. She could have missed it, coming in in the dark, I thought, but when I got home, it was still there. I knocked on her door, but she wasn't there. How long she was gone this time, I wasn't sure. All I could do was wait.

The first day passed, and then the next, and the next. At night, I watched headlights from the highway slide across my bedroom wall. I wanted to be angry at her, but I was worried too. She'd told me, on returns from past disappearances, about the kinds of things that happened when she was gone. The beatings, the assaults, the narrow escapes. While I was lying safe in bed thinking angry thoughts about her, she could be somewhere getting hurt.

What little food we had went quickly, though I didn't touch the brownies. Halfway through the first week, the toilet paper ran out.

It was easy enough to pocket some of the free meals I got at school. Easy enough to unscrew the toilet paper roll from the stall and put one of the industrial-sized rolls in my backpack. In class, I started to feel like my teachers were looking closely at me, that they could see in my face somehow what was going on. My stomach pinched all the time, from concern, from hunger, from heartache, and from fear that a social worker would show up and knock on the door. Worse, Ben's dad called once or twice to see about the next visit.

"Where's your mom?" he asked.

I wanted to tell him I was wondering the same thing, but I held my tongue and said she had gone out for cigarettes. He accepted my half-truths, but I knew he would call back. To be safe, I stopped answering the phone.

Since I was alone, I turned the thermostat up until I could comfortably sit around in my underwear. There was no telling how much longer the utilities would be on if she didn't get back soon. The walls got damp and the windows fogged up again, as if the house was sweating her out.

In the humidity, the corner of the Mother's Day card had started to peel. To preserve it, I moved it to her room. The blanket she'd tacked up over the window kept the room dark and cooler than the rest of the house. I posed the card on the desk beside her bed and closed her door.

By the next Sunday, I had run out of the dish soap I was using to wash my clothes. What food I'd taken from school had run out too. Even the batteries in the fire alarm were dying, causing the little disk to emit a piercing, high-pitched beep at an interval that seemed perfectly matched to the span of time it took my heart to settle from the last beep. The closed door to her bedroom felt just as loud. As long as it was closed, I felt like she might be in there. Like she could have come back and slipped in while I was pacing on the other end of the house, or climbed in through her window. Every day, the idea seemed more possible until, finally, it was unbearable. I opened the door.

Even away from the worst of the humidity, the Mother's Day card had curled even more. It was so warped that the front flap had peeled open and I could read the message I'd written inside. I wrote it because she had accepted this tiny house from Grandpa even though she hated taking things from him, so we could have some stability. I wrote it because, despite everything, she was trying. I wrote it because she needed to hear it. The card said, "I'm proud of you."

The words bulging out at me felt like mockery. Suddenly, the heat was unbearable. It made me want to tear off my skin and the rest of the house while I was at it. I took three big steps across the room and snatched the card, crumpled it in my fist, and threw it away in the kitchen trash. Then, because it hadn't been satisfying enough, I took it out and plunged it back in, where it uncurled itself again, revealing: "proud of you."

For another week, I waited. My clothes smelled sour. I could hardly think of anything except what I might eat next. On the last day, I stood outside and watched the end of the driveway, willing her, as I had so many times before, to please come home now. Cars kept passing and none of them were her. I went inside and called Clay.

"My mom left and hasn't come back since last week," I said, blunting the truth just a little.

"Hold on a sec," he told me, and put the phone down. While I waited, my heart raced. I'd never breached the unspoken rule not to tell people about how bad things were. Saying the words out loud felt like unleashing a curse, which I could never take back.

"I told my mom and she's gonna come get you," he said when he got back.

"Oh!" I hadn't expected this. "Is that . . . okay?"

"Yeah," he said. "Just pack some clothes."

I threw a few things into my backpack and then sat in the living room to wait. When the headlights finally shone through the window, I had a moment of pause. What if it was my mom? What if I'd only needed to wait a little longer? I walked outside and squinted into the lights.

CHAPTER 10

Promise Land

Clay's family, the Smiths, lived in a nice house in a residential neighborhood at the edge of a cornfield. To me, their family was the image of middle-class life. Diane and Kenneth, his parents, had full-time jobs that allowed them to afford things like gaming consoles and concert tickets for their two sons. A tree out front, a flourishing flower garden, a basketball hoop at the end of the driveway, along with a stone with the names of all the family members, including the dog, carved into it. Neighbors chatted at the edges of their yards and came together for potlucks on holidays. Inside, the wood floor was covered by large Turkish rugs. Framed family photos lined the walls. There was a delicious smell in the air that I still can't exactly put into words—not quite sweet or savory, something like a faint hint of celery. A giant TV just inside the front door on a heavily knickknacked buffet. A wood stove in the family room.

When I was a kid, I loved the movie *All Dogs Go to Heaven*. I studied the way the protagonist moved, how she clasped her hands and looked up through her eyelashes. If I could just emulate that, I felt, someone might see me being lovable and love me, make me a syrupy stack of waffles in front of a bay window on a sunny day the way the nice couple in the movie did for Anne-Marie in her rag dress, with her rosy cheeks and bright blue eyes. Now here it was, the put-together family taking me in. A dream come true.

In the summers, Diane and I liked to float in the aboveground pool. The water stayed cold even when the day was so hot you could barely breathe. She floated on one inflatable raft, and I floated on another. It was safe out there, with the sun slowly killing us both. Kenneth brought us ice-cold drinks and then went back inside because his whole head turned red if he stayed in the heat for long. If Diane dropped her transition lenses, I'd dive down and get them, rising up next to her and reaching over to put them on her, upside down and dripping. She'd splash me and call me a goon, and I'd wade back to my own raft, laughing, and climb on. We settled, rotating in comfortable silence, her reading a warped magazine and me thinking, I want to tell you.

I'm getting ahead of myself.

THAT FIRST NIGHT, after Diane picked me up and I went to shower, she washed my backpack and the clothes I'd been wearing. In case of cockroaches. I washed my hair with their nice shampoo and conditioner and scrubbed my body hard with a washcloth lathered in their nice bodywash. I put on their pajamas and went into the room where Diane had laid out clean bedclothes. My stomach twisted all night long—and that whole first week. Sharp pain, like a jumble of silver pins pricking me from the inside.

Luis, their older son, was deployed in Iraq, so I slept in his vacant room. His guitar, which I'd seen him play on their front porch swing, sat propped in the corner of the room. He had a black comforter and a picture of him and his friends sitting in a rain puddle tacked to the wall. These were sacred items in a sacred place, I understood, so I tried to sleep flat on my back with my arms at my sides. This is how I moved around in that house in the beginning. A museum guest, careful not to disturb anything. Sure that soon enough I would have to leave.

When Diane took me back to the house by the highway to get more clothes, the smell of cigarette smoke knocked me back. I'd never not been cloaked in it. Now that I was clean, I saw everything as if for the first time: The shriveled wad of mildewed clothes I'd left in the washer. Tracks on the walls from where condensation had dribbled and dried. Candle wax melted on the carpet. Our box TV on a rolling microwave cart in the middle of the living room. Gnats around the sink and trash can. My eyes opened to the nakedness of our squalor.

After I had been with them for a few weeks, Diane and Kenneth offered me the dream. I could live there. There was no way they were sending me back to someone who would leave me alone for this long. Yes, I said. Yes to the dream.

CLAY AND I were friendly and cautious around each other.

"You two can't be living under the same roof and playing hanky-panky," Diane and Kenneth told us.

I still ached with young love, but kept it to myself. My greatest fear was overstepping, and what could be more of an imposition than pursuing someone who did not want me and betraying my saviors' trust? To be safe, I relegated myself to the role of pal. It was easy enough to make myself stop hoping for something I told myself would never happen. Manageable heartache, banter, careful distance. Until we were alone after school. Me, sprawled on the floor, watching the TV. Him, on the couch, watching me. Pretending I didn't notice. Convincing myself he had to be looking somewhere else. Closing my eyes to enjoy the feeling of a clean rug and slow my heart. His slow crawl across the room, face close to mine. He kissed me and I kissed back and back and back, muttering when we separated for air, "I'm sorry. I'm sorry." Afterward, we sat side by side on the couch, his hand awkwardly on my knee. I urged myself to ask, What now, to verbalize my guilt and hope, but nothing came out. Diane and Kenneth came home from work. Neither of us confessed.

After that, I was sure Clay would leave his girlfriend, but they stayed together. It had been a mistake, I decided, and I was stupid to believe it meant anything. Then it happened again. Me, keeping my hands in my lap, and him, leaning over, gradually, slowly, to mouth at my shoulder. Then again, and again. Passion followed by shame, and no ground to stand on and ask him why or what it meant.

I HAVE GRIEVED for the teen version of myself. She didn't plot herself into that house to seduce the boy who broke her heart. She wanted to be good. She wanted to go on long bike rides and walk around the thrift store with Diane. She wanted to help Kenneth chop vegetables for dinner, singing Meat Loaf together at the top of their lungs. She wanted to walk the dog and do her homework and notch her height on the doorjamb of the laundry room.

When she lounged on the couch with her eyes closed, she was only listening to the wind chimes tinkling outside the screen door, relishing the spots of sunlight dappling her skin. Breathing in deeply, enjoying the fragrance of home, her newly discovered sense of smell, powerful in the absence of smoke. She didn't intend to entice. Her body was a beacon, whether she wanted it to be or not. It called the boy over to climb on top of her, and then it went with the motions, the way she had learned far too early. The thrill in her belly, which soured and pinched in the moments following, was a confirmation that this was what she was meant for. This was what love looked like, how it felt. The most she could ask for.

Am I Not Your Own Donkey

Maybe he resented me for the guilt he felt about cheating, or because I was a permanent fixture in his home, an inescapable commitment. Maybe I annoyed him. I know better than to try guessing other people's motivations, but when you spend a good chunk of your life watching other people's moods like a shepherd checking the horizon, the habit becomes reflexive, protective. A change in breathing, furrowed brow, slammed door, coyote tracks. Hide, fawn, run, fight.

Whatever his reasons, Clay could flip the switch from sweet to uncaring so unpredictably that I never knew where I stood on any given day. A new side of him emerged, so different from the boy who used to walk along the train tracks to nap the afternoon away with me. Now, if I felt him looking at me and looked back, his expression could be one of lust or contempt. No way to track which it would be. One day he might tell me he wanted to spend the rest of his life with me, and the next I was presumptuous for leaning against him while we watched TV. The safest route was to let him make the first move, gauge the mood, and then adjust accordingly by either loving him back or keeping myself small and unassuming.

He was difficult to read. I sometimes got it wrong. Got shrugged off or berated. Once, while he was bent over looking for something in the closet, I playfully honked his butt. A "goose," my grandma would have called it. He whipped around, shoved me onto the bed, punched me hard on the shoulder, and left the room. I lay there for a moment, shocked and embarrassed. My arm throbbed. I wasn't thinking, How could he hit me? I was thinking, Why am I like this? A grabby, hyperactive little monkey who forgot herself. Unlovable.

THERE WERE OTHER punches on my shoulders, pinches, his white fist pounded on my legs, headlocks, armbars, crimping and mashing my fingers. Once, I stepped on his foot while he had pins and needles, and he swung his arm out and caught me in the gut. Sometimes he clamped his mouth around my arm just above the wrist and bit down until I thought the bone would break. Love bites, I called them. When someone loves you so much that they look at you and it shakes them up inside, and they just have to act on it. The love bites left behind deep ridges in my skin, dotted with tiny beads of blood. Before they faded, I liked to slot my own, smaller bite inside of his so that when I pulled away, the spit and red skin and rings of teeth marks looked like some beast with two rows of teeth had gotten ahold of me. The slow fade, over the course of days and weeks, from red to green and then sickly yellow.

The violence was easy to write off as sibling roughhousing. That's how we were supposed to see each other, according to Diane and Kenneth. Brothers and sisters, perverse as it was to think of us that way, squabbled. They hit and called each other names. No big deal. It's not like he was hitting me in the face, I reasoned with myself. I couldn't call us a couple and I couldn't call what was happening violence. I even laughed sometimes as I was being hurt, played along, kept my inside voice as I asked him to please stop. Getting loud or saying sternly, "I'm serious," ruined the fun. It made me a bad sport and a killjoy.

"Jesus," he'd groan, dropping whatever limb he'd captured. "I'm just messing around."

What hurt worse was how he spoke to me. When he wasn't in the mood for me. If I got brave enough to ask him what I meant to him. When his girlfriend came over to hang out and he wanted to prove to her that I was nothing. The sharp edge in his voice and disgust in his eyes when he told me to get out of the way or shut up or go jump off a bridge. That my body was shaped weird or my skin was getting too dark from being out in the sun.

"I'm sick of you," he'd say, shaking his head. Looking at me like I was the nastiest thing he'd ever seen. "Keep acting like an idiot and see what happens."

Then, when we were alone, he would apologize. Tearful confessions about how he didn't want to turn out like his dad, who could go into silent furies so oppressive that no one wanted to walk through the middle of the house where he sat in his recliner with his jaw set. He recognized that he wasn't being good to me, and he wanted to change. He was going to change. A repentant hug turned into a squeeze, his mouth on my neck, and me giving in. At the end, when I tottered off to clean myself, I rewound it in my mind, tried to fit certain hand placements, certain exhalations that could have been certain words, certain fistfuls of hair that could have been caresses, into loving meanings. A catalog to keep me from withering when he turned cold.

If I just loved him well enough, I convinced myself, it would all change. Put my head in the lion's mouth to show my complete fidelity. The crueler he was, the more I cooked him food, rubbed his back, posed myself just the way he liked. Love brewed and swelled inside me, and I beamed it at him, hoping he felt my dedication. Love so big it left no room for anything else. Not dignity or God or even my little brother, whom I barely talked to during that time. Even The Barn was sold while I lived with the Smiths. I went over to help with the move, a years-long process of packing every single thing, down to the curled *Marmaduke* comics clipped from newspapers in the '90s, but I remember basically none of it. All I ever thought about was getting home to Clay.

I was possessed by love. I loved the trail of goose bumps that bloomed when I ran a finger along Clay's arm. I loved to press down the veins on the back of his hand and let go, see the blood halt and rush. Or lay my head on his chest to hear the thumping before he shrugged me away, too intimate. Each time he kissed me or laughed at one of my jokes, I knew it was working.

He talked to me about things he never talked to other people about. How he worried about Luis in Iraq, but also that everyone liked Luis more than him. How Diane hated him because he had always been so difficult, throwing tantrums at the babysitters' until they wouldn't watch him anymore, kicking the principal of the elementary school, breaking things.

"I'm a piece of shit," he'd say. Self-deprecation disguised as penitence, but really it was a challenge for me to prove him wrong, to convince us both that his insecurities were my responsibility. One I rose to because love had always felt incomplete if it wasn't abject.

"I don't think you are," I said, stroking his hair. The only person who understood him. Us against the world.

By the time my mom returned, there was no way I was going to leave. I don't remember her explanation when she called to say she was back, if there was one. That world felt so far away. Now she wanted me to go back, to come home.

"I'm staying here," I told her, my heart racing.

"Like hell you are," she said, and I hung up.

I hoped she might just forget me. She had done it before. The phone rang and rang while I paced. She left voice mails demanding that I answer, saying she was coming over.

"You want me to answer and tell her to fuck off?" Clay asked.

"No."

"Well, I'm calling my mom to let her know."

I put my arms over my head and squatted on the ground, trying to breathe. This had been inevitable, I knew. My time with the Smiths was always temporary. There had never been a chance that I'd really stay. I'd gotten too comfortable.

"My mom says to lock the door and wait for her to get home," Clay said, kneeling next to me. He looked concerned. "I'm also going to get my dad's shotgun."

"Please, don't." I imagined the barrel pointed at my mom, my mom backing away from the porch with her hands raised. The fear and defeat. The betrayal.

When my mom got there, she pounded on the door and yelled for me to come out, to pack my bags, to get my ass out there. I hunched near the door and chewed on the knuckle skin on my thumb.

"Come on," Clay urged me. "Let's go in the other room. You don't need to hear this."

I couldn't not listen. I didn't want to go back home, but I felt my mother's desperation. What a monster I was, within arm's reach of the doorknob to let her in, but too cowardly to do it or even tell her I was sorry. What a horrible daughter. She left before Diane got home, but came back later with Grandpa.

"She needs to come home and take care of her momma," he said from the yard. He had on his usual wrinkled business shirt and navy slacks. His duct-taped shoes left indents on the grass that I itched to smooth back out. Mom sat in the car and wouldn't look at us.

"She is the child," Diane told him. "It's not her job to take care of her mother."

Still in her work clothes, she stood in front of me, shielding me. I appreciated her, and also wanted her not to challenge them. Once Grandpa got involved, I knew it was over. People didn't tell him no. Besides, it *was* my job to take care of Mom. I knew, by other people's standards, that this wasn't how parent-and-child relationships were supposed to work, but we were different. Whether it was right or not, she needed me. I was abandoning her.

"Please, Brittany." Mom had gotten out of the car. She leaned against the open door and smiled at me sadly. "Please come home."

It was hard to say no, and it got harder each time I had to repeat it. Yes was so easy. I could get in the car with them, resign myself to the inevitable, and be free of this horrible tension that made my body curl in like a handmade card. But if I just held out a little longer, it would be over, and it would be worth it.

"I'm sorry," I said.

Anger flashed across her face for a second before she glanced at Diane and smoothed her expression back to crestfallen. My stomach twisted at the sight of her tucking her tail between her legs. How she must have felt with her baggy sweatshirt and chapped hands in front of this woman with a wedding ring on her finger, an anniversary necklace hanging on a thin, gold chain, and a yard where stone statues of Danish children smooched on a miniature bridge.

All at once, I wanted to thank Diane and shout at her not to look down on my mom. I wanted to tell my mom that I didn't think I was winning anything here. I wanted to yell to the neighbors who were surely peeking through their blinds that one time my mom brought me a sheet cake and a helium SpongeBob balloon at school even though my birthday wasn't for another week, and even though the principal followed her, saying she couldn't just barge in during the school day, all because I was sad that my birthday was during spring break and I wouldn't get a class celebration like other kids. I wanted to tell them about the off-duty police officer she tried to fight after a screening of *Saving Private Ryan* because he came up to us in the lobby and told me I had talked too much during the movie. I wanted to tell them about her patiently watching me choreograph my own dance to the theme music of *Bonkers*, how when I got to the part where I tried to incorporate the Charleston Step and leaned too far forward and fell and busted my face, she didn't even laugh, just held her shirt on my nose to stop the blood and told me I was a great dancer. She was a good mother, I wanted to tell them. She's just lost.

My mom left and I stayed, but it wasn't over. She called and showed up when she knew Diane and Kenneth were at work. I couldn't eat because my stomach was tense. When Clay and I fooled around, I barely felt anything because I was so anxious that she would ring the doorbell at any second. I begged him not to tell his parents, afraid that they would realize I was too much trouble and send me away.

"I'm sorry," he said after a day when she showed up and stood on her toes to look through the window at the top of the door. "I have to tell my parents. She can't keep coming here."

The next time, Diane opened the door and stepped out. Mom backed down the steps.

"Kristie," she said, no-nonsense. "Do not show up at my house without calling anymore."

I went to the bathroom. I didn't want to watch. I hated myself for not bearing witness. Thankfully, she left without a fight and stopped showing up out of the blue. The calls continued, and when I was too guilty and tired of saying no anymore, I agreed to sit on the porch swing with her and talk while Diane and Kenneth were home. She brought Grandpa again, who complained about "rats in the house" when he saw the ferrets through the screen door. He sat on a wicker chair and Mom and I shared the swing. They looked out of place.

"I'm not here to ask you to come home," she said. "I just want you to promise you'll still come visit."

Grandpa leaned forward. "You oughta come home."

"Daddy, it's okay," she told him. She looked back at me, smiling again. A sweet smile.

"I'll still visit," I promised.

She held out her pinky. "Pinky promise?"

I twisted mine around hers. "Pinky promise."

Before they left, Grandpa helped Mom write out a document giving the Smiths third-party custody so they could take me to the doctor if I needed it and sign school papers. I thought things were all squared away, but the school papers stirred up trouble. At the beginning of sophomore year, when I went to the office to turn in my permission slip for a field trip, a secretary asked why I didn't have a parent's signature. I explained the situation as well as I could, but she kept asking questions about why I lived with another family and why they had third-party custody.

She was a white woman with blond hair piled tall on her head, the signature Pentecostal crown, and she had always been inordinately short with me in comparison to how she smiled and joked with other students who came into the office. It would be years later, in a moment of random reflection, before I realized that her dislike of me may have had more to do with my stark brownness in that school than anything I might have done. Another unanswerable thing. When I refused to give the juicy details she wanted, she called social services.

"So," Diane started when she got off the phone with my case-worker, "they're going to come look at the house and make sure it's a good environment, and they want to talk to you."

Social workers had never been so thorough, in my experience. It would be a real kicker if the first time they pulled me out of a home was when I'd found a stable one. Kenneth and Diane had good jobs. The house was clean and safe. The only concern was that Mom might use the system to force me back home. Diane called her to talk it out.

"Here's the situation," she told me after. "You're going to have to tell the social worker that you and your mom didn't get along, that you got into fights all the time and you didn't want to live with her anymore."

"But that's not what happened," I said. "That makes me sound like I'm just a brat instead of her leaving me!"

"I know." She sighed. "But if we tell them that, they might take you away for neglect, and then we won't be able to keep you here. The state would have you."

The social worker came and looked around the house. In the fridge, the towel cabinet, under Luis's blankets. He checked off things I couldn't see on a clipboard, and then we sat on the porch swing for the interview. No crayons or construction paper for me to draw a butterfly.

"So, you and your mom didn't get along so well, huh?" he asked me.

"Nope," I said.

"You know"—he tapped his pen on his leg—"a lot of teens fight with their parents. That's no reason to leave home. Some kids have it way worse."

"Yep," I said. I couldn't bring myself to commit to the part of spoiled child, but I didn't need to. It was easy to see myself the way he saw me: selfish, immature, ungrateful.

He tapped his pen again, and then stood up. Dismissed me. Left. I stayed on the swing with my fists clenched until the urge to scream passed.

Then I was safe. I didn't have to leave. I had this feeling, like after a long car ride, when you're standing on solid ground but still feel the forward movement. I was waiting for the ground to start rolling out from under me. The longer it didn't, that feeling I always had, that leaving was imminent, got further away. So did my mother.

She still tried to convince me to come back. Once, she turned up at my school and had me called to the front hallway, where she bounced with hyperlight in her eyes.

"I just had a job interview at McDonald's!" she told me, and I saw that she had lipstick on her teeth. She wanted me to see how hard she was trying.

"That's great!" I said, wrenching the sound of genuine excitement out of myself. Once she was gone, I went into the bathroom and bit down on my arm until my jaw ached.

She even bought me a car my junior year, a used Ford Taurus for $1,000. Dark blue, her favorite color. The transmission blew a few months later while I was driving Shirley back home after a weekend visit, and I spent my first few checks from my after-school job at Dairy Queen to have it fixed.

When the gifts and gestures didn't convince me to come back, she became angry again. "Why don't you go get emancipated since you want to leave me so fucking bad!" she howled once, the tendons in her neck sticking out.

I kept my head down, thinking about how I'd already looked up emancipation on the Smiths' computer. I could never go through with it, I thought, but hadn't I?

THE FIRST TIME I tried to end things with Clay must have been sophomore year of high school. I told him I was done one morning before school. I was tired of hiding in my room when his girlfriend came over, and how he talked to me when she was around, and how he talked to her on the phone at night in low tones he had once used with me. I hated the twisted, spiteful person I became at the end of the school day when they walked to the bus together holding hands and kissed goodbye. How I seethed with satisfaction that he was cheating on her with me. I didn't want to be that person, to feel so pathetic all the time, so I told him I wanted to be done.

"I guess I'll break up with her." He sighed and texted her.

"I didn't ask you to do that," I said. Secretly, I was pleased.

That weekend, they got back together. When he told me, we were up late, watching *Bram Stoker's Dracula*, a movie I loved because Dracula's hair reminded me of the way women at my grandma's church wore theirs. I stood up and walked into the kitchen to put my dishes in the sink. He followed and blocked me in the laundry room.

"You're going to have to get used to her," he said.

I tried to duck under his arm, but he blocked me again. "Let me out."

"No." He moved to keep me from slipping around him. "Not until you understand that this is how it's going to be."

"I don't have to accept anything," I said, and tried pushing his arm out of my way. My hands trembled. I wanted out. Diane and Kenneth were in bed. I thought about calling out for them, but then I would have to explain why we were having this argument.

Finally, I sat down on the ground and put my arms over my head. He sat next to me. His confidence and easy smile made it all worse. He already knew how this conversation would go because he wouldn't let it go any other way. All I could do was follow along. Nothing I said mattered, and I wasn't physically strong enough to get away. No matter how angry or trapped I felt, he was at least a foot taller than me and had demonstrated many times how easily he could subdue me with moves he'd learned in his martial-arts class.

"Why am I not enough?" I whined, and hated my own voice.

He rubbed my back, and I hated his touch even more. "It's not about that."

The only way out of the laundry room was to swallow my pride. I played my part, he let me go to bed, and I continued sleeping with him. In the middle of the night, he would shake me awake and lead me quietly, quietly to the other side of the house, where I got into position on my knees with my cheek to the ground, facing the dark hallway to watch for an approaching figure. Always quiet, always, be quiet, when I already wasn't making a sound.

Even when we were somewhere no one would hear, the car parked in the middle of the field, my hands creating ghost prints on the trunk, stars bowing out above us. Or in the pit behind the cemetery where generations of teenagers past had dragged tires for seats and left empty cigarette packs and crinkled beer cans bleached by sun and rain, my knees grating on a graffitied stone slab. Or, after he moved into the storage room at the other end of the house to make room for Luis, in his windowless, over-air-conditioned bedroom with me flipped on my stomach or tugged to the end of the mattress or with my wrists tied to the frame. Until I realized that if I turned around, I didn't have to bother contorting my face to feign pleasure. I could let my muscles go slack, rest my forehead on whatever surface I was being pressed into, and wait for it to be over.

This isn't to say that I didn't have my own desires. I was a teenager, and when the urges came, I instigated. If I changed my mind at any point in the process, I kept it to myself because I believed that I was obligated to finish what I started. I wanted to feel wanted and held. Sex simultaneously satisfied and heightened the want.

On days when I'm feeling forgiving, I grant him understanding because we had plenty of sex that I was enthusiastic for, and he was only a teenage boy who couldn't have known there was a difference between those times and the times I simply went through the motions. If a "no" or "stop" was once or twice ignored, there was always the possibility that I'd said it too quietly.

Then I remember the times I kept my body stiff or gave excuses or said an apologetic but clear no. His explosive anger. Accusations of my disloyalty or waning love, the only possible explanations. Me, bowed forward, looking at my olive hands, my pink palms, promising and apologizing, until I learned that "no" was not worth the trouble.

The only person I talked to about any of this was Shirley. For hours at a time, we watched TV together, measuring the delay in air times by trying to match up the dialogue. Waiting for moments when no one else was around to talk frankly. Here and there, we got visits, meeting halfway between us in Indianapolis, driving back to her place or to the Smiths'. We'd go on long walks or sit in the van in her parents' driveway, where we could talk in private.

"I'm like, the other woman," I told her in the faux saucy voice we used to ease the pressure of vulnerability.

"He needs to make up his mind," she'd say, and I'd noncommittally agree. Not ready to admit that I was anything other than desperate for his love.

Shirley and Clay had known each other since elementary school. Even rode the same bus. When she visited, they got along well. She got the same roughhouse treatment as I did. Pinches, dead-arms, headlocks. Once, when she was visiting, he kept a lighter lit until the metal was hot and then pressed it against her leg. In retrospect, I wish I had stood up and snatched the lighter away or at least made a fuss. I was so used to that kind of thing. We all just laughed and laughed.

His affection for Shirley could flip as suddenly as it did for me. He might snatch the phone from me and scream into the receiver, or give me the cold shoulder as I packed for a visit with her, or call me relentlessly while I was at her house and force me to listen to his furious silence while she sat beside me drawing lewd photos in a notebook to try to make me laugh. There were friends I stopped talking to because he accused me of either cheating with them or wanting to, but when he told me that Shirley was a bad influence, I refused to budge. One of the few things I never ceded.

CLAY AND I had inside jokes and a favorite section to sit in at the local Chinese restaurant. You have to know how much sweeter a firm hug or kiss on the forehead feels in between pockets of rejection and contempt. You have to know that I was allergic to the ferrets and the dog and the kitten we found that had survived the dog attack that killed all its siblings. The kitten curled around my neck at night and I would wake up with a constellation of evenly spaced claw marks on my shoulder from its kneading and the sensation that my lungs were turning to pumice. The animals inflamed my asthma the way nothing else ever had, and I contracted bronchitis roughly once every few months. Ironic, how much worse my lungs fared in the absence of everyday secondhand smoke.

My coughing and wheezing could get so bad that I couldn't sleep and my inhaler would only help for a moment. I would get out of bed and go to Clay's room, where he was usually still awake, in the habit of staying up until the sun rose. He'd come with me to the kitchen and boil water, holding my hair as I took wracking breaths to get steam into my shriveled lungs. Rub my back, saying, "You've got this, Bert." Sit with me in the living room while I drank hot tea and trembled from the albuterol. Tuck me in on the recliner because I could only fall asleep sitting up. Brush the hair off my sweaty forehead. Love me.

I can't feel it anymore, but I know I used to.

Nehushtan

After the Exodus, God's people were hungry and afraid. Generations of suffering made them doubtful of miracles, so when the journey to the Promised Land was pitted with skirmishes and thirst and the exhaustive and absurdly specific demands of God, they reached for the idols they knew to supplement the uncertainty. For this, God commanded them to kill one another and then go, depleted, into the desert again. In the desert, God battered his people, testing them and burning them and opening the ground to swallow them. Their Promised Land He took back from them, decreeing that only the next generation of children could enter.

When they complained, God sent snakes to bite them. Everyone who was bitten perished from the venom. They prayed, begging for him to take the snakes away, but he refused. Instead, He ordered Moses to create an image of the serpent and post it where everyone could see. Anyone who was bitten could look upon the bronze snake, an inversion of their old idols, and be healed.

You could look up at Nehushtan, your body covered in bites, and see love, if you had no other choice. Under enough pressure, your mind could let go of logic and indignation. If seeing did you no good, you could close your eyes to the contradiction of a mercy built on cruelty. You could follow that snake into the wilderness.

Pale Horses

I tried to end the relationship after Clay broke up with his girlfriend for good. After the other girls I found out about through messages or when I had to ride with Diane to pick him up from another girl's house. After I asked if he was going to hang out with me one weekend and he looked at me like I was a mite and said, "You act like we're together or something."

It was never as simple as just breaking it off, even when he broke up with me. He would come back, or hide in my room until I went to sleep and then stand at the foot of the bed and cry, hitting himself in the face. Or drive around the back roads, speeding up every time I tried to get out, pressing the auto-lock at any stop signs, letting go of the wheel so we drifted closer and closer to a fence post, a telephone pole, or another car, until I screamed, or whispered, Okay.

On the way home one night after a late movie, he sped through the back country roads so fast that catastrophe felt inevitable. It was a test and a demonstration of how far he could push the limits without consequence.

"Please," I begged, clutching the armrest.

He ignored me, his jaw set, grey-blue eyes fixed ahead.

The horses seemed to come out of nowhere. One moment the headlights illuminated only the narrow road and the dark woods around us, and then a horse stepped out onto the faded blacktop. Then another, and another, and another. Clay slammed on the brakes, only a few feet from them, a whole family of horses. Unsettled dust swirled in the light of our beams, making them look otherworldly. They finished crossing and disappeared into the trees. I thought, Take me with you.

Make Me Dwell In Safety

In the beginning, I loved him. I loved him so much that there wasn't room for anything else. Not dignity, not holiness or chastity, not loyalty to my mother or to Ben, who I'd left behind. My mind had become accustomed to love earned through tribulation. The ebb and flow of hurt and comfort lighting up my grey brain in splashes, irresistible. By the time I surfaced for air and realized I wanted to get away, I couldn't, and so I dove down again, pumping my arms to a mantra of love love love, until I felt it again.

During the honeymoon phases, it wasn't that hard. Honeymoon love feels the way ripe cantaloupe tastes. Wet, sweet ecstasy on a dry throat. A taste I tried to keep on my tongue, convince myself it was still there even as it faded, got rubbed away by all the apologies and explanations. Until the next fight, when he would scream at me or punch the wall or locker or bed, or tell me he hoped I got raped. Accuse me of cheating so often and so fervently that I came to the conclusion that there was something inherently disloyal about me. My unclean thoughts, my lukewarm devotion.

Then I couldn't sustain the love anymore and I went on long runs and bike rides by myself just to get out of the house. If Diane went into town, I went with her. When Kenneth made dinner, I sat on the counter or offered to help. As long as they were around, I was safe. I believed I couldn't tell them what was happening. He was their son first. If we couldn't live together, I would have to leave.

I wanted to be honest. I had this terrible fear of them thinking I had conned my way into their house. This was my dream home, my dream family, and I thought I was the one poisoning it.

Diane gave me plenty of opportunities to come clean. She asked me outright if Clay and I were sneaking around, and I lied to her face. We'd had a few close calls and been caught before in a state of half-dress. Diane once found nude photos of me on Clay's digital camera while cleaning his room.

"I want you to put this in the camera and look at the pictures you took," she told me, holding up the SD card and the camera.

I knew right away what was on the card. I remembered posing myself over and over to try to get the perfect picture, and then sitting with a towel around me, deleting photo after photo in a cloud of self-loathing. How I hadn't even wanted to take a picture in the first place. Now Diane wanted me to look at the final products and feel a more appropriate kind of shame.

I took the camera and SD card from her and tried to do what she asked, but the display showed an error message.

"Try taking it out and putting it back in," Diane said. Her voice was still stern.

The SD card was lodged in the camera. I couldn't get it out. Diane tried too. She sent Clay for a pair of tweezers and then sent him back to his room. We both pried at the SD card with the tweezers until it finally popped out and then I put it back in the right way and opened my nudes.

"I just want you to look at those and think about them before you delete them," Diane said, and then stood behind me.

I looked at the pictures of myself contorted into ridiculous poses for what I hoped she would deem an appropriate amount of time and then hit "delete." I knew she wanted me to feel shame, and I did.

"Go to your room," she told me, and I added the implied "and pack some clothes" myself.

"Your free ride is over," Kenneth told me from the doorway as I packed my things, feeling the imminence of The Barn like a cold stone in my gut.

Then they told me to unpack. A long lecture, a re-up on a promise not to be romantic, and a seed planted in my head that my place in the house would always be tenuous. They already knew—about Clay and me sneaking around, not about the quiet, noxious way it had twisted—but they didn't want to send me away, so the deception lingered beneath our relationship.

I wanted to throw it off and just be family, which was hard enough for me already. Diane and I went on errands together. We liked to get Starbucks and browse the local flea markets and see movies at the tiny theater in town that showed only PG-13 movies. We read all the Jodi Picoult from the library together and ranted about the characters' choices on long bike rides in the country. Ours was like the mother-daughter relationships in movies, curling each other's hair, doing Richard Simmons workout tapes together. Except I didn't know how to relax into it, and I didn't know how to be mothered.

"Why don't you call me and Kenneth Mom and Dad?" she asked sometimes.

I could not tell her, because Mom and Dad are categories that I could not survive again. I deflected and joked, "Why don't you call *me* dad?" Or shrugged and shut down. I shut down all the time, and I didn't even understand why. Questions about why I was being quiet or chewing my knuckle or how my visit with my mom and Ben had gone would leave me blanked out, unsure of what to say and annoyed about being expected to produce a response. "I don't know," I would repeat over and over to simple questions.

At The Barn or any of the other places I'd lived, I had always been afforded, by nature of neglect, space to come and go as I pleased, physically and mentally. If I was overwhelmed, I could disappear into the woods or tuck myself into some corner out of the way and drift off to a fantasy. The Smiths, on the other hand, were attentive.

"Where are you going?" Diane or Clay or Kenneth would ask me if I tried to slip outside.

"On a run," I'd say, trying to keep my irritation from my voice.

"Where to? Want me to come with you?"

"Just down the road. That's okay."

"Be careful. I worry about you out there by yourself. Somebody could snatch you up or run over you and not stop."

I'd scream in my head for them to leave me alone, aware even as I did of my petulance and ungratefulness. "I'm always careful."

The countryside was beautiful. Fat clouds hanging in the blue sky. Fields stretching out all around me. That corner where I always picked up speed to get past the smell of dead animal. Hills that sloped so sharply, every ascent felt like a gamble that a car would crest too fast to dodge. Relief when the road evened out again and I was still in one piece. Road rash and sore knees. Vigilance and movement, a familiar cycle. The only place where I didn't have to answer to anyone, just move out of the way of passing cars. Where I could grit my teeth and growl out loud. Not a scream that would alarm some-one, but a strangled groan just forceful enough to express some of my rage. Until the hair-ripping, helpless fury that I otherwise never acknowledged passed, and I could go back and be the quirky, fun version of myself that I wanted to be for them and for me.

Who Dares Open The Doors Of Its Mouth

As a member of the family, I was invited to come along to the Indianapolis airport when Luis came home on leave. We grouped with the other families, watching them reunite and waiting our turn until Luis came out, face pink under his patrol cap. I stood off to the side, unsure of my place in all of it as they hugged and slapped each other's backs. He had Diane's mouth and Kenneth's nose, I noticed. Thinner and with shorter hair than when I'd met him before he enlisted.

"So, you're my new sissy?" he asked me in what I would come to know as his goober voice. Facetious, but in a friendly way. I smiled, and he ruffled my hair. He had a way of making a tense situation feel effortless like that.

Luis was easy to get along with. He was charismatic, quick with jokes, and had good taste in music. When he went into town, you always knew he was back when you heard the bass in his car from down the street. Not wanting to displace me from his old room, he moved into the one right next to it. Through the walls, I could hear him laughing out loud at a movie or some lyric in a song. He seemed to be on the move all the time. Coming and going into town, bouncing his leg, playing guitar on the front porch swing and singing in a put-on raspy voice that Diane hated because she wanted to hear his real voice. When he went back, I wrote him letters to send with everyone else's, drawing little doodles on the margins, imagining him reading it on the other side of the world.

On the other side of the world, he hit an improvised explosive device while driving an armored car. He was honorably discharged, given a Purple Heart, and sent home a little quieter than before.

"I'm a damn war hero," he'd joke, sliding on sunglasses and swaggering with a cigarette dangling from his lip. But we caught him staring into space sometimes. Someone in town called Diane and said they'd seen him sitting in his car at the city park, no music at all, just looking straight ahead.

PTSD was a diagnosis I knew of but hadn't really thought too much about. It explained the way he jumped and almost punched me the night I walked out of the bathroom and unintentionally startled him. It also explained the nightmares that I clawed my way out of some nights, covered in sweat and sure that Mark or the devil or the Reverend were at the foot of my bed. Afraid of slipping back into the same dream, I'd get up and tiptoe to the living room, where I'd find Luis watching *Roseanne* reruns on low volume. He'd nod at me and I would settle in on the couch across from him to watch the colors on TV move around until I nodded off again. Some nights, he made us food, peanut butter curry and rice, and I would sit on the counter listening to whatever quiet song he played on his portable speaker.

Diane worried about Luis when he moved out. She wanted him to use the GI Bill to go to school, but he seemed happy working as a bouncer at a bar in Bloomington called The Bluebird. After live shows, he brought CDs and posters home to Clay and me.

"Quit spending all your damn money on vinyls and go to school!" Diane would scold him, but he always found some way to make her laugh and forget the conversation for a while. He visited often, to do his laundry and for mandatory military drills that he hated.

"I just want to be done with them," he'd say, pulling at his uniform. Even after he broke his arm stage-diving, he still had to attend, standing off to the side in his cast, watching young men at the start of a journey that had left him with trauma and permanent hearing impairment. As soon as he could, he covered his body in tattoos that he hadn't been allowed in the service. Like charms to keep them from taking him again.

"Oh, Luis!" Diane yelled the day he came by with a fresh aloha monkey tattoo. Kenneth belly-laughed when he saw it, and then eventually so did she. They couldn't stay angry at him. Not even after his whole household got bedbugs and we had to drive to Bloomington to help him clean. We put all of his things in totes—bedclothes, books, DVD collection, clothes—and drove to an all-night laundromat. For hours, we washed and dried loads of laundry and sat on the sidewalk out front combing through everything for apple seed–sized intruders.

"You guys really don't have to stay," he'd say as the night got later and later. Clay and Kenneth eventually left to take care of the animals, but Diane and I stayed.

When all that was left was to wait for the dryers to finish, Luis and I sat at a scuffed Formica table in an exhausted daze. Diane had gone outside to call Kenneth and let him know that we would be on our way back soon. The dryers hummed and I closed my eyes, relaxed in the warmth.

"I feel like a real asshole making you stay here all night," Luis said, breaking the silence. "Your neck is going to feel like shit tomorrow if you fall asleep like that."

"You didn't make me stay," I told him. "I wanted to. Besides, I've slept worse places."

I had meant it to sound reassuring, but to my own ears the words were melodramatic. You idiot, I thought, he's been to war!

"Jesus, Brittany," he said, earnest concern in his voice.

I crossed and uncrossed my legs.

"Do you want to talk about it?" he asked, and I was surprised that I did.

Luis was the only one in my new family who could stand to be around my mom. When she showed up, talking too loud and bearing thrift-store-bin gifts, he never told her she should leave. He'd offer her a cigarette and ask about her day. When she was gone, he never made fun of her. He was probably more welcoming to her than I was, wrapped up as I was in the shame that ran over me when she was around. The only thing I dreaded more than her visits was going to visit her.

I had held up my promise to visit from time to time, though I did so as infrequently as I could. The visits ranged from holiday parties where aunts and uncles pulled me aside to say they were glad I made it out, to theme-park trips where a disagreement about whether or not to get a line-skip pass—Ben and I didn't want the people waiting in line to resent us—could escalate into a shouted lecture on ungratefulness that started at the beginning of the line, continued throughout the duration of the roller coaster, and, on our way out, earned knowing, disapproving looks from the very same adults whose very same expressions we'd been trying to avoid.

For non-holiday, non-outing visits, we got together at the little house on the steep hill where my grandfather continued to let my mother live. I hated being there. Now that I'd gotten away, going back was that much harder. Like sitting down after walking for a long time, and then getting back up to walk again with knees swollen from the rest. The smoke, the little bits of toilet paper and hair gathered in the corner of the bathroom, repelled me. Much worse were Ben's sad eyes that said, Why did you leave me here alone, and Mom's desperation for everything to go perfectly so that I would come home, see that she was doing better, that we could be a family just as well as any welcome mat, front and backyard, water and ice dispenser on the fridge, aboveground pool family could.

I tried very hard not to show my misery at being there, though my skin crawled the entire time. Any sign that I wasn't completely relaxed and at home could send Mom into a spiral. She would jump up from the couch where we'd been watching a movie and turn over the TV tray holding her Mountain Dew and ashtray, then storm to her room, slam the door, and wail, "Even my fucking kids are against me." Leaving Ben and me to clean up the yellow-grey slush and then sit holding hands, wondering in whispers if we should finish the movie or if it was safe to leave. The sound of the front door opening would bring Mom back out, her face puffy but ecstatic, to make us some food. "There has to be something to eat here. Let's order a pizza!" So we'd stay and watch the movie, always missing some chunk in the middle, or play a card game, or roll craps, or work on a 1,000-piece puzzle while the classic-rock station played on the TV and her smoke wrapped long white ribbons around us.

As the sun set and I watched both their eyes dart from the clock to me, tracking my own glances at that same clock, I'd pepper in yawns and drooping lids to work myself up to comment on how much homework I had or some early-morning obligation. Always careful not to say, I think it's time for me to go home. Even though I wanted to go home, even though calling it home still felt like overstepping, even in my own head. Always avoiding my brother's pleading gaze, which urged me, on a silent sibling frequency, to stay another twenty minutes, ten minutes, five minutes, please don't go, until I'd extended my stay late enough to be in danger of an overnight. Always the falling faces and dragging of feet and visible winces if the goodbye was too quick. Always culminating in a torturously long hug and too-warm kiss on my face from my mother wherein I did not reciprocate adequately or the discomfort in my stomach leaked into my limbs, causing me to stiffen against my will, and she would ask, Why won't you love on me?

To which I could only respond by wrapping my arms around her neck and giving a squeeze-hug until she was satisfied. To which I could not respond, Are you asking because you want me to say it or do you truly not remember? To which the thought of any response at all created a pressure in my head, like the wobbling silence before a train makes itself known, so loud I could not hear or close my mouth, could only swallow and move my fingers as the prickles of blood returning to them moved up my arms and neck and down my back and hips and legs and into my feet, leaving me a buzzing thing too big for any house.

At the end of the visits, when I got back, I would take a shower to wash away the smell of smoke and the invisible stamps of affection. Rub too much shampoo on my head, scour my body with the roughest washcloth, get on my hands and knees and push the water to the drain with cupped hands, wrap the day's outfit into a ball inside the towel so it wouldn't touch the other items in the hamper, and climb into the bed that was getting easier and easier to call my bed. Diane or Kenneth would come to the room, offer me dinner, ask how it went, and I'd give them the performance I hadn't been able to afford my old family, saying, "I'm all right, just tired."

On these nights, Clay would leave me alone, or if he came, I kept my eyes closed and my breath heavy, pretending to be too deeply asleep to be roused as he shook my shoulder or mouthed my neck, my chest, my inner thigh, sighed in aggravation into that part of me I was trying to forget. On these nights, I stayed awake and fought back the images that answered my mother's question, Why won't you love on me? On these nights, I bit down on my clean arm, inside the scars from earlier bites, until it stung. On these nights, I crept from the bed and down the hallway, past the living room, where the dog and ferrets in their cage and smiling family faces in their frames watched me, through the kitchen, with its gingerbread-man theme, to the laundry room, where I would curl up next to the furnace, a towel between me and the hot metal, to finally fall asleep. That room was enclosed and just the right amount of warm, and it rumbled, like a car. Like I'd never left the car.

In laundry room dreams, I nested on a trash bag full of all the clothes we owned. Mom and Mark up front, highway lights sliding in orange waves over the car, nowhere particular in mind, our favorite nighttime radio host, Delilah, playing songs about love. In the laundry room dreams, we never stopped driving, and the sun didn't come up, and gas station lights never reached in and hurt our eyes. We didn't need to park on the side of the road, or at a truck stop, or under a bridge with the doors locked to catch some shut-eye. We didn't talk about money or the next move. I didn't know yet that he wasn't my biological father. We didn't stop at a motel and I never saw them tangled in each other in the blinking bedside lamplight, and they didn't see me seeing them and pull me from my thin blankets into their bed to tangle me too. They didn't pass a pipe back and forth or sleep for days or pick, pick, pick, pick the skin from their faces, and he didn't yank her by her hair from the passenger seat and leave her blinking on the shoulder as we left, only to return later, once she'd learned her lesson. In laundry room dreams, my mother didn't carry me on one hip in the middle of the night to the car, put it in neutral, glancing at the rearview mirror every few moments, until we were far enough away, and then spit blood out the window as she started the engine. We didn't spend the next few years bouncing from shelter, to shelter, to him, to friends, to family, to strangers, to cars, to cars, to cars, headed nowhere at all. Just Mom and me, in the front seat now, on a midnight cruise to wherever you want to go now, Britters, just pick a place on the map, and I would trace my fingers along the little capillary lines tangling each other and think of a song that someone, somewhere had sung to me,

Down the road to Sleepy Lane
There goes Brittany Lee Anne
Lots of toys and games to play
Down in Sleepy Lane

CHAPTER 11

Down The Road

My escape came, as it does for so many, with a college acceptance. Ball State University, two hours away in Muncie,
Indiana. College had never seemed possible to me before, but during
my senior year, the guidance counselor, my academic decathlon
coach, and my English teacher all encouraged me to apply. When
the acceptance package came in the mail, I called everyone into the
kitchen.

"You only got in because you're Mexican," Clay said. "They have
to fill a quota."

"Clay!" Diane chastised him.

"I'm just messing with her," he said, but the seed was planted, and
would sprout any time I was in class feeling intimidated or unable to
raise my hand. Not supposed to be there.

I knew I had to tell my mom and Ben about the news too. When
I called, my mom shrieked with joy. I held the phone away from my
ear as she let loose a stream of "Yes! Oh my God, yes! I'm so proud
of you!" The three of us went out to celebrate at a local fried food
place and I did my best not to look uncomfortable.

That summer before I moved, and for the next few holidays when
I was back visiting, I worked at a local domestic violence shelter. My

job was to attend the desk, monitor the cameras, dole out medicine, and answer calls from women who were fleeing abusive situations. Before I could approve them to come, I had to run them through a questionnaire with questions like Does your partner own a gun? Has your partner ever threatened to kill you if you leave? Does your partner break your things? All the while, not thinking of how I would answer. The residents called me Miss Brittany and would come to the desk to talk about their court cases, their kids, the overbearing shelter rules. They liked to spend time in the library right next to the desk, pulling up music videos on YouTube and quietly singing along. At the end of my shift, I'd hand over my keys to the next person, go out to my car, checking the back seat before getting in, wave at the camera to let them know I made it out safely, and then sing along to my own music on the way home.

If I Am Silent, What Pain Leaves Me

On move-in day, we all drove up together with the family car packed full of my things. Since the campus was small, I'd decided to leave my car behind for Clay to use. My dorm room was a tiny white square with two beds, two dressers, and an older radiator that knocked when Kenneth turned it on to test it. After we moved everything in and Kenneth and Diane went to turn in the move-in cart, Clay gave me a ring. A thin gold band and a heart inlaid with what looked like diamonds. I slipped the ring on and sat on his lap, wrapped my arms around his neck.

"It's just a promise ring," he said. "I want to get married someday, but not right now."

Before they left, we went out to eat. Clay and I had been planning to tell them we would be dating now that we didn't live together, but when the time came, he got up and went to the bathroom.

"I can't be there," he texted me. "It's too awkward."

So I told them by myself. Kenneth looked uncomfortable. Diane sighed.

"He's my son and I love him," she said, "but I would never pick him for you."

He was too rough, she warned me, and I was too laid-back. I couldn't stand up to him. She was right. The feeling of being wanted, the wax and wane of affection and neglect, satisfied a hunger that nothing else ever touched. A line ran from that pleasure center in my brain down to my body, which had learned so early on to go limp, be compliant, when someone touched me. Reason was no match. Truth couldn't reach me.

I spent my first two and a half years of college detailing where I had been every day over the phone with Clay. Who I had talked to, and why. Apologies for not answering when I was in class, apologies for a guy asking me out even though I told him no, apologies for taking my ring off to shower and letting people think I wasn't taken. Confessions about outfits I wore and small talk I made that I could have kept to myself, but he always knew when I was hiding something.

I went to class, to work, and back to my little room, keeping mostly to myself. I attended a single meeting of the Latinx Student Union, finally ready to embrace my heritage, but everyone seemed to know one another and I wasn't sure how to jump in. I felt like a fraud and an interloper, so I left and never went back. It would be years before I started to untie the knots of self-hatred and internalized racism and find community. At the time, I didn't feel fit to be around anyone. On a whim, I joined the hall council in my dorm and spent every meeting with that same interloper feeling, like I was too strange, too wrong, to be around people. Obligation kept me there, but a combination of social anxiety and adherence to Clay's jealousy kept me on my toes, unable to relax. If he knew I was going to be out with my fellow council members, he called and demanded to know what we were doing until I apologized for going out at all and my new would-be friends looked everywhere but at me.

"I'm never going to get away," I told Shirley when she visited.

Ball State was closer to where she lived than Martinsville had been, so she was able to come stay in my dorm whenever she had time off work. We spent the days eating fries from the grill downstairs and watching my tiny TV. Once, I tried smoking weed with her, but it sent me spiraling and she had to get behind me in bed and hold me until I fell asleep. I told Clay the story the next time he came to visit, thinking he would find it funny.

"Are you fucking serious?" he demanded. I flinched.

"What?" I asked, as if I hadn't already accepted my guilt.

"You go to college and you start doing drugs!" he yelled, and punched the roof of the car five or six times in a row.

I stayed quiet, hands tucked under my legs. After a while, he calmed down and we both apologized. Progress, I thought.

In those last couple of years, we had fewer fights. Those we did have resolved faster and with what seemed like more self-awareness on his part. We were maturing together, I thought. It didn't occur to me that it was easier for him to keep his cool now that he didn't have constant access to me, and I had perfected the art of calming him like a veteran circus wrangler with an unruly bear. We no longer argued over messages he was sending to other girls because I wasn't there to find them. Now the only disputes we had were over his insecurities about me being at college. He was convinced that I would leave him for someone I met there, that I had only chosen the school to be closer to Shirley instead of him, that I would change into someone he didn't like.

The truth was, I was changing. I was shedding the vestiges of a religious, rural, insular upbringing. In classes and online, I was exposed to perspectives about race, class, sexuality, gender, and mental health—topics previously broached only in derision or contempt. Facets of myself that I'd tried to repress bubbled up. The Bible my grandma had given me sat beside my pillow, touched only when I accidentally bumped it while trying to get comfortable. A shock of guilt when I remembered it there.

Losing your religion feels like being bayoneted and trying to hold your guts in as they slip out of you. Christianity had been instilled in me, compulsory and unquestionable, since early childhood. The threat of eternal damnation and suffering, paired with unconditional, divine love. A push-and-pull dynamic that I was already primed for by the models of abusive relationships I had. Wrath because He loved us. Even though I never felt the religious ecstasy I was told I should feel, I maintained a base-level commitment to God. I prayed before every meal and at bedtime. I put on conviction that I knew, deep down, I really didn't have. If for no other reason than to stave off the absolute horror that gripped me when I thought of letting go.

"If I can't believe in God, then I don't want to live," I'd cried to Clay when the first wave of the crisis hit. As time went on and I had less exposure to consistently enforced spiritual terror, backsliding became a more and more survivable possibility. Also, an ethical choice. The teachings I'd grown up with were full of misogyny, homophobia, racism, and general closed-mindedness that I finally had the room to consider and reject. After what felt like forty days and forty nights, I called Shirley and told her that, if God was real, I wanted nothing to do with Him.

"Amen!" she shouted. She had shed her own commitment to Mormonism some time before and then waited with sad but respectful patience for me to join her.

This shift in my ideology made it harder to return home on breaks. Back to Martinsville, where I worked a second job in the summer at a gas station and patrons hit on me or demanded, "Where are you from?" or "What are you?" I was surprised at how blaringly not okay it all seemed now.

"You're turning into a total feminazi," Clay groaned. It was the catchall term he used to shut me down when I started talking about things that needed to change.

We argued often about ideological differences, which he seemed to enjoy for the opportunity to get me worked up and then point out how emotional and thereby irrational I was. A dynamic I was annoyed by but no longer convinced about as I realized that, as with God, my relationship with Clay was not sustainable.

VISITING MY FAMILY had been uncomfortable since I'd moved out, but now there was the added complication of keeping my secularism to myself. Most of the time, I could use the excuse of not being able to make the two-hour trip or that I had to work, but for Christmas, I knew I had to be there. That first Christmas after losing my faith, I was home for break and wheezing my way toward bronchitis once again.

"You don't have to go," Kenneth offered, but I drove over anyway. It was cold out already. I felt it in my lungs. The party was at my grandma's new house on the hill, which had no proper-noun name but did have an incredible view of the fields and Martinsville's lights off in the distance.

The new owners of The Barn had covered the black wood with beige vinyl siding. I drove past it, up the steep hill and the steep driveway, and sat in the car for a moment, preparing myself, taking a puff from my inhaler.

My mom greeted me at the door, looking smaller and older than her forty years could possibly have made her. Her bright blue eyes sunken into her face, a neck tic that she'd recently developed jerking her head to the side every few seconds. Ben, taller than both of us now and with a pale mustache growing in, stood behind her.

"Ayyyye!" the Means family intoned behind them, the traditional greeting for every person who came in late. I smiled, determined to stay on the right side of that tenuous line between having a good time and sinking into the despair of being back.

From the first enthusiastic, held-too-long hug hello, the smell of cigarette smoke seeped in and set in motion an asthma attack that would build and build despite my many trips to the bathroom to use my inhaler and brace myself on shaking arms against the sink while I gasped in the mirror, not just for oxygen but also in shock that the blasts of albuterol that usually worked were not helping. When it got bad enough that I couldn't muster a laugh at my uncles' corny jokes,

I told Mom and Ben, between wheezes, "I'm sorry... but I have to ... go. I can't ... breathe."

"Do you want to use my inhaler?" she offered.

The thought of putting my mouth on something she regularly put her own mouth on between drags off her Marlboros made me internally recoil, but instead I told her, "I have ... mine. It's just ... not working. Thank you ... though."

"It's not working?" she asked, raising her voice.

I darted my eyes to see who was turning to look. Historically, my mother had always had some kind of health or personal crisis when we were all together, and I didn't want to be the new pariah of the family gathering. Even though I'd resented that they'd made her cries for help into a running gag, I didn't want the looks in their eyes and slightly upturned mouths that said, Like mother like daughter.

"I'm fine," I assured her, even as the next inhale came with a squeak. "I have ... a nebulizer at ..."

I paused, not for breath, but because I knew that calling the Smiths' house "home" made her flinch, and not even on the surface the way she did sometimes to appear wounded. It happened in the back of her eyes where she kept herself. Ben shook his leg from where he was sitting. He wanted to ask me to stay too, I could tell, but he wouldn't.

"Okay, yeah," she said, with practiced, transparently fake cheeriness. "You do what you need to do."

As I got up to leave, hoping to make a quick and quiet exit, my mother informed everyone that I was having an asthma attack and requested that they all gather around me and pray. The family surrounded me and laid hands on me. My mother, my uncles, my aunts, even the children who could only reach up to touch my leg or stomach, all bowed their heads and closed their eyes. Ben and I shared a blank glance before he folded his hands in front of himself and closed his eyes too. Out of respect, I bowed my own head and followed suit.

As they recited their prayers and "Jesuses" and spoke in tongues, I felt my lungs shriveling further from their touches and from God and the smell of those among them who smoked. When it was over, they all looked at me with holy glee and my mother looked at me with hope that the prayer would immediately cure me and I could stay. Ben slipped away toward the bathroom without looking my way at all.

Out in the car, I didn't have enough air to scream, so I clenched my seat belt as hard as I could in my fists instead. I knew I needed to let the car heat up, but I was afraid that if I sat there long enough, someone might come out and offer a follow-up prayer or prolong my departure in some other way. I drove away and the frigid air rolled into my lungs and froze them too stiff to expand or expel.

By the time I realized that it wasn't my headlights dimming but my eyesight, and that my grip on the steering wheel wasn't weak from the cold but from a lack of oxygen-rich blood to my extremities, I was a mile away from my family and almost a mile from home. This far out from town, an ambulance would take too long, and I was afraid of losing consciousness and driving through someone's house. Without air, I couldn't plan or think beyond a fear of hurting someone.

I want my mom, I thought, but my mom was back at the party where I'd left her. Where I'd probably ruined her night. What I wanted was a version of her that had probably never existed, a fantasy nurturer I had idealized before I was old enough to really know her. The woman who lived in her body now went to church every day and loved it. She called me to talk about her latest health crises, to complain about never having time for herself since moving in to take care of Grandma, to pray for me. I didn't know her at all either.

Want my mom, I thought anyway, my throat aching now too. I wanted to get out of the car and get back in on the passenger side, look up at her. She'd wink at me and reach over to turn up the radio. That one song about standing on a bridge that they played on the radio nonstop the year I turned nine and we drove to Tennessee in a blizzard. After the third or fourth time they played it, Mom said, "God damn, did the DJ fall asleep?" But then the throaty slide of the cellos matched perfectly with the flurry falling outside in the dark. The road just kept going and the song kept playing. Eventually we had learned all the words and we sang them too.

Mom leaned forward and squinted through the frantic wipers, murmuring, "Isn't anyone trying to find me?"

I'd finish, "Won't somebody come take me home?"

Then we'd both belt out the line, "It's a damn cold night!" except I'd say darn instead of damn.

We sang it with our own lyrics, in goofy soprano with crossed eyes and in baritone with opera hands. We sang it serious and were surprised when it caught in our throats. We tried to change the station and listen to other songs or reports about the severity of the blizzard, but they didn't feel right, so we changed it back. We let it play through in silence. Then we broke the tension by chiming in at full volume on the "yeah-eh-yeahs" and pointing and gesturing with flair at one another for the "I'm with you" part.

The song made the danger outside feel fake, like it was scenery in a movie on the way to a scene that was guaranteed to come. The snow kept coming down and we were barely moving at all, crawling past semis that had stopped and turned on their hazards. Finally, Mom found a streetlight and parked a few feet in front of it so other drivers would see our big blue station wagon. We folded down the back seats and laid out our blankets to sleep until maybe the roads would be cleared.

"Can we keep the song on?" I asked as she tucked me in.

"I'll leave it on while you fall asleep," she said. "But I don't want to kill the battery."

With the volume on low, she crawled under the blankets and held me against her. The storm wailed outside and pushed cold through the windows and under the blankets in little searching fingers, but I curled myself into the tightest ball I could and pressed into her. When she sang the song, I could feel it rumbling in her chest, mixing and rattling in all the cigarette smoke that she never seemed to be able to breathe out completely. The sound put me to sleep.

Mom woke me up, panicked, when she didn't feel me beside her. I must have rolled away in the night.

"Brittany?!" she called out, patting the flat blankets where I'd been.

"I'm here," I said and crawled over to her. Her hands found me in the dark and pulled me back in. She rubbed my shoulders and brushed back my hair, even reached down and squeezed my feet.

"I'm okay, Mom," I told her. "I'm sorry I scared you."

"It's okay," she said, but I could still feel her heart pounding.

Impatient, I wanted to wiggle away, but didn't.

"I thought I was gonna lose you when you were born," she said. This was a story I'd heard before. I could recite it myself, including tone changes at specific moments and where to pause. My umbilical cord had gotten wrapped around my neck. When I came out, she'd tell me, "You looked black and blue, and you wasn't breathing."

Instead of handing me to her, the nurses carried me over to a table in terse silence and didn't respond to her cries to let her see her baby. I was dead. When they told her, she'd dropped her sweaty head back on the pillow and asked God please not to take me. Please. They worked on me for a while and then, when she heard me cry for the first time, it was the most wonderful sound she'd ever heard. I imagined the grim reaper in the delivery room, reaching for my body with one bone hand, scared away by my scream. She'd usually end by saying, "You had this gorgeous full head of black hair. You were so beautiful." I knew the story, but I loved the sound of her voice as much as she must have loved the sound of mine coming back to life, so I didn't interrupt.

Years and states later, after swerving off the road and drooping in the passenger seat of my own blue car, I wished for the song to come on again so we could sing together and I could listen to the smog vibrations in her chest until I slipped away. My mother wasn't in the car with me, though. She was back at the Christmas party. She was having a good time, I hoped, despite the fact that I'd left. At least one of her kids stayed, I imagined her saying, hugging Ben to her side as he kept an eye on the door, also hoping I would come back.

On the unplowed shoulder, I considered letting myself drift off. The car rumbled underneath me as if it was also shivering. Air came out of me in alarmingly small clouds, billowing out smaller each time and accompanied by the familiar teakettle whistle of struggling lungs. My body calling over the grim reaper, again, like it had for my birth. It would have been easy to let myself be taken. A relief, actually. Like falling asleep. Watch the snow build up on the windshield. Let myself relax and think of something lovely. Hot food, or being carried. The song.

Instead, I thought of how my mom sat close to me all night at the Christmas party, as if trying to re-create the front seats of the station wagon on the couch. How I had broken whatever spell might have been brewing by telling her that the smell of smoke was making me wheezy.

I opened my eyes and pushed myself up in my seat. If I died in the car tonight, my mother would always think that it had been her fault. She would think of me telling her that her smoke was making it hard to breathe. I would be leaving her twice and she would think both times were because of her.

I reached into my pocket and felt the cool metal of the albuterol canister, the rounded edges on the mouthpiece cap. It would only help for a second, but a second of breathing was better than a second of not breathing. I took it out of my pocket and shook it, uncapped it, put the mouthpiece in my mouth, and pushed down. All I could take in was a fraction of the medicine, and my attempt to inhale sounded like a croak. It felt like nearly nothing. Only the taste of chemical. Still, I put the inhaler back in my pocket and got out my phone as I shifted the car into drive. It rolled forward and I hoped I could steer straight. With shaking hands, I dialed home.

"Need the . . . nebulizer" was all I could get out, but it was enough. When I finally got there, I left the car running and staggered up to the front door, inside, and to the kitchen table, where the nebulizer was chugging and my foster family hovered, wavering in front of my eyes like a mirage.

CHAPTER 12

A Place To Rest

During my junior year of college, I rented my first apartment. The building, which loomed over the cracked blacktop parking lot of the church next door, looked like three white trailers stacked on top of one another. My unit was in the basement at the end of a dark carpeted hallway, past a water heater that exploded that first winter and spewed boiling water everywhere, forcing me to climb out my window and hoist myself up to ground level to get to class. Exposed water pipes snaked along the ceiling from one side of my apartment to the other. They clunked and clanged at unpredictable moments, waking me in the middle of the night. The day I moved in, a cockroach fell from the ceiling and landed in my hair. I called the landlord and cleaned the place from top to bottom with bleach, but that night, I wrapped my blankets around me and slept sitting up in the center of the bed for fear that more bugs might crawl on me.

Despite all this, I loved the apartment. It had rounded archways between rooms, a seahorse painted over the light switch in the bathroom, and a built-in bookshelf in the bedroom with a hidden reading light. I scoured yard sales and dumpsters until I found furniture I liked, dragging each new piece across town and down the stairs, into its perfect spot. I bought plants at the campus greenhouse sale and put them in the windows, where they grew crooked and leggy reaching for the sun. I put out my trinkets, taped up pictures. The last thing I needed was a couch.

"Why do you need a couch?" Clay asked me.

It seemed like a staple of a living room. A place to sit and do my homework or watch my tiny TV.

"You just want to have people over," he said.

No, I told him. There wasn't anyone I knew well enough to invite over other than Shirley, who had moved into the apartment next door.

"Probably some guy from class."

I didn't talk to any guys.

"I bet," he scoffed.

There was no convincing him when he came up with scenarios to be angry about. The couch wasn't just a couch anymore. It was a symbol of me moving away and getting too comfortable. When he visited, we laid down blankets in front of the TV, in the spot where a couch would have been. We ordered Chinese food and watched whatever movie he'd brought. Before it was over, he pressed himself against me in the way that meant he wanted sex, so we moved to the bedroom and I bent over the bed and clenched the blanket in my fists as my knees slammed into the wooden frame over and over. Lying in bed afterward, my stomach ached in the old familiar way that I had come to assume I would always feel when sleeping next to another person.

"I think I'm going to leave tonight," he said. "So I can avoid morning traffic."

"Are you sure?" I asked, half hoping he would change his mind and half hoping he wouldn't. "Do you think you'll be all right driving so late?"

He shrugged. "Probably. I just want to get home."

"Okay," I said. I kept my face and body as neutral as possible. If I seemed too hurt or too relieved, he might get angry. "Will you at least wait until I fall asleep?"

He tucked me in and then lay down on top of the blankets and spooned me. After a while, I pretended to be asleep and felt him slip away, heard him collect his stuff and leave the apartment. Alone, in the dark, I couldn't get comfortable. I pictured him moving along the highway in my old car, the road stretched out in front of him, moonlit and quiet. My body ached to move.

The relationship was over, but I continued wearing his ring the same way I had kept my old Bible beside my pillow. If I kept up the routine, I still believed, the devotion would manifest. This had worked for years. I would sit on the toilet afterward with the spirit leaking out of me, telling myself that there had been a loving meaning in the way Clay held his hand on my throat as he thrust into me. That this was the way life was, so I might as well enjoy it. We weren't even fighting anymore. He hadn't yelled at me in months. Our bad times were behind us. If I left now, I thought, I would be wasting the years of hardship that had led to this stability.

Then, one night in April, when Clay called and screamed at me, called me a whore, sneered as he told me he'd had sex with someone else, I had a revelation. This would never change. No matter how long the calm lasted, no matter how many talks we had, it would always come back to this. I would spend the rest of my life waiting for wrath.

"I'm done with you!" he spat. "I'm fucking done."

I didn't say anything and he hung up. He expected me to call back and apologize, atone, beg. The way I always had. Instead, I turned off the ringer and went to sleep. Not even the pipes woke me up. The next day, I had dozens of missed calls and messages. As I got ready for class, he called and I answered. His voice was cold.

"Are you ready to talk now?"

"I didn't know there was anything to talk about," I told him. "You broke up with me."

"Oh, so you really think it's over?"

I was silent. The old aversion to saying no.

His voice grew high-pitched, panicked. I couldn't do this. Was I serious? Dude, really? I couldn't fucking do this! Please!

"I have to go to class," I told him, and hung up.

I floated to campus and sat through my classes not hearing anything, my chest cleaned out. The world bigger. Shaking. Missed calls and messages accrued all day. Paragraphs of apologies and threats. My body screamed at me to comfort him, but I resolved not to give in. When he realized I wasn't going to respond, he messaged that he was driving up to see me. I thought of how flimsy my door was, how easy to kick down, even if he hadn't had that spare key. I stayed on campus for as long as I could, trying to get some work done while I stalled, but I couldn't focus.

My hands trembled as I walked down McKinley Avenue, past the Museum of Art and the student center. I cut across the church parking lot, did a wide lap of the building looking for his car, my car. I didn't see it, so I went inside, stepping carefully through the hallway in case he was waiting around a corner. At my door, I waited, listening in case he was already inside.

Water trickled through the pipes overhead, but otherwise it was quiet. My pulse pounded as I searched the apartment. Sparse as it was, there weren't many hiding options available. I was thorough anyway, checking under the kitchen table, the storage space beneath my bed, and the closet, where all three of my outfits hung. He wasn't there, yet. I looked for something I could put in front of the door, but nothing was heavy enough.

All I could do was wait. Maybe hide, but then again, the options were few. I tucked myself in the closet anyway and tried to think of anyone I knew who would let me come over and wait out the storm. I couldn't go to Shirley because he knew she lived next door, and shame kept me from admitting to her how scared I was. A few faces flitted through my mind: classmates I'd worked with on group projects or hall council; someone who'd smiled at me in passing in the technology building. The truth was I hadn't made any friends at college. I wasn't allowed to. Now, unless I wanted to go find a single-occupancy bathroom on campus to sleep in, there was nowhere for me to go.

My phone lit up. A call from Diane. My stomach clenched. It could be him using her phone, but I answered anyway.

"Bert?" It was her. She sounded tired. "Ya there?"

"I'm here," I said.

"Did you really have to do it over the phone?"

I said nothing.

"You don't plan on taking him back this time, huh?"

"No." I let the silence hang. "Is he okay?"

"He's really, really not."

I paused. "Is he actually driving up here right now?"

She sighed. "No, he ain't. He's here. But I don't think I could stop him if he decides to."

That night, I slept as lightly as I could. Every creak of the building woke me. The pipes' clanging propelled me from the bed entirely. I jerked awake intermittently to no sound at all, sure that I was going to look up and see Clay standing over me in the orange light filtering in from outside. In the morning, my stomach was pinched and my muscles were sore. I went to my campus job and jumped every time someone entered the student worker room. Clay had driven me to work on past visits. He knew where to find me.

For the next few days, fear ruled my routine. I searched my house at night, half-slept, left cups lined up in front of the door to alert me if anyone came in, looked over my shoulder as I walked to and from campus. I tried to relax in Shirley's apartment, comforted by her supportive rendition of CeeLo Green's "Fuck You," but I could only think about him waiting for me when I went back to mine. I sent Clay a single message about how my decision was final and took one call based on a promise that it was only to say goodbye. He kept that promise, and the barrage stopped, but I knew he could change his mind at any second, the way he had before.

Diane called me near the end of the week to tell me that Clay had crashed my car outside of a gas station in Martinsville. He was all right, she said, but the car was totaled. I was relieved that he was okay, and that the destruction of my car—my first car, that I had sunk hundreds of dollars from part-time jobs into—meant that he couldn't drive to me.

"You broke my boy's heart," she told me.

For the millionth time, I wanted to tell her about how things had been. Then she would understand why I had to leave. I thought of all the times she'd told me not to get involved with him or asked me if things were okay. All the times she'd stayed up all night talking with me and I'd held everything unspeakable inside. It was too much to explain now and too late, so I said nothing.

New Rituals

For $100 on Craigslist, I bought a bright red microfiber loveseat that fit perfectly in the space I'd kept open for a couch. It was cute and comfortable and could easily be pushed in front of the door at a moment's notice to impede an intruder long enough for me to climb out the bedroom window. When I started bringing people home from the bar, we threw our coats and purses onto it before moving to the bedroom. I'd show them my secret reading light and then they'd initiate a sequence of kissing to foreplay to penetration that quickly became predictable in the way college sex does. Still, I loved deconsecrating my body, the way I passed the point of no return, the way I could bury my face in between legs, slide my hand from hip to waist to ribs to breast, rub thumb over nipple, feel the tension and release roll through them the way I'd only ever faked. How their backs arched off the bed like they were full of the spirit.

Afterward, the spell that had allowed me to touch and be touched would leave and I became awkward, unsure of how to transition from intimacy to parting ways. The most difficult of Midwest goodbyes. Like the woman who I thought had left when I was in the bathroom. I walked to the kitchen butt naked and chugged half a gallon of apple juice in the cold light of the fridge before I realized that she was sitting in the dark at the kitchen table ashing her cigarette into the decorative pineapple-shaped bowl I'd found at the flea market.

"I have asthma" was all I could think to say, and she apologized, stubbed the cigarette out, and asked if she could borrow some pajamas. I spooned her through the night, growing wheezy from the smell of smoke on her, and then left early in the morning for work. When I got home, she was gone, but she had left a sweet note and the butt of her cigarette still in the pineapple bowl. I held the note against my chest and did a little spin around the living room, feeling romantic, but then I was left with the empty apartment.

This was the catch. When I slept with people, they eventually left, and then I held the dissonance of relief and absence in my lower stomach. I was alone. I would lie in my bed and say into the dark, "This is my home. I am home." It was tempting to go out into the hallway, turn, and knock on Shirley's door. She was often audible through the wall, crooning like a lounge singer as she made dinner, but I couldn't make myself reach out. I would fall asleep, but then jerk awake, sometimes upright in bed, or somehow on the couch, once or twice even standing in different parts of the apartment. My body wanted to move. I'd grab a blanket and go to the kitchen to sit beside the fridge, a hulking green rusted machine that hummed like a car if I held the freezer drawer open long enough. I would lean against it, close my eyes, and build a dream to carry me away.

The dream was that much of my life had been a dream. That I was still in the car with my mom and Ben on a rainy night. We had all been hypnotized by the steady rhythm of the windshield wipers. Blurred white letters on a green sign telling us where we were about to be and how to get there. All of the exits we took hadn't come yet. All the times we'd been shouted at had instead been the boisterous voices of radio jockeys. Every fist raised against us just a trick of the lights in the rearview mirror. The smoke that choked us and stole her singing voice was just our breath fogging up the windows, cleared with the press of the defrost button. The meals we scrounged were just gas station snacks settled at the bottoms of our stomachs. Once the rain let up and we woke, rubbing the crust from our eyes, passing the bottle of Listerine back and forth, stretching and popping our limbs, I would navigate us toward different turns than the ones we'd made. The feeling I'd always had—no matter how bad the place and situation we were leaving—that driving meant we were moving toward something better, would finally be true.

The Flood

My little apartment was a short walk from campus. Every morning, I woke up at five, springing out of bed to go to the gym and swim laps. Hair still wet from the shower, I'd run to the bus for work. After my shift, I went to classes, then back for another shift. By the time the bus dropped me off at the stop where pretty red cobblestone gave way to cracked asphalt, I was practically crawling in through my door, pressing my face into the thin carpet. I cooked spaghetti for dinner nearly every night, finishing my homework as the noodles boiled on one of the two working burners. Shirley might pop in to complain about work or I'd sit outside on the basement steps with her while she smoked.

On the weekends, when I wasn't dog-sitting or cleaning or doing yardwork or some other campus gig, Shirley and I walked five minutes to a cluster of bars to play pool and drink. We'd get drunk—cheap beer for her and pear cider for me—and then walk home with our arms linked, singing old Fall Out Boy songs into the night. Laughing so hard we'd fall down on someone's yard and let the dew seep into our clothes.

"I fuckin' love ya," she'd say, kissing my forehead, and then swat my butt as I walked into my apartment to collapse in bed butt naked and then wake up at five again to head to the gym. I slept so good on those nights, limbs loose and happy in the dark.

After that first year, Shirley moved down the alley into a house with her boyfriend and some of their friends. I missed being able to open my door, turn directly to the right, and knock on hers, but I was glad she wasn't there for the summer night when it rained so hard that the window boxes filled up and water started to rush inside. A trickle at first, then a stream, and then a waterfall. I moved as much as I could up to my bed or the tiny kitchen counter. High ground. Grabbing a large plastic bowl I used for popcorn, I ran outside, wading through the water, to try to bail the window boxes out.

"Please," I yelled, filling and tossing bowls of water over my shoulder. Hopelessly drenched in the downpour. "Please!"

When the rain finally let up and I had drained the boxes down to an inch or so of water, I went back inside, where a loud gurgling sound drew me to the bathroom. Rancid, dark brown water had bubbled up out of the tub drain and spilled over the side of the toilet. I dialed the landlady and left tearful messages until she called back, snapping, "I *know*."

The next day, I cleaned up the muck, washed the walls, and hassled the landlady until she begrudgingly hired someone to shampoo the carpets. Still, my apartment felt tainted, a curse that hung in the air along with the smell of sewage. Its homeyness, the pride I'd felt when hosting or hanging up my sheer white curtains that blew so prettily in the breeze, was gone. I sat down on the stained carpet and wept.

After that, I spent a lot of time out, studying at the library, staying the night with hookups. I was surprised, but not bothered, when I came back for a change of clothes one day and realized that mushrooms had begun to grow in the corner of my bedroom. I plucked them and cleaned the spot with stringent chemicals, but they kept growing back.

Begging And Thanking At The Same Time

To maintain my funding, I had to write a letter to the financial aid office once a year detailing my situation. They wanted to know why my FAFSA didn't include information about my parents' income. Having answered this many times for general and departmental scholarship and grant applications, it eventually started to feel like I was writing a story about something that happened to someone else. Some girl who'd moved in with a family after her mom left her.

After writing the letter, I would go in and have an interview with a financial aid officer. Every year, I sat in the office while they read the letter and then asked me questions about my home life that were questionably pertinent to my scholarship and loan qualification.

"So, your mom just left you?"

"Yep."

"That must have been so hard."

"Yeah, it was, but I'm here now."

I understood inherently that there was a show I was meant to put on. A level of suffering I was expected to convey. If the financial aid officer asked me whether I still talked to my mother, I could not be short or refuse to answer while his pen hovered over the signature line to approve my independent student status. I also could not answer honestly, could not say that sometimes I pretended to call my mother and cry to her about how hard everything was and then listened to the silence and imagined what she might say to me, except I could never conjure the right words because I had never actually heard them.

"You know," they all said to me, in some combination of words or another, "a lot of people in your circumstances turn out really bad. But look where you are now!"

Then they would scratch their signature on my form and I would thank them, practically bowing, and leave the office. Down the long, narrow hallway, thinking about turning out really bad and loving people who turned out really bad.

At the other end of the hallway from the financial aid office, Ball State had counseling services that were free for undergraduate students. This information was made available on the syllabus for every single class I took, but I glazed over it as if it was only pertinent to other people. I was struggling enough as it was to stay focused and present, to keep myself on the Dean's list every semester and almost never miss a class, even if I spent classes with my hands clenched between my knees to keep them from shaking, my mind wandering and wobbling and warring, not hearing a word.

When I think of that time, I imagine myself walking through the halls of the Robert Bell building, my eyes trained ahead, my body bent forward, while a seven-headed beast made of light pulls itself along with dripping clawed arms, reaching for my back. I was so determined for nothing to be wrong, I thought I could will the beast away. I wanted to be what the financial aid officers thought I was—someone impervious to being touched by the things that had happened in my life. I would go into a bathroom stall and bite down on my arm until the pain chased away the intrusive flashbacks and crushing sensation of doom. Smooth out my clothes, open the stall door, wash my hands, go about my business.

"Your arms are looking toned as hell," Shirley told me one night as I was stirring a pot of spaghetti. "I need to learn to swim."

"Thanks," I said, handing her the wooden spoon to take over so I could grab the sauce. "I had a nightmare the other night that I went to the pool, but instead of jumping in, I stood on the starting block, screaming to the lifeguards for help, and they just sat there and watched me with blank faces."

"Bitch!" Shirley shouted, splashing the wooden spoon in the spaghetti water. "Go to therapy!"

This seemed like as good of a reason as any to go. My relationship to therapy up to that point had been run-ins with CPS and cautious sessions with school counselors that I used primarily to get out of class. I'd never been able to share honestly in a session without fear of legal repercussions for my mom or other people in my life. As with prayer, I said my part dutifully, while keeping pieces of myself back and knowing in my heart that there was something wrong with me.

Now there was no reason not to tell the whole story. My counselor was a young woman who had a common name with a unique spelling. We sat in an incredibly small office with furniture that looked like props meant to be broken during a wrestling match. At the beginning of our first meeting, she informed me that we had a limited number of free sessions and I did the math in my head, trying to mete out how I would allot my life into segments. My mind reached out for the scholarship application script and its safe, polished distance. She listened attentively and I barely heard myself because I wondered the whole time whether I was going to tell her what I had remembered and was trying desperately to forget again. The images and sensations that came to me at unpredictable times. In class or at work or while I was swimming, leaving me thrashing in the water, gasping for air.

I don't remember the words I used to tell her what happened that night at the motel. What I remember is the feeling in my body once I said it, like static everywhere. Now I couldn't un-say it, and I couldn't un-remember it anymore. At the end of the session, I walked out into the hallway that led to the financial aid office. I left the building and passed the gym, passed the student center and the church and my apartment and the river and the highway and all the cornfields and the trees and the clouds.

"Where do you want to go, Britters?" my mom asked me.

"Anywhere," I said.

Monster Repellent

Our bodies give us what they can, when they can. After Ben was kidnapped, sometimes he would get so angry, he'd clench his whole body and shake. Years later, in therapy, I learned about progressive muscle relaxation, a practice where you tense and release muscles in different parts of your body in tandem with slow breathing, to ease your anxiety. I'd lie on the floor in the dark and squeeze my arm muscles, my core, my legs, and then let go. This is an act of love for yourself. Telling your body, something is scaring you. I believe you.

When Shirley was little, she used to be afraid of monsters in her room. When she told her dad, he didn't tell her that monsters weren't real. Instead, he sprayed cinnamon air freshener in each corner of the ceiling, telling her that it was monster repellent.

Shirley's dad didn't consider that her asthmatic lungs would struggle in the monster repellent. Just like Ben's body didn't know or care that the shaking made him a spectacle. It squeezed and turned red, and he survived.

Our bodies and our parents aren't perfect machines. They miscalculate and relent to selfishness and exhaustion. They lose track of the difference between their plans and ours. Their desires and ours. Their survival and ours. Their love and ours.

I love my body for the ways it has tried, succeeded, and failed to take care of me. I love my mother. I love my mother.

Friends With Benefits

Somehow in that packed schedule of therapy and hookups and classes and work, I met my beloved. At first, he always seemed to have some kind of hand injury. Scraped knuckles, a thumbnail regrowing, old scars. I thought maybe he got into a lot of fights. Then I saw an injury firsthand. We were walking across campus after a particularly rainy day and, as we passed by a puddle, he stopped and pointed at it.

"Look how the clouds reflect in the water!" he gasped. "It's so beautiful, I just wanna—"

Leaning over, he mock-punched the puddle a few times. He's a goober, I realized. He reached up to adjust his backpack straps and we both noticed that his knuckles were bleeding.

"Oops," he said. "Didn't realize it was so shallow."

"Is that what's always happening to your hands?" I asked.

"Huh?" He looked at his hands like he'd never considered them to be particularly accident-prone. The thumbnail, he said, had come off after he slipped and hit it with a hammer while adjusting his dorm bed. A tiny pink line marked the spot where he'd crashed his bike as a kid. That discolored patch beside his pointer knuckle was a burn mark from bumping the top rack in the stove as he took out a sheet of cookies.

The winter we fell in love, we started a tradition of finding and collecting discarded doors. There was a weird amount of them in dumpsters and out on curbs. If either of us spotted one, we'd wait until nighttime and then come back together to carry it to a gas station near my apartment with a wide, alley-facing back wall, where we'd prop them up.

"If we slip on this ice," he would say as we carried a heavy wooden door in small, careful steps over the frozen ground, "we'll be dead as a doornail."

"Stop," I'd say, laughing, "you're gonna make me drop it!"

"If you don't like my jokes, well, there's the door."

At the time, we were trying to be friends with benefits, but the benefits were turning out to encompass spending nearly all our time together. I didn't want to get into another serious relationship, but I also felt like something was missing on the rare nights when he didn't stay at my apartment. We both knew we needed to talk about it, but it took a few months of mutual, oblivious brooding and anxious attempts at confessing our feelings before we sat down for a picnic and relationship talk. Neither of us can remember what we ate or said exactly, but we talked for a long time, moving from the picnic back to my apartment. We lay on my living room floor, talking well after the sun went down. In the dark, we worked out what we wanted and needed. Both of us had been through difficult long-term relationships that we didn't want to replicate.

No monogamy, we agreed. We'd both been hooking up with other people since we started our friends-with-benefits situation and it didn't take away from how we felt about each other. We worked out boundaries and rules by asking crucial questions such as: What if we get jealous? Should we tell each other when we meet someone? Do you prefer to know or not know the details of a date? Who do you think is a better kisser, Goku or Piccolo? The sun came up and we started dating, moved to Iowa together, adopted a little black cat, and moved again to Albuquerque.

Our little cat is a flat-faced abomination we named Baby Jeff, after my beloved. Every day since we picked her up from the shelter, Jeff cleans the goobers from her big, orange eyes. She sits between his legs with a puckered expression while he runs a folded-over wipe through the gross little crevices where a nose ought to be. He's so gentle with her. With both of us. It makes my throat ache.

At first, I didn't know how to be loved gently. It felt like a long con. If he was in a bad mood, I'd feel the old, familiar anxiety, but also anticipation for the cycle to play out the way I was used to. The push and pull. It never came. Instead, he told me, "My mood is not your responsibility." A hard lesson to learn, and a harder thing to really feel. Even now, after years, I occasionally find myself trying to read his neutral face for warnings. Some sign that I should pack my bags or grovel. Sometimes I ask for reassurance, and he gives it freely, but by now, it's my responsibility to put away those expired reflexes.

When it's time for bed, we both get hyper in anticipation of falling asleep next to one another. One of his classic jokes is to get a running start, jump, free-fall into bed, and pretend to be asleep, snoring and all, upon impact. It makes me laugh every time. Baby Jeff curls up next to me and kicks until my shirt is out of the way so she can rest her soft paw pads against my stomach. In the morning, I wake up sandwiched between the two of them, and a dust devil of terror and joy swirls around me. I've never had this much to lose.

My beloved has impeccable physical comedy. He's a poet. Regardless of what I'm wearing, when I come out of the bathroom after getting dressed, Jeff always says, "I love it when you wear that." He plays guitar for me when I'm in the shower. His hands are covered in stories. He loves me without trapdoors.

Go Up, Thou Bald Head

When I first started college, Ben was in his own cycle of moving around as he finished high school. He called me from Jon's, from friends' houses, from his grandma's.

"You're so close to being able to go to college!" I told him when he called one night after a fight had broken out where he was staying.

"Does it get better once you're out?" he asked me, voice raw.

I thought of my nightmares and the dreaded, ranting calls from Mom, how I stole food from the cafeteria and held down two campus jobs along with side gigs to get by. The way the muscles in my side clenched so hard sometimes I couldn't breathe. The feeling that something terrible was coming so strong I nearly screamed in the middle of a lecture.

"Yes," I lied. "You wouldn't believe how much easier it all gets."

Ben finished high school and got a full-ride scholarship to a university an hour away. We called each other often, finally on the same page about everything.

"I know how you felt now," he said, after going back for break the first time. "I'm sorry I was such a dick. I didn't realize how hard it is to be there once you've left."

We talked about what we'd been through in the time we were apart, what we'd been through in the time we were together, the funny stories, the hard stories, about God, about Mom. Manipulations and unhealthy attachments that we now recognized for what they were.

"Remember how your dad used to tell you Mom didn't love you?" I asked.

"What?" he sounded confused. "He never told me that."

"But Mom said—ohhh."

"Yeah."

We talked more than we had in years. He called me one night of my junior year, crying, so stressed that his hair was falling out. Perfectly circular bald patches had appeared on his head, seemingly overnight.

"It'll probably grow back," I offered.

"That's not the point!" he snapped, raising his voice.

Classes were overwhelming him. Mom's calls. His dad relapsing. His friends all seemed to have regular upbringings and just didn't get it. There was the financial aid bureaucracy. The nightmares. It was all too much.

"I don't get it," he said and sniffed. "I made it out, Brit. Why am I not okay?"

"I think," I responded, choosing my words carefully, "we were in survival mode for so long, and it sucked, but we had that adrenaline or whatever it was, to keep us going. Now the immediate danger is gone, so all our coping mechanisms have dropped out and we're left with the aftermath."

"Yes!" he said, sadness pushed out momentarily by the excitement of recognition. "That feels like exactly what it is!"

"Yeah, I'm pretty smart, I guess."

There is power in learning the name of a demon. Ben and I got into therapy around the same time, but he took it a step further and changed his major to psychology. The day he graduated, I sat next to our mother in the packed IUPUI stadium. When he walked across the stage, we both stood up and screamed so loud that people in front of us turned to get a look at the unreserved women. By the end, Mom was tired and took off as soon as she got a chance.

"I'm surprised Mom didn't stick around," Ben said later that night as we did celebratory shots. "She's usually not so quick to skedaddle."

"What are you talking about? She's been skedaddling our whole lives!" I slurred, and we laughed so hard we cried.

One Way It Ends

Every year, on the day Ben was kidnapped, I make sure to call or visit. In March 2017, I planned a weekend for him to come stay with me. I was excited for him to see my new apartment, a one-bedroom with wood floors and a sunroom full of plants. In preparation, I cleaned, prepared a hot meal, and bought a bottle of wine from the gas station a few blocks away. A few months later, I would be moving out of Indiana for grad school, and I wanted to show him the stability I had set up for myself before I left it behind. While I waited, worried about him making the drive, my phone rang. It was Clay.

"Luis is dead," he told me.

It had been years since we'd seen each other. In that time, Luis had started to struggle with drugs. Injuries from the war plagued him, but the VA left him in the waiting room for hours and hours at a time only to hand him highly addictive pain meds that didn't solve the problems. The medicine gave way to heroin, a sweet syrup that laid cool hands on him and took away the pain, and twenty pounds, and the shape of his voice. Then his life.

Are you sure? I wanted to ask. Maybe I did ask. It had happened maybe twenty minutes earlier. Still recent enough that it felt like they should be able to put him back, fix it.

When Ben arrived, I hugged him close, feeling the weight of his body, so much taller than me now. I told him about Luis and he offered to drive me back to Martinsville the next day so I could be with the Smiths. We ate our dinner and watched a movie, though I don't remember what it was or if Ben was impressed with my apartment. Late that night, I went to the doorway of the living room and watched his chest rising and falling from the nest of blankets I'd set up for him on the couch. His brow furrowed in his sleep. I closed my eyes and listened to his breathing.

As promised, he drove me back to Martinsville the next day. A two-hour trip, the back end of which led us through old familiar parts of Indianapolis. That gradual shift from city to rural. Past the White River and the cow fields, past The Barn.

"What do you think the inside looks like now," I asked, watching it disappear behind the trees.

"Cleaner, probably."

At the Smiths', we hugged goodbye and Ben drove away. My chest tightened as I watched him turn at the end of the street and pull out of sight.

I wish I remembered more from that time. When I push, I can recall lying in bed next to Diane while everyone else was at the other end of the house. Crying in the dim room, holding each other. Days of picking through Luis's things, smelling his colognes, laughing at the notes he had scrawled and left in his pockets. Leaning over his body to clip his fingernails. Sitting in comfortable silence on the porch with Kenneth before everyone else woke up, both wiping our faces as the chimes tinkled in the chilly morning wind. The military recruiter who paced in front of the coffin at the funeral and ranted that the boys he enlisted were like his children, and how I had maybe never wanted less to bear witness. Hunkering by the firepit in the backyard, drinking E&J by myself until Clay came out to check on me.

"You okay?" he asked, sitting across the fire so it looked like he was burning.

I nodded. "Just wanted to be alone."

"I don't think any of us should be alone right now," he said, and I felt that old irritation rise up at not being able to hide away from this attentive family. I took a deep breath and let it out. They're not trying to be pushy, I told myself. This is just the way they know how to love each other.

We talked about nothing for a while, about Luis, and about the safe parts of old times. Him, mostly looking at the fire or at his own hands. Me, taking gulps of my drink that sloshed my mind away from my body, which wanted to run away, climb over the privacy fence, and disappear into the cornfields. The need to run built up inside me, making my knees ache, making me angry.

"You were terrible to me," I slurred. He didn't look up. "Do you know how much I hated myself?"

"I know," he said. The fire popped as steam escaped from the logs. "I was abusive and shitty, and I'm sorry. I know that's not enough, but I'm sorry."

I gripped the hard plastic armrest of my chair and tried to breathe, wanting violence. His apology scared me. It was so much easier to think of him in a binary, as only someone who had hurt me. Since I'd been back for the funeral, he'd been gentle with all of us, almost a different person. I looked down at the white scar on my arm from where he'd once sliced me with a folded piece of aluminum foil, just to test its sharpness. I thought of his face when he'd done it, curious and youthful. The man sitting across from me now had sunken cheeks and sad eyes. There was nothing I could pull from him that would fix what had happened.

We sat next to the fire until it was almost out. When we stood to go back inside, my head swam and I stumbled.

"I'll get my mom," he said, and ran inside.

Diane came out and said something, but I couldn't hear what. I looked back at the firepit as she pulled my arm over her shoulders to keep me upright. I want to go back, I tried to say, but I couldn't hear what I was saying. My voice sounded like nothing. The firepit and the empty chairs around it looked like nothing. My legs were like liquid as we stumbled into the house and she lowered me onto the couch in the family room. I closed my eyes and let myself go away, and Diane, who had watched Luis thrash on the hospital table as the doctors tried and failed to resuscitate him, shook me and pulled my eyes open, but I was so languid in that dark, warm room of my mind that I couldn't tell her, I'm okay.

IT OCCURS TO me that I may just as easily have slipped into addiction, especially considering my genetic predisposition and the way my mental unwellness has occasionally driven me to desperation for release. A way to push a button in my mind and make it all feel okay, nearly irresistible.

When I drink during social occasions, I find it easier to talk and joke and laugh. Alcohol turns off the constant ticker tape of hypervigilance and overthinking and allows me to relax, but, by whatever fortune of brain chemistry, I don't struggle with alcoholism. Spirits have never quite caught on inside me. This is not evidence of any superior moral strength, but a fluke exemption from a disease that has ravaged and destroyed people I love.

Luis is dead. My mother is alive, but swaths of her life have been swallowed by trauma and drug use. I am alive, but the past lives in my body and sometimes I fall inside myself and get lost in it. None of this had to happen, but it did, so we keep living, or we don't.

To The Clouds

Through a string of misfortunes that are not mine to tell, Luis's ashes ended up in the trunk of an impounded car on the other side of the country a year and a half after he died. Diane called the lot and asked if someone could send them back to Indiana, but the owners refused. The car would be scrapped by the end of the week, they told her. This final indignity broke her and Kenneth's hearts. It was like losing him all over again. Before they could tell me no, I bought a plane ticket.

It was my first time flying. Iowa to San Diego. Takeoff was delayed to de-ice the plane, but once we were in the air, I watched the quilt of the Midwest turn into the orange and brown West, and all the people in their cars going wherever. When we landed, it was sunny and in the mid-seventies.

San Diego was the most beautiful place I'd ever seen. The palm trees, the sweet smell of flowers. Plants I didn't recognize growing on the medians between roads where people drove like God was screaming at them.

First thing, I went to the impound lot. I resisted the urge to physically attack the owner, thinking of a saying Grandma had always told me: You win more flies with honey than with vinegar. Feeling acidic, I smiled and followed them to the car, where I dug through the trunk and pulled out what was left of a complex, beautiful life. A man who chewed his breakfast cereal too loud and knew all the words to every song from *Grease*. Ashes in a bag, stuffed inside a can, all I could bring home.

The flight home was early the next morning, so I called a car to pick me up at a nearby overlook well before the sun was up. While I waited, I sat Luis carefully on the fence that bordered the cliffside. I stepped back and took in the scene, wishing that the magic of the black sea crashing below and the full moon glinting off his dented gold tin urn could alchemize him back to life. I wished he would mock me for being so sentimental, reach over and pinch the fat on my upper arm, call me shitbird.

I thought about how he'd belted out songs in his car, aviators reflecting the road, tattooed arm resting out the open window. How he looked like someone who would never die. How I wanted the drive to never be over.

THE NIGHT I almost died from the asthma attack, Luis was also home for Christmas. He sat with me, his leg bouncing under the kitchen table while the nebulizer booted up. Watching my face, leaning forward like he wanted to help but knew he couldn't. I'm older now than he was when he died. Sometimes, when I miss him, I close my eyes and hold my breath and remember his hands gripping his knees, waiting for me to breathe. I hold my breath until I can't stand it, and then I keep holding it. I go back to that night when my chest burned and my vision blurred. I was scared that my lungs were closed up too tight to take any medicine, but I hunched over and wracked in as much of it as I could until my chest started to open and fill with the cold vapor. It felt like crystal-clear water rushing into a dry riverbed.

When I exhaled, the albuterol came out in thick white plumes. I gasped it in and closed my eyes. It reminded me of a time when I was very little and Mom and I had driven through heavy fog. She told me, "It's a cloud that fell down from the sky," and rolled down the windows so I could touch it. To me, it just felt wet. I was disappointed that clouds weren't like big magic pillows you could rest on, but I didn't say that. I was old enough by then to know that she was giving me what she could. Instead, I sat on my knees, stuck my head out the window, and opened my mouth. I wanted to eat the clouds. Mom stuck her head out her window and did the same, chomping and pretending to swallow big gulps of it.

"Maybe now we can fly!" I suggested.

She asked me, "Where to?"

I closed my eyes, but I couldn't imagine anything better than this.

CHAPTER 13

A Level Highway In The Desert

A few months ago, I sounded my final barbaric "ope" over the roofs of the Midwest and set out across the country with Jeff. We were tired of the cold winters and wanted to start somewhere new. Our plan was to hire movers and drive to Albuquerque together in one vehicle, but the devil has many faces and one of them is greedy moving companies. The morning we were set to leave, the moving company doubled the price quote and we found ourselves renting a last-minute U-Haul and purging as much of our stuff as we could to make it all fit. Plants, clothes, furniture. Everything that I'd spent the last few weeks packing and thinking, How did I ever let myself accrue so much?

Boxes were stacked in the living room so that we had to walk through narrow pathways to get around. My heart raced at the disorder and at trying to choose what to leave behind. Fright mounted until, on the way to take a small end table that I loved out to the curb, I stumbled and broke a planter that I also loved. It was small, ceramic, and intricately painted. Jeff had brought it home with the groceries one day after I'd mentioned how a rectangular planter would fit just right in the front windowsill. Now it was in two pieces at my feet, soil and succulents spilling out.

Anger is the emotion I am least comfortable with, and when it comes, it comes in great big, sudden waves. This wave toppled me. I threw the end table across the backyard before picking up the two halves of my planter and slamming it down on the ground, shattering it into irreparable pieces.

Jeff came outside to see what had happened and, just as suddenly as it had arrived, the anger fell away.

"I'm sorry," I said, and then sat on the ground and burst into tears.

He crouched in front of me and waited. There was a cut on his knuckle from misjudging the width of a doorway.

I pressed my face into my knee. "It just feels like all the times I had to leave a place and I couldn't take anything with me. I know it's not the same. It just feels—"

I couldn't find the words, but he understood. He went inside and grabbed the broom and dustpan. When he came back out, he helped me off the ground and handed them to me.

"I'm not going to clean this up for you," he said, rubbing my shoulder. "I love you."

While I swept, I thought about the times in my life when people I loved had broken things out of anger. Grandpa breaking the TV. Mom breaking a phone. Theresa's boyfriend breaking the light fixture. There was always someone else I loved there to come in and clean up after them. Always someone to explain their behavior away or apologize on their behalf. I thought of how much easier it might have been if Jeff had swept the patio for me and let me go inside to calm down. How I might have felt inside the house, relaxing, knowing he was out there squatting on the ground and cleaning up my mess. What paths both of our minds might start to form without us even realizing, and despite our best intentions. How sometimes the most loving thing you can do for someone is let them clean up their own mess.

After I swept everything up, I finished carrying the end table out to the curb. When I looked out later, someone had taken it. There was nothing left to feel about it. There and gone. We left around midnight, Jeff in the van and me in the U-Haul. We held each other for a long time outside on the dark street, and then started our separate drives.

The drive from Iowa City to Albuquerque is just under seventeen hours. Within the first hour, it started to rain. The rain fell heavier and heavier until I could barely see past a few yards. This is one of my favorite driving conditions. Late at night, leaning forward, entire body tensed. Music turned up so loud that I could feel but not hear my voice cracking as I sang along. Pitch black on all sides. Hyper-vigilance utilized to its full capacity.

Once the storm cleared, the air felt purified. I was alone, dancing in the green glow of the dashboard display. One hand on the steering wheel, the other wheeling and clawing in the air. Howling the lyrics of "Hasta Que Te Conocí" and starting the song over to howl it again. The road slid underneath me, a conveyer belt. Every now and again, a splash of red gore, a bloodstain. Animal bodies crumpled like laundry on the shoulder. There and gone too quick to process. Racing through the night, headed elsewhere, like being chased.

When we got tired, we stopped to sleep at hotels. I sank into the bed closest to the door, my lower back unraveling even as my head buzzed with desire to keep going. In the morning, back on the road, the other cars made me nervous with their unpredictable moves and close proximity. Eventually, the sun relented to the moon. The cars dwindled until I could be alone again. Turn up my music, raise my voice. Nothing, nothing, feels better than being on the move.

Farmland gave way to different farmland, then open expanses, green mountains, orange earth. I entered Albuquerque under a sky so big, it took my breath. The city is spooned by the Sandia Mountains, named for the pink glow the stone takes on at sunset. Junipers, ponderosa pines, and mixed conifers line the slope, forming the rind. Within a few months, Jeff and I would take a tram to the top. We'd hike to the peak and look out over the whole, beautiful city. Our bodies full of air and endorphins. A moment of enormous joy that I'd want to stuff in my mouth and eat, so I could keep it. For now, I navigated the U-Haul through unfamiliar streets. Anxiety roiling in the space between my heart and stomach at having done something so uncertain and irreversible. I pulled up to the new house. Tan stucco, empty and quiet. I turned off the truck, hopped out, and hummed with momentum.

All Creatures That Crawl Along The Ground

Imagine that the water has receded steadily from the Earth. For the first time in over a year, you step off the Ark and onto solid ground. You sway, your legs flexed on instinct that's no longer necessary. The animals come behind you, trumpeting and praising. Above, a bow of color, refractions of sunlight, not yet a covenant. An altar is built and one of each clean animal is burned in offering. Its pleasant aroma pleases the Lord. He gives you the world.

At night in the vineyard, you rest your head on flat, dry ground and gaze up at the unquestionable stars. Even now, you smell the offering. To your mortal nose, the scent is not sweet. You shake your head to rid yourself of the bleating, the desperate thrashing bodies and flapping wings of animals that survived the ruin of all life only to be slaughtered in the true end. Your crop grows in earth made fertile by the bones of sinners.

Metaphor Is Useful And Limited

It has always made me happy to imagine things as other things. What I can't process head-on, I can see from the side, from up in the fantastical sky, and then I come back down with a better idea for a blueprint. For you, I will try to say this straight. I had no home, so I tried to make a home in my body. Other people exerted their power on my body until I no longer felt at home there. This isn't fair, and I am trying. On my worst days, I want to destroy my body and fly free of it. On my best days, I am grateful. Most days between, I clean my house desperately and obsess over the shape of my stomach and my legs and the soft pad under my chin because the rituals of upkeep give me a sense of control that I am simultaneously desperate for and aware does not exist.

I want to tell you that I am okay now, but sometimes I'm not sure. There's a pumpkin on the table in front of me while I write. I grew it. The day I poked the seed into the earth, I felt good. An air balloon spinning through the sky, never looking back. Investing in a place where I knew I would live long enough to see the fruits and vegetables and gourds of my labor. I had the thought, Maybe it's all really behind me. The same trick early spring plays on me every year before the dying throes of winter claim March and April. The seed sprouted and turned into vines. Each day, I went outside and marveled at how much they had grown overnight. The vines were thick and spined, stinging my hands when I attempted to lift them. They grew and grew until they took over more than half the yard and I had to step and hop strategically to navigate around the gigantic leaves.

One morning, while watering the garden, I had the thought, I could kill myself and lie down under these leaves, and no one would find me. I hadn't been sad or upset about anything particular leading up to the thought. I shook it off, but the idea persisted and then unfurled into a feeling. The feeling raged inside me and the pumpkin vines grew out of control. My garden no longer brought me joy, but still I pulled the weeds and watered it and sat with my hands deep in the soil and my heart beating dully, promising, for myself and Ben and you that I would stay, stay, stay. Some days full of rage at the obligation. Until the feeling receded and I parted the leaves one day to see tiny, pale green bulbs topped with pointed flower buds, like newborn gnomes.

Only one survived into a full-grown pumpkin, bigger around than me, before the first frost killed the entire web of vines. I sawed it off the vine, hefted it inside, and put it on the table in the sunroom where I write, and I'm amazed at how long it has lived. Eventually, it will get soft and I'll roll it into the river or smash it with a hammer from the garden shed, and bad days will come, and I'll survive them, and I'll grow new vines maybe in some other yard, and I'll stand outside in the early morning watering the garden with my chest full of airy joy, thinking, Maybe it's all really behind me.

The truth is, I spent so long imagining a perfect future so I could get through a profoundly imperfect present. I'd close my eyes and build beautiful houses where nothing could ever go wrong. I needed that to hold me up, but now I have to let it go. The world will never be entirely safe. Troubles will come, loved ones will die, and landlords will reject my offer of free eggs in exchange for an exception from the terms of my lease. Now I'm the cloddish adult who controls my life, so I have to stop waiting for perfect conditions and trust that I can handle what comes. Planting a seed is easy. Tending to it so it can grow is the hard part.

All The Wild Animals Play Nearby

Jeff and I like to go on long walks. We used to run together in the mornings, but at the advanced age of twenty-nine, it's better for our joints if we meander at dusk. Since we moved to Albuquerque, we have favorite neighborhoods to wander through. There are so many nice houses with beautiful front yards around us. We start walking, stopping sometimes to marvel at the red yuccas and lavender and prickly pear cactuses that look like cartoon hands whose fingers got slammed in a door.

"I want some of these in our yard," I tell him.

"I'll plant you a million," he says.

"Ew, promise me we'll never paint our house a color like that."

"I promise."

Not always, but fairly often, a stray cat will find us and come up to rub on Jeff's leg. They always go straight to him. Dogs, cats, an injured bird once. He pets them and I try to use my breathing techniques to fight back covetous thoughts because I've always wanted animals to be charmed by me the way they are by him. I can't blame them, though. He'll look up at me from where he's squatting to pet them and flash a dimpled smile. Even the dimple is ridiculous, technically a scar from the time he got hit in the face with a golf club as a child. Hit in the face with a golf club and it only made him more handsome.

"You look amazing in this lighting," he'll say, looking like the statue of David, and then take a picture of me wherein I look like a newt being held for ransom.

After the animals wander off, we keep going. We leave the neighborhood and wander to a nearby commercial district to watch the sunset hit the mountains. They go pink and black, and then fade into night sky. The neon lights come on and we point out places we might visit if we weren't such homebodies. We walk until we get tired, and then turn toward home.

I heard once that it was irritating to ask your partner, "What are you thinking?" but we ask each other all the time. It prompts us to share memories that resurfaced for no apparent reason, places we want to go, books we read once but can't remember the titles of, recipes we want to try, old conversations we thought of new responses to. He talks about the vastness of space, and I listen, rapt, even though I get cosmic vertigo when I think too hard about how small we are.

When we get home, sometimes we go around the block a few more times just to keep talking. It's almost hard to make ourselves go inside. I'll pause in the driveway and make up some reason to stall. The sedum looks droopy. A receipt blew into the bushes again.

"What if we go around the block one more time?" I ask when the sound of the key in the door makes me want to run.

"How about we go in and I'll make us some food?" he counters. "We can watch something or play a game."

We go inside, and I rest my head against his back while he cooks, and his heart sounds like the tempo of a long walk.

Questions With Answers That Change

How do you begin to undo the knots of trauma, the patterns that the brain is designed to hang on to? How do you retrain your mind to come to conclusions other than catastrophe or miracle when you had only extremes modeled for you? How do you maintain hope when you have a string of good months interrupted by sudden, shriveling regression? How do you cope when it takes untold effort to function at a level that other people maintain and surpass with apparent ease?

Recovery is different for everyone. What works for you might not work for me and vice versa, but this is what I've done. When the sensation of doom crushes me into the corner of my bed and I can't move from the fear, I tell myself, I am here and now. Even when I can't feel it, I tell myself. When I can't be understanding and instead am flooded with rage, I let myself feel it for as long as it needs to be felt, but I don't let it overstay. I breathe. I go to therapy. I take medicine when my coping skills aren't enough. I write love letters to my friends when I'm struggling to love myself. I go salsa dancing, reveling in the beauty of bodies that look like mine. I go to the local pool and swim laps under the sun until my limbs feel like rubber and then I cling to the side of the lane and gape at the Sandia Mountains, panting and shaking. When terror and rapture wrestle inside me because of how much I have to lose, I let them coexist in my mind.

My covenant is to look back so I can understand a better way to move forward.

Taking Ben Up The Mountain And Not Killing Him

My brother is coming to visit. As soon as his school lets out for break, he'll fly from Indiana to New Mexico to spend the holidays together. It'll be the first time he's been here and I'm excited to show him around. Until now, Jeff and I have procrastinated on hanging up some of our decorations or getting those last few pieces of furniture to bring certain rooms together. Now I'm populating empty spaces with plants and paintings and maps. Desperately searching for a forty-two-inch side table to fill in that catchall space in the bedroom.

Logically, I know that he'll get here and say something playfully disparaging about the place, like how it's too close to a busy road or that the swamp cooler is an eyesore. Still, I hope he'll be at least internally impressed with what we've built. It's a little goofy for me to try to impress him based on my own standards, but I also have plans for impressing him based on his own. For instance, my brother loves a beverage. Take him to a grocery store and he inevitably gravitates to the tea aisle or to the glass-bottle soda pops. He'll leave with at least three different six-packs of whatever intrigued him and make you sample at least one of each. I've identified the nearest restaurants with agua fresca varieties and stores that have expansive beverage options.

Ben also loves a trinket. Everywhere he goes, he accrues treasures to put in his office for his clients to fiddle with, or gifts for friends. In his house, he has a wide assortment of miniature and novelty things such as a little zen sand garden, a magnetic hourglass, several tiny lava lamps, a pendulum, and some of those plastic baby hands. His office at the school where he counsels has googly eyes of various sizes on every one of his supplies, including staplers and his phone, and two giant ones on the side of the desk where the students sit. Even though he won't be able to take much back on the plane, I've scouted at least four different shops to take him to.

"I found another place to take you," I tell him when he calls me on the drive home from work.

"Ohhh, what's it like?" he asks.

"That's none of your business!" I tell him.

His work commute is nearly an hour, so he calls me to fill the time. Some days, he sounds exhausted. He sounds like someone who understands what can happen to children at that age and feels the full weight of his responsibility to help them. I know they're in good hands. I'm glad they have someone who cares about them the way he does. And I worry about my brother.

"Would anything help?" I ask him on hard days, knowing I'm too far away to do any of the material things I want to do. Make him food, tuck him into bed, poorly play guitar at him until he wakes back up, furious as a bull.

"No." He sighs. "I'll be fine."

"Are you sure? Want me to talk like Popeye?"

". . . Okay, fine."

So I talk like Popeye and scout out stores with treasures I hope he'll like. I make a karaoke playlist and buy cake mix and wrap a pen shaped like a french fry in wrapping paper. I clean the house like I'm preparing to host royalty. When Ben gets here, I'm going to take him up to the mountain, where he can look out over the city and the desert. See how beautiful it all looks when you're far away. The nodding onions and golden asters and western wallflowers that we might once have made into potions. How terrified your body feels of falling, tensing and overcorrecting so you sway like a stalk. When we come down and our feet are tired, I'll take him back to my clean house with its plants and comfortable furniture and stocked fridge. We'll sit together on the couch and I'll ask him, Where to now?

We're Here

I try to remember the first place I ever was and can only see the road. The passenger seat under me, a texture like stiff animal fur cut very, very short that I would run my fingers over both ways to prickle up and then smooth back down. Corona cherry car freshener in a cat-food-sized can. And Mom, driving. At eye level, I see her arm extended out to steer us, white like a pillow and covered in soft hair. No sense of where we're going, no urgency to find out.

Now we all have to leave the car. This has always been my least favorite part of a trip. I used to pretend to be asleep so she would lift me out of the car and carry me. My cheek on her shoulder. Her hand on my back. Eventually, I got too big for that, and then I kept getting bigger. We're getting out of the car now.

But we could sit with our legs dangling from the open door for a moment longer. Feel the car air pulled out and replaced with outside air, fresher and cooler. Lean sideways against the seat and close our eyes, just linger. Run the tips of our fingers along the rubber weather strip.

"Door ajar," the car reminds us on repeat. If we don't close the door, the battery will die. We have to leave the car, knowing that nothing will ever be as sweet as the promise of a destination. We have to step out onto solid ground.

ACKNOWLEDGMENTS

MOM, I MADE this book for you. I made it the same way you made me, getting it wrong and getting it right, and so, so full of love. Thank you for giving me life. Thank you for making me, the navigator.

Ben, shut up. Thank you for being so gracious even though you were angelic and god-sent and Mom found me in the garbage. Thank you for reading every draft and suggesting so many titles with your name in them. Thank you for all the phone calls and messages. This book is yours as much as it's mine, but it's actually mine. Don't freaking touch it.

Shirley Jean Rice, I hate your stinking guts. You make me vomit. You're scum between my toes. Love, Alfalfa. But really, thank you for being my constant. Thank you for pacing the Earth into a more beautiful rotation. I'm so excited for all the ways we're going to grow together before we die at exactly the same time. For crying out loud, you know I love you. And your stinky little son too.

Jeff, my treasure, thank you for making sure I ate while I wrote. Thank you for loving me the way I need to be loved. Thank you for listening and building a life with me. Thank you for everything about you. I love you so much, I could just crap. Baby Jeff, you can't freaking read.

Hafizah and PJ, thank you for guiding me through this whole confounding process. Thank you for advocating for me and not letting me get lost. I appreciate all of the rounds of feedback and the sound advice you gave me when I was overwhelmed. Eternally, thank you.

Anna, my incredible editor, thank you so much for helping me bring this book home. Thank you for understanding my story so thoroughly that I could trust it was in good hands and finally allow myself to relax my grip on it.

Thank you to Zibby Owens and the Zibby Books team for giving this book a home and doing all of the hard and compassionate work to get it to this point. There are so many of you to thank for so many huge things, but please just imagine that I'm astral projecting into your homes and blasting powerful beams of gratitude that nearly break your windows.

To my NWP cohort, thank you so much for reading the early fetuses of this thing and loving this socially anxious bumpkin. Thank you for the cosigns and the parties and giving me new ways to see and love the world. Special, love-filled thanks to T. M. Tucker, Aracely, Alexander, Darius, Nico, Gyasi, and Amelia.

To Inara, thank you so much for your warmth and wisdom. Thank you for always listening and telling me what I didn't know I needed to hear. Thank you for seeing the beating heart of this book and helping me see it too.

To Kiese, thank you for more than I even know how to say. Thank you for making sure we care for each other and ourselves. Thank you for showing me what's possible, how writing can be tender and when it needs not to be. Thank you for that time you called me weird. I hold it as one of the dearest compliments I've ever received.

To Jill, Cathy, and Kenny B, thank you for believing in me when I was barely even aware of myself. Thank you for helping me understand that writing is a kind of home.

To the rest of the Means family, thank you for being weird enough that I could fill a whole book. Otherwise, I might have had to write a novel, and I don't know if I have the chops. Thank you in different and overlapping ways for giving me homes, lessons, and stories. Thank you for loving me and each other.

To the Smith family, thank you for taking me in and loving me like one of your own. Thank you for giving me stability and comfort, even when I didn't always know how to accept it. Thank you for being my home.

My dear friends, thank you for understanding that I'm cramming you into a paragraph to save space! Rachel, thank you for mind-melding with me so completely that it scares me sometimes, for the art days, and for making life, from one side of the country to the other, so beautiful. T. M. Tucker, thank you for being the best conversationalist I've ever known, for all the music and the genius essays, and for trying so valiantly to help me be stylish. Sarah, thank you for guiding me like a will-o'-wisp through this whole process, and for being so brilliant and funny. Jackson, thank you for how you take care of everyone, but thank you even more for taking care of yourself. Liam, thank you for being a good sport about this joke where I pretend this is your name. Ashton, thank you for being the best kind of freak, and for bringing the best snacks to the tent. R. M. Kidd, thank you for being my go-to horror connoisseur, and thank you for always being willing to go on the long tangents to wherever. I love you all so, so much.

A moment for my grandmother, grandfather, brother, cousin, and uncle, who used to live in the world with us, and now live inside us.

To the people I almost certainly forgot on the page but not in my heart, an apology and personalized thank-you is forthcoming. I'm sure I will wake up in the middle of the night with your face in my mind here soon, absolutely drenched in shame sweat. Does that make you happy? Is that what you want?

ABOUT THE AUTHOR

BRITTANY MEANS is a writer and editor living in Albuquerque, New Mexico. A graduate of Iowa's MFA Nonfiction Writing Program, Means has worked with Inara Verzemnieks and Kiese Laymon. She has received several awards for her work, including the Magdalena Award and the Grace Paley Fellowship. Her other talents include doing horror movie screams and baking ugly but delicious cakes.

www.brittanymeans.com